YALE SOUTHEAST ASIA STUDIES, 3

Political Ideology in Malaysia

Reality and the Beliefs of an Elite

by James C. Scott

New Haven and London | Yale University Press

1968

Library of Congress catalog card number: 68-27766

Designed by John O. C. McCrillis,
set in Baskerville type,
and printed in the United States of America by
The Colonial Press Inc., Clinton, Massachusetts.

Distributed in Great Britain, Europe, Asia, and
Africa by Yale University Press Ltd., London; in
Canada by McGill University Press, Montreal; and
in Latin America by Centro Interamericano de Libros
Académicos, Mexico City.

Published with assistance from the foundation
established in memory of Amasa Stone Mather
of the Class of 1907, Yale College.

To the Memory of my Parents

Parry M. Scott, M.D.
Augusta B. Scott

Preface

This is a study of political beliefs in a new nation. It is not, however, a case study in the customary meaning of that term. What I have done is to suppress the unique and particular character of the Malaysian experience in the interest of accentuating those political beliefs and experiences that are common to many relatively poor new nations. Those concerned primarily with comparative political studies will find this perspective a valuable one inasmuch as it explicitly suggests temporal and spatial comparisons that merit research. Those interested primarily in Malaysia will hopefully be compensated for the lack of much mention of that nation's quite special circumstances by a greater appreciation of what Malaysia shares, at a fundamental level, with other developing nations.

When I had spoken at length to a number of civil servants, I became aware that their views of human nature and of human conflict—both of which were crucial for their political attitudes—were not markedly different from the views of people from poverty-stricken portions of the Western world. That is, their views seemed to flow less from something in their culture per se than from something in their environment. Throughout my treatment of their political beliefs, I have stressed that these beliefs are reflective of certain assumed environmental restraints—e.g. material scarcity. I have thus tried to place their beliefs against the background in which they arise and which gives them meaning. This kind of contextual analysis not only leads to an appreciation of how ideology might change but also avoids the danger of evaluating such beliefs from the observer's context in which they may appear unrealistic or even pathological—but solely because of the imposition of an alien context.

Because of my concern with democracy and the conditions under which democratic values are likely to thrive, this study devotes considerable attention not only to the nature and extent of democratic beliefs among Malaysians, but to their sources as well. Here again I have endeavored to see these beliefs in a context that includes the realities of poverty and social cleavage which beset most new nations. Malaysians who might otherwise appear to the observer as pseudo-democrats are seen now in context as democrats facing dilemmas that would sorely try their Western counterparts. My evaluation of democratic beliefs in Malaysia therefore reflects the fact that such beliefs require more commitment when the social and physical environment is hostile than when—as in the West—it is supportive of democratic beliefs.

My desire to develop propositions of comparative value led me beyond the basic interview data to limited sample surveys among Malaysian elites and comparisons with findings based on similar instruments in the West. It was inevitable that some of the individuality of the interview respondents would be lost in this quest for broader theory. If the effort to sift out what beliefs these seventeen individuals share has thus occasionally made them appear two-dimensional, this is more the result of the analytical perspective than of any lack of appreciation for the great human variety in the sample.

Rather than write the conventional historical opening chapter, I have instead introduced Malaysia in a more impressionistic fashion that might facilitate a fuller understanding of the setting for this study than a historical narrative. In Part I the analysis focuses on ideology in the broadest sense, while Part II is largely devoted to democratic beliefs in Malaysia.

The kindness and generosity of seventeen Malaysian civil servants have made this study possible. They welcomed me into their offices and homes and spoke candidly of themselves and their nation. Although I cannot acknowledge them by name, they are aware of how very grateful I am for their friendship and assistance.

I am particularly indebted to officials of the Staff Training Centre, Civics Training Centre, Postal Training Centre, National Productivity Centre, Audit Department, and Bank Negara and to their trainees for allowing me to administer research questionnaires. Their interest and willingness to help me are typical of the hospitality and openness which I encountered wherever I went in Malaysia. I wish to thank the Federal Establishment Office, and Ishak bin Haji Pateh Akhir in particular, for helping me get in touch with the seventeen civil servants whom I interviewed.

While in Malaysia my wife and I had the good fortune to live in Kampong Baru, a settlement reserved for Malays in Kuala Lumpur. Our neighbors responded to this strange intrusion with such hospitality and graciousness that we shall always cherish our time among them. We owe our knowledge of, and fondness for, Malay culture to the people of Kampong Baru. We owe a special debt to Mazli bin Som, who suggested that we join this community, and to Che'gu Sa'id, a member of the *kampong* committee, who kindly gave his consent. In addition our friend Zaharrudin bin Mohd. Nazir nurtured our facility with the Malay language and made many translations from the Arabic script for me. Both he and Zulkifli bin Ya'akob assisted me in innumerable ways throughout the research. Ron Provencher, our anthropologist neighbor in Kampong Baru, was generous in the time he spared introducing me to the literature in his field bearing on my work.

Finally, I join a long list of foreign scholars who have profited greatly from the assistance and scholarly interest of the History Department of the University of Malaya. Special thanks are due its Chairman, Professor Wang Gung-wu, who, in spite of a pressing schedule, never failed to offer his encouragement as well as friendly, sensitive critiques.

The intellectual debts I acquired at Yale's Graduate School are so many and varied they defy full accounting. Nevertheless, I wish to thank Karl W. Deutsch, Harry J. Benda, Carl Landé, and Robert Dahl for making graduate education the exciting enterprise it should be.

Robert O. Tilman has taken great pains to clarify both my thinking and written expression. I could not have asked for a more sympathetic critic or a more devoted mentor. The insights of Joseph LaPalombara have also contributed a great deal to whatever merit this study has, and I thank him for his many attentive comments. My research, like that of many others at Yale, originates from the work and teaching of Robert Lane. His broad concern with the development and maintenance of political ideology has inspired me to attempt a similar exploration in a non-Western area. I only hope that my efforts here begin to justify the care and generosity he has lavished on my development as a scholar.

Gayl Ness and James Guyot each read the manuscript with a sharp analytical eye, and I have tried to incorporate many of their suggestions into the text. I am grateful, too, for the considerable editorial skills of Ann MacLean which are in evidence throughout this work.

With such intellectual resources at my disposal, it is obvious that the shortcomings of this study must remain my own responsibility.

My wife shared the satisfactions and burdens of this project from beginning to end. Were it not for her considerable editorial skills, the reader would scarcely be able to find his way through the text. Her understanding of a distracted—even slightly deranged—husband was at times the only thing that sustained me.

J. C. S.

Contents

By the way, Odili, I think you are wasting your talent here. I want you to come to the capital and take up a strategic post in the civil service. We shouldn't leave everything to the highland tribes. My secretary is from there; our people must press for their fair share of the national cake.

Chinua Achebe, *A Man of the People*

Kemajuan kampong kachau dengan kemajuan perut. [The welfare of the village interferes with the welfare of my stomach.]

A Malay villager explaining why community projects had failed in his village.

I. Malaysia and the Study of Ideology

1

The Setting

THE COSMOPOLITAN PYRAMID

The drive from Malaysia's modern, air-conditioned university outside Kuala Lumpur to my interview in the city with Ja'afar bin Musa takes a scant fifteen minutes. In that brief span alone any skepticism about the cosmopolitan character of this administrative capital is quickly dispelled. The satellite town of Petaling Jaya occupies either side of the broad, new Federal Highway leading to the city. It is barely saved from resembling the drab suburban sprawls of Western cities by its red tile roofs and the surfeit of orchids thriving on sunny front lawns. Here, in this neatly laid out residential area, live a good portion of the professional men, higher civil servants, and businessmen who work in the city. Distinguished largely by their comparative wealth and often by English education, Malays, Indians, and Chinese live here side by side and share common middle-class concerns about the education of their children, the installment payments on their new cars, and their domestic help. This class of industrious, educated, nouveaux riches is in large measure a product of the colonial past. It is this class, with its skills and learning, which for the moment at least is entrusted with the building of a postcolonial nation.

Not more than five hundred yards farther along the Federal Highway toward Kuala Lumpur live some of the presumably ultimate beneficiaries of this postcolonial society. They are Malay squatters who have established a small *kampong* or village on the higher ground beside the highway. Their poverty is mild compared with that of Javanese villagers in Indonesia, or even when compared with the lot of their rural kinsmen in thousands of kampongs scattered throughout Malaysia's countryside. But it is poverty nevertheless. Women dressed in *baju kurong* must fetch water from across the road in five-gallon tins secured to either end of a long pole. The kampong houses are hastily built fragile affairs, for these are squatters, and one day they will have to move on to make way for some new building needed by a new Malaysia.

But already these squatters benefit in some measure from the new Malaysia. The Ministry of Labor helps the men locate jobs, the Welfare Department looks after the handicapped and needy, and the Ministry of Health tries to cope with the medical problems of the kampong. Long lines of neatly dressed village children—boys in blue shorts, girls in blue sarongs—dawdle on their way to the Sekolah Kebangsaan (National Primary School) two hundred yards down the road. The school itself is an unpretentious frame building with a small play area surrounding it. Boasting neither the air-conditioning nor the bold modernity of the university, it nevertheless is equally symbolic of the new Malaysia. Chances are the children studying here will know the Malay roman script and the national anthem before their parents. Their generation is the first that will be more than 50 percent literate and the first to be instructed en masse in the heady ways of nationalism.[1]

That such benefits as these were not entirely absent in pre-independence Malaysia should not obscure the fact that the relationship between rulers and ruled has changed in a fundamental way. For the first time, the kampong folk have a measure of power, however tenuous. The mere giving or withholding of their votes makes a difference in the fortunes of greater men in the State Assembly and Federal Parliament. Their small measure of power over these *orang besar* (big men) ensures that services will continue to expand and that when they are forced to move, a new piece of land and building materials will be offered them by politicians anxious to please. To be sure, the chief beneficiaries of the power the British left behind are represented by the middle class of Petaling Jaya, but the kampong Malays enjoy their own modest share as well.

On the outskirts of town, a multitude of small but prosperous stores and restaurants owned by Chinese and Tamils cater to their daily clientele. The scene is familiar, for the Chinese, and to a

1. Total school enrollment increased by over 400,000 to 1.39 million from 1956 to 1962, and the rate of increase has accelerated since. Moreover, the number of pupils in English language schools more than doubled, from 199,689 to 406,480 in that same period. *Malaysia, Buku Rasmi Tahunan, Official Year Book, 1963* (Kuala Lumpur, Government Press, 1964), p. 532.

much lesser extent the Indians, dominate small commerce and industry in Malaysia and, indeed, in much of Southeast Asia. Just across the road are the modest cement quarters built by the government for the largely Tamil labor force of Malaysian Railways. Originally brought to Malaya by the British, they, together with their countrymen who were imported to tap rubber trees in vast plantations or work on the roads for the Public Works Department, have forged a strong trade union movement. Through their organization they have wrested a share of the new nation's economic pie, as have their neighbors, the Chinese shopkeepers, who benefit from the increasing wealth of their clients.

Kuala Lumpur is a boom town in a boom nation. Construction gangs of Chinese girls mix concrete or scurry about carrying baskets of stone and sand for the new office buildings which rise on every hand. With the starched cloth sun visors they wear, they could easily be mistaken for a crew of welders who have momentarily tipped back their face shields. While the commercial skyscrapers on which they labor are the most dramatic evidence of Malaysia's new wealth, the construction boom has left its mark on more modest edifices as well. Across the street a Sikh cloth merchant helps hoist a bright new sign above his entrance, and two doors down the modern facade of a popular Chinese restaurant receives its final touches.

The prosperity that makes all this activity possible has come about comparatively recently and rests on shaky foundations.[2] Who would have thought fifteen years ago that television sets would be within the reach of a modest civil servant, that those who then

2. The foundations of Malaysia's prosperity are shaky both politically and economically. Political problems will be examined later, but it goes without saying that any new nation set amidst the turmoil of Southeast Asia and troubled internally by communal tensions cannot take its security or stability for granted.

Economically, Malaysia has the best rate of economic growth in Southeast Asia over the past decade. Nonetheless, the economy is still largely dependent upon natural rubber for foreign exchange earnings, and the rising costs of production, coupled with both a downward trend in the world price and the competition of synthetics, do not augur well for the future. Replanting schemes designed to raise per acre yields and diversification into palm oil and other products offer some hope for the long run, but they do not appreciably affect Malaysia's present vulnerability as a primary producer to world market trends. Cf. Gayl D. Ness, *Bureaucracy and Rural Development in Malaysia* (Berkeley, University of California Press, 1967), pp. 66–69.

aspired to a motorcycle now own a car, while those who hoped for
a new bicycle now ride proudly on their Japanese motorscooters?[3]

Amidst this new wealth there is some uneasiness. A prosperous
Chinese shopkeeper still takes care to fill his huge earthenware
pot to the brim with rice each year—just in case. He hopes good
times will continue, but he is not foolish enough to act as if they
will, for he has a long memory. He recalls only too vividly the
drastic fall of rubber prices in the late 1920s that made his father
a poor man almost overnight. The family had slowly recovered
some of its former wealth by trading in gold when the Japanese
occupation forced them to flee Kuala Lumpur and take up subsistence farming. Even today, when he is rich beyond his father's
fondest hopes, he remembers what happened and sets aside enough
rice for his family's needs in the event everything else is lost.
The war with Indonesia, the breakup of Malaysia, communal
riots in Singapore—all remind him that his prosperity is a tenuous
achievement.

There is a lot of money to be made in any boom town, but
it must be made quickly, for no one knows exactly when the
vein of gold will give out. The trick is to get as much out as fast
as you can before the opportunity disappears for good. The
premonition that a pain economy will return is precisely what
gives this and every other boom town its frenetic character.

CHE' JA'AFAR BIN MUSA AND THE SELANGOR CLUB

The Ministry of Information, where Che'[4] Ja'afar works at an
important job, is just off the center of the old town. Across a wide
padang, or green, from the Ministry's offices lies the Selangor Club,
a rambling Tudor structure looking self-conscious and out of place
in its tropical setting. A brief decade and a half ago it was a spot
to which Englishmen could retire in the company of their countrymen for an evening of dancing, billiards, and amiable conversation, free from the rigors of their administrative or business affairs.
Like hundreds of identical sancta sanctorum throughout the once
vast British Empire, it was not so much a symbol of racism as

3. Between 1955 and 1962 the number of private motorcars more than doubled
(from 53,545 to 112,843), while the figure for motorcycles increased almost fivefold
(17,999 to 88,207). If anything, the rate of importation has increased since then.
Malaysia, Buku Rasmi Tahunan, Official Year Book, p. 528.

4. Comparable to "Mr."

of public school snobbery extended to colonial peoples.[5] It was only in 1952 that General Templer, a grammar school product appointed head of operations against communist insurgents, made a symbolic dent in the colonial social system by threatening to turn the august club into an army barracks unless Asians were admitted immediately. Today the barriers to membership are really only financial, and Asian ministers and higher civil servants pass freely through its portals. But ironically, that is all that has changed; the style of evenings at the Selangor Club remains essentially the same—only the members are new. Whether what has happened at the Selangor Club is seen as a credit to the British or a credit to the Malayans does not matter here as much as what it says about the colonial history of Malaya and the civil servant we are about to meet.

From behind an enormous desk Che' Ja'afar presides over a smallish room filled almost to the ceiling with old files dog-eared by countless reverential clerical hands. The piles of folders seem almost an essential structural feature of the building. The impression is given that if one of them were removed hastily, the entire ceiling would immediately collapse. Peering out owlishly through a slot created by two columns of files, Che' Ja'afar smilingly bids me to be seated and sends one of several office boys scurrying off to fetch coffee. He is a middle-aged Malay, and although he has risen quickly in the civil service, he feels frustrated by younger superiors whose very presence limits his future chances. Under the circumstances he has turned his thoughts to retirement and the quiet pastoral life he hopes to establish for himself and his family. The relaxed, affable manner in which he speaks of his boyhood, his job, and his political ideals always makes our regular two-hour interview seem shorter than it really is. He obviously welcomes this diversion from the normal bureaucratic chores.

If Che' Ja'afar were suddenly to find himself chatting with the former members of the Selangor Club during its halcyon days, he would not feel much out of place. Like the colonial elite, he is well educated, and what is more, his political ideals are entirely British. Even if the conversation turned to the prospects for democracy in Malaysia, Che' Ja'afar's comments would be quite in keeping with the company. In particular, he is saddened by

5. James Allen, "MCS: Fact and Fiction," unpublished manuscript, p. 22.

the opportunism of politicians, by the inability of the Malays to compete with the Chinese, and by the lack of civic consciousness and national loyalty among his people. "The people I work with have no fixed idea—we're all British trained. We think things here haven't reached the standard we expect. Maybe we expect too much, though."

His whole tone is one of regret rather than condemnation. Where the British might feel some compulsion to exaggerate Malaysian shortcomings to justify Western rule, Che' Ja'afar labors under no such psychic handicap. He and his colleagues would readily agree with many an Englishman's appraisal of democracy in Malaysia, but for them the appraisal is a cool-headed and realistic one in which animus toward the subject people plays little or no role.

Perhaps the most striking aspect of Che' Ja'afar's political views, however, is the almost complete absence of anticolonial or anti-British sentiment. The same is more or less true for the other sixteen civil servants I spoke with, but since Che' Ja'afar expresses himself more explicitly than the others, I have chosen his views to portray an essential element of the setting for my later discussion. The familiar declarations issuing forth from Afro-Asian meetings do not speak for Che' Ja'afar, and he is quite clear about it. In his personal case, some training in England itself may help account for his views, but for many young men from British colonies a similar experience has had quite the opposite effect. When talking of the crisis in Southern Rhodesia, he speaks of the "low level of civilization" of the Africans and concludes, "I wouldn't want a quarter of a million whites to be governed by seven million half-civilized blacks."

While some of the racial myths of colonialism seem to have rubbed off on Che' Ja'afar, I should hasten to point out that he considers himself a nationalist and a patriot and is proud of Malaysia's independence. What is missing are the traces of bitterness one might expect to find—the standard diatribes of colonial rule. Instead, he feels the British governed Malaya "impartially" and even muses, "perhaps I was unconsciously pro-British myself." This comes from someone who gave serious thought to entering politics himself during its nationalist phase.

How is it that for Che' Ja'afar and others, being a nationalist does not mean being anti-British or anti-West, and being proud of independence does not mean vilifying the whole of colonial rule? I would like briefly to suggest here that the cause for this anomaly is to be found largely in the nature of Malaya's colonial experience.

Malaya was colonized rather late compared with, for example, Burma, Ceylon, and India, and a good many of its constituent states were governed in a way that preserved, perhaps artificially, much of the precolonial power structure. The human suffering attendant on economic dislocation, which characterized lower Burma's colonial history,[6] was much less severe in Malaya. Education policies in Malaya did not produce the large unemployed, alienated, educated elite who formed the core cadre of nationalists in many other colonial nations. With the exception of the Chinese, who by and large considered themselves temporary residents, the great bulk of the English educated were absorbed into the administrative structure of the colony.[7] Finally, unlike India, which for the greater part of its colonial history was governed by an alien elite with an unshakable conviction of its right to rule, British rule in Malaya was barely consolidated when doubts about the white man's burden had begun to sap the confidence of imperialists. The relative brevity of colonial rule, a measure of indirect rule, the lack of overwhelming economic hardship, the absence of a substantial, unattached "shadow" elite, and the early loss of the colonial raison d'être all conspired to make Malaya's colonial experience comparatively untraumatic. The basis for large-scale bitterness just did not exist, nor were there many unattached intellectuals available to organize it.

The nationalist movement was slow in coming, and when it did arrive after World War II, the issue that touched it off was the British Malayan Union proposal, which Malays felt threatened their political rights vis-à-vis other communities. Inevitably a split developed in nationalist ranks, and a more Indonesian oriented, populist faction of Malays, including Islamic reformers under the leadership of Dato Onn bin Ja'afar, pitted itself against a liberal democratic, Western-educated group of moderates who drew considerable support from the ranks of the civil service. That

6. See J. S. Furnivall, *Colonial Policy and Practice* (New York, New York University Press, 1948, 1956).

7. James Scott, "Education in Malaya," unpublished paper.

the latter group won was made possible by the vagaries of colonial history as mentioned above and some timely concessions by the British in the face of Malay opposition to the Malayan Union proposals. British concessions made it unnecessary for the Malays to turn to more radical political leadership, while the struggle against a powerful communist insurgency required close cooperation with the British lest there be nothing at all to hand over after independence.

By the time independence was granted in 1957, the British were already old hands at giving way graciously. There was no long, bitter struggle against the colonial regime, which could have produced the enduring hatreds and humiliations that cast long political shadows. The transfer of power was almost purely an administrative transfer, as the local political leadership was virtually identical in education, outlook, and social background with the local bureaucratic elite. One could say of Malaya as has been said of Ceylon that

> the 1947 transfer of sovereignty consisted of the replacement of conservative, moderate, aloof British civil servants by conservative, moderate, aloof British educated Ceylonese notables who, to more nativistic eyes at least "resembled the former colonial rulers in everything but the color of their skin." [8]

Is it any wonder that Che' Ja'afar could emerge from the colonial period without any of the crystalizing experiences of a long, anticolonial struggle which would have made him more acceptable in the Afro-Asian fraternity? For him, and for the political elite as well, independence came naturally—enough conflict to be a source of pride and self-respect, but not so much that he cannot retain a good measure of respect and admiration for his former colonizers.

When the beliefs of Malaysian civil servants are examined in more detail, it will be useful to recall Che' Ja'afar's lack of bile. Through his eyes, an essential portion of this study's setting has been portrayed. To broaden this setting still further, we must meet another civil servant.

8. Clifford Geertz, "The Integrative Revolution," in Geertz, ed., *Old Societies and New States* (New York, The Free Press, 1963), p. 121.

LIM FONG SOON AND THE NATIONAL MOSQUE

On the way to Mr. Lim's house, one passes the high minaret of the recently completed National Mosque. Audaciously modern to more traditional eyes, it is a source of enormous pride to Malays throughout the country, not least to the muezzin, who rides an elevator to the top of the minaret for his five daily calls to prayer. Rural Malays from every part of the nation come in chartered buses to pray to Allah and admire *their* national mosque, while the Malay-dominated Alliance Party government hopes that the experience will still any suspicions that too much is being done for the Indians and Chinese and not enough for the Malays. The hope is not at all naïve, for as Che' Mustapha in the Health Department remarked about the prospects for democracy in Malaysia,

> It depends on the result of what democracy has brought to the citizens of this country—that's why the government wants results immediately, so that the people can see. Many people who are illiterate—they have to see—the Mesjid Negara [National Mosque], the museum—the new roads; those people believe this is democracy—not to work or contribute to it— but they believe these things stand for democracy.

Impressed by the power and wealth of *their* government as symbolized by *their* mosque, Malays are indeed more firmly bound not only to the present government but also to democracy. The loyalty of the Malays in this instance is not achieved without some cost. Long before the mosque's completion, grumblings could be heard from Chinese and Indians about the price of such a monument, notwithstanding frequent grants to Buddhist and Hindu temples. Nothing illustrates better the precarious business of politics in a multiracial society than the National Mosque— what is given to one community is perceived to have been taken from the others.

Mr. Lim is a senior member of the new class who lives in the middle-income residential area of Petaling Jaya. His progress up the bureaucratic ladder has been slow but steady, and he now finds himself holding a high post in the Railways Department. Presently responsible for the quality of passenger service in trains and answering complaints from the public, he appears somewhat overwhelmed by the pressure of responsibilities that he never anticipated being given.

Like many other civil servants, Mr. Lim prefers to be interviewed away from office anxieties in the relaxed atmosphere of his home. His pleasant house is rented from the government and precariously guarded by an aging, phlegmatic mongrel more concerned with a losing battle against ticks than with the approach of strangers. Mr. Lim and his wife greet me at the door and at once place a cold Tiger beer on the inevitable glass-topped table surrounded by four rattan chairs. Both my hosts dress Malay style, Mr. Lim in a sarong and Mrs. Lim in a colorful *sarong kebaya,* for they are "Straits Chinese" whose parents were born in Malaya. They call this country their home, although at the same time they regret the decline of Chinese culture in the Malayan Chinese community.

Calling a place your home is not necessarily the same as feeling at home there. Mr. Lim is well aware of this paradox, and for precisely that reason I have chosen him to illustrate one of the personal consequences of living in a multiracial society. Time and again during the interviews he voices his concern over the uncertain future of his family and of the Chinese community as a whole in Malaysia. Greatly worried about the most recent political issue between the Chinese-dominated People's Action Party and the Malay-dominated Alliance Party,[9] Mr. Lim whispers twice with great feeling, "We feel very apprehensive." When Malays shout at Chinese in the Parliament House to "sit down and shut up," he regards it as a foreboding of similar events on a larger scale outside Parliament. His anxiety is coupled with skepticism about the religiosity of the Malays and also with a morbid concern about the fatal concoctions of bamboo hairs and ground glass Malays are reputed to prepare for enemies. Mr. Lim's apprehension about the Malays and about the fragility of the multiracial society he calls home appear to be generalized into a fear of politics. Asked if he likes to discuss politics with his friends outside work, he answers, "We shouldn't talk about politics even with our friends—we don't know what can be conveyed to the

9. Our discussion occurred before the split between Malaysia and Singapore on August 9, 1965.

authorities." The undercurrent of fear is strong when he speaks of politics, and its effects on his political style cannot be underestimated. It is, unhappily, an inevitable element of the setting in a multiracial nation like Malaysia.

It would be a mistake, however, to see Mr. Lim's uneasiness about the Malays solely in the light of the tensions generated by a fragile, multiracial nation. Communal animosities may provide a convenient focus for his anxiety, but he finds other targets as well. Everywhere he looks in today's Malaysia, "The big fish eat the small fish and the small fish eat worms." The public only feigns respect for civil servants in order to take advantage of them, political parties "fizzle out and work only for their own personal gains," and the industrialist "cares only for his own pockets." As Mr. Lim surveys it, this world is "all governed by 'vitamin M' [money]," and selfish interests are apt to lurk behind even the most innocent facade. The strains of multiracialism help direct and organize his suspicions, but this is only the most prominent facet of his generally misanthropic nature.

The present racial composition of Malaysia's population of about seven million is roughly 3.4 million Malays, 2.6 million Chinese, and .8 million Indians.[10] Until independence, British colonial policy established some special Malay privileges, some of which are retained, while the increasing numbers of Chinese and Indians were largely dealt with as if they were not permanent residents. The net result is that there has been precious little overlapping of interests which might soften political differences. The Chinese are largely urban laborers or businessmen, Buddhist or Christian, and Chinese speaking, while Malays are for the most part rural agriculturalists who profess Islam and speak their own tongue. The history of relations between the two groups has been broadly characterized by a mixture of active and passive coexistence (mostly the latter), marred occasionally by communal violence—most notably immediately after World War II and again during September 1964 in Singapore.

What collaboration has occurred has been for the most part

10. Projected from the figures given in *Malaysia, Buku Rasmi Tahunan, Official Year Book, 1963*, p. 43. The figure for Malays includes a small number of aborigines as well, and the figure for Indians includes those of both Ceylonese and Pakistani origins.

among that thin upper stratum of Western-educated Chinese, Indians, and Malays, many of whom are civil servants. Working with each other at some short-term sacrifice and under great handicaps, they have managed thus far to keep the fabric of the nation tenuously whole. This stratum alone has the common experiences of English education and modern, urban occupations that permit some common outlook and interpretation of events. Politics outside this stratum would have to be treated almost as three different political systems, each corresponding to a racial group, conducting "international relations" with one another at arm's length within the Federation of Malaysia.

Even among this small elite to which Mr. Lim belongs, fear plays its role. If they collaborate because of common Western ideals and education, they collaborate as well because the Chinese fear submersion in a Greater Indonesia and the Malays fear a similar fate in a Greater China. Never absent from their political thoughts is the obvious fragility of their nation, the awareness that the future is uncertain and that all could be lost tomorrow or the day after, and a general apprehension that cool heads may not, in the end, prevail. For most of their adult lives, after all, they have lived in an atmosphere of political crisis: first the Japanese occupation, then the return of the British, then the communist threat during the Emergency, and most recently, *Konfrontasi* with Indonesia. Their fear has an ample basis in the realities of the Malaysian experience quite apart from any personal or collective pathology. These pressures can lead to an emphasis on conciliation and compromise in politics, as typified by Prime Minister Tengku Abdul Rahman, but they could also lead, at the personal level, to autism or to a messianic style. If Mr. Lim favors either of these alternatives, it is autism, but the purpose in introducing him was simply to illustrate a portion of the background against which any discussion of political ideology in Malaysia must take place.

Che' Ja'afar has served to illustrate an important effect of Malaya's colonial history upon current beliefs, while Mr. Lim's views underscore the ideological consequences of the nation's multiracial character. Malaya's particular colonial experience tends to make politics milder and less explosive, while communal feelings have the opposite effect. These factors do not, however, by any means cancel each other out, for each is relevant to a different area of experience and beliefs. The reason for introducing them so soon is that, although not entirely unique, they seem to be in some respects peculiar to Malaysia and therefore important. Although this study is largely concerned with finding patterns of belief that are common to recently independent nations and must therefore eschew many of the unique qualities of Malaysia that would merit study elsewhere, these two eccentricities are of such prominence in the landscape that the picture would be woefully incomplete without them.

2

An Orientation and a Method

THE WESTERNIZING ELITE

The purpose of this study is to examine the ideology of a Westernizing elite group of civil servants. If one were to ask Mr. Lim and Che' Ja'afar if they were part of a "Westernizing elite," they would probably be discomfited and shyly decline the honor. Nonetheless, they have a consciousness of this role that becomes apparent when they speak of the responsibilities of civil servants and the future of democracy in their nation. Both realize that a great deal of Malaysia's future depends on them and others like them. They believe that as more and more Malaysians become like themselves—educated, civic-minded—the better off their country will be.

Looking at the newly independent nations ten or even five years ago, one's impression of the process of change might well have coincided with that of Mr. Lim and Che' Ja'afar. The new states were being governed, as they had been governed under colonialism, by an alien elite—alien by virtue of education and acquired Western beliefs and ideals. By an irony of history their very anticolonialism and, often, anti-Western orientation, had its roots in the West. The bankruptcy of colonialism was shown not by its failure to satisfy traditional cultural values but rather by its hypocrisy when measured against Western ideals. That the new elites were "indigenous-aliens" who enjoyed legitimacy in a nationalist world should not obscure the fundamental fact that a great gap separated them from the masses whom they ruled—a gap produced by Western education and values.

The cultural process involved in the immediate postcolonial period was not far removed from the colonial process. Quasi-Western values were now diffused directly from the capital city of the ex-colony rather than from the metropolitan capital as before. In a sense, the source of imposed cultural change had shifted, but the direction of the change remained the same. The basic problem of the new situation was whether the "indigenous-alien" elite could succeed in changing the values of enough of the important sectors of their populations so that the process could continue. If the new elite failed to retain its legitimacy, if the masses became mobilized before they became sufficiently acculturated or "domesticated," then the Westernized elite would be replaced by a more truly indigenous group whose significantly different vision of the future would presumably change the process altogether. The contest was thus between two social processes—acculturation of the masses by Westernized leaders, and the mobilization of these masses as a political force.

Malaysia is still the scene of this contest, the outcome of which is far from decided. It is therefore important to ask, what are the values that the elite hopes to diffuse? Are they Western? If so, in what ways and with what selective emphasis? If these values are not entirely Western, then what other values and beliefs does this new elite represent? The outcome of the contest depends, for the elite, upon its numerical strength, the power it exercises, and, most fundamentally, on the values and beliefs it stands for—that is, its ideology.

If the contest in Malaysia is still being joined, it has proceeded far enough in many other nations to allow a preliminary assessment of the strength of the contestants. Nigeria and Algeria, to mention only two, are nations that have seen their initial political elite cast rudely aside in favor of new rulers who, notwithstanding the fact that they are sometimes less anti-West in their policy orientation, represent more truly indigenous values.[1] It may well be that the

1. Occasionally this metamorphosis can occur as a result of a change in the style of an elite rather than as a replacement of one elite by another. Nkrumah in Ghana and Sukarno in Indonesia, notwithstanding their unique qualities, became "symbol manipulators" who drew increasingly upon the indigenous culture for their raw material. While both were more consciously "ideologizing" than the new elites of Nigeria or Algeria, the decline of Western styles and values (making no value judgments) is evident in all four nations. The term "symbol manipulators" comes from Herbert Feith's impressive study, *The Decline of Constitutional Democracy in Indonesia* (Ithaca, Cornell University Press, 1962).

Westernized postcolonial political elites have already been given their brief, historical opportunity and have failed, although there is some indication that this judgment is premature.[2] One fact, however, is clear: the eclipse of the Westernized postcolonial elite seems to be a general phenomenon in Africa and Asia, whether it represents a temporary or a permanent decline.

It may seem that the decline of this elite group considerably dilutes the significance of the present study. But the decline is, in a sense, more apparent than real, because for the most part, it entails the eclipse of the political and not the bureaucratic elite.[3] In fact, the new, more indigenous leaders have an even greater need for the experience and skills of civil servants than their more Westernized predecessors, who often shared a common background and training with these civil servants. The more indigenous elites in these nations often preside over roughly the same development programs as their predecessors, even though the atmosphere for planning and executing such programs may have drastically changed.

It is not really so amazing that the inertia created by bureaucratic plans and programs can often survive changes in political leadership; the West itself is no stranger to this phenomenon. But I would suggest that it is more pronounced in new nations, where the bureaucracy has generally broader responsibilities than in the West, and where new political elites are likely to have vaguer policies and less experience in translating their diffuse notions into concrete programs. The civil service remains, often by default, the major center from which plans for a new society emanate and by which they will be executed. Given this continuing central role for the bureaucracy, the ideology of civil servants remains of crucial importance for the future of the postcolonial

2. The election victory of D. Senanaike over Mrs. Bandaranaike in Ceylon signaled the return to power of the more Westernized group of professional men and civil servants that had steadily lost ground under the regimes of Mr. and Mrs. Bandaranaike. This, I believe, was the first reversal of the trend I have described, although Indonesia's post-Sukarno military rulers may qualify as well.

3. For a more detailed argument along these lines, see William J. Foltz, "Building the Newest Nations: Short-Run Strategies and Long-Run Problems," in Karl W. Deutsch and William J. Foltz, eds., *Nation-Building* (New York, Atherton Press, 1963), pp. 117–31.

world regardless of political changes. The long-term chances for the creation of an open, participant society and for economic development depend, in large measure, on the beliefs and ideals they represent.

A study of the ideology of civil servants is important in still another sense. I remarked above about the common background and training shared by members of the initial postcolonial political elite and the higher civil servants. The similarity of these two groups was especially striking in such nations as India, Ceylon, Nigeria and Senegal, while not at all relevant in countries like Algeria, where a long, violent struggle for independence precluded its development. Nonetheless, the experience of the former nations parallels that of the bulk of the postcolonial world. Using this similarity in outlook as a tool, it may be possible to find in the beliefs of civil servants some of the reasons why the Westernized political elite seems to have fared badly. Although it is not a primary purpose of this study to use the ideology of bureaucrats as a Trojan horse to evaluate the ideology of political elites, a knowledge of civil servants may help to understand why politicians, of similar training, experience and outlook, failed to establish their own legitimacy and to enlist wide popular support for their plans. The key to the failure of these politicians may lie in the common ideology they shared with higher civil servants.

It should be quite clear now that this study of ideology among civil servants in Malaysia is undertaken less for what it can tell about the uniqueness of the Malaysian experience than for its value in clarifying the role of ideology in postcolonial settings. If I sometimes fail to do justice to Malaysia's peculiarities, it is not because I am unaware of them, but rather because the concern here is a broader one. I feel that there is enough similarity between the colonial and postcolonial experience of most new nations to allow some modest generalizations about the ideology of elites.

THE SAMPLE

Obviously, in order to talk about the ideology of civil servants, it is necessary to talk *to* some civil servants. Using a random table

of numbers, I selected the men to be intensively interviewed from
the 1964 Federal Establishment List (Senarai Pegawai-Pegawai
Persekutuan)—a roll of senior bureaucratic posts and their present
occupants categorized by ministry and department.[4] The term
"senior bureaucracy" requires some explanation. Bureaucratic
posts in Malaysia are divided hierarchically into four divisions,
with Division I posts the highest category and Division IV the
lowest. The Federal Establishment List includes all of Division I
and some Division II posts. The list itself approaches the status of
the Bible or Koran for civil servants, whose copies, studied rever-
entially, are filled to the margins with notations of promotions
and retirements that might affect their own anxious progress up
the bureaucratic ladder. Altogether some three thousand Division
I posts are listed,[5] and from among the incumbents of these posts,
seventeen were selected for intensive interviews by the random
process described.

Several initial exclusions from the Establishment List were necessary.[6] First, with regard to monthly salary, those earning less
than seven hundred Malaysian dollars per month (U.S.$233)
were excluded, as were those earning in excess of M$1400 (U.S.-
$466). The reason for not interviewing those earning less than
M$700 was that they constitute the lowest ranks of Division I, and
I wished to draw the sample from a higher elite. Excluding those
above M$1400 was regrettable, since it omitted la crème de la
crème, but it was felt that this small group of civil servants held
such high and heavy responsibilities that they would be both less
willing to talk frankly and less able to spare the twelve hours or
so needed for the interviews. Numerically, this group is quite
minute, since in most ministries only the permanent secretary and

4. Significant exceptions to this method of listing are the Malayan Civil Service
(MCS), an elite corps restricted mostly to the Malay community by law, whose members can be posted to any ministry; the Malay Administrative Service (MAS), a
"junior" MCS restricted exclusively to Malays; and the Executive Service, not restricted to any community, whose members can be similarly posted anywhere.

5. Projection from figures in Robert O. Tilman's study of the Malayanization of
the civil service in Malaya, *Bureaucratic Transition in Malaya* (Durham, North
Carolina, Duke University Press, 1964), p. 70.

6. The List itself excludes Division I civil servants who are members of a *state*
civil service, e.g. Johore Civil Service or Kedah Civil Service, rather than of the
federal civil service.

two or three others have such exalted status.[7] Furthermore, among those receiving more than M$1400 per month, there are still many expatriates whom I obviously did not wish to interview.

As I was primarily interested in civil servants as a sector of the ruling elite, I omitted from the sample the professional and technical degree holders such as teachers in the Education Service, doctors in the Medical Service, engineers in the Public Works Department, and so on. This limitation of the universe from which the sample was drawn increased the chance for Malays to be chosen and decreased the chance for Chinese and Indians, who are more likely to be found in the professional and technical branches of the civil establishment. The effort to select bureaucrats with broad responsibilities thus eliminated a good many more non-Malays than would be the case if the sample were drawn from among all Division I posts. More obvious reasons dictated the omission from the sample of not only a considerable number of expatriates (mostly British) still serving Malaysia but also the few women holding responsible posts.

The kind of research this study represents is a novelty in most young nations and is apt to arouse some initial suspicion. In order to minimize this anxiety at the outset, I reluctantly excluded civil servants in the following ministries with heavy internal security responsibilities: Home Affairs, External Affairs, Defense, and the Police Service. Together with the omission of holders of professional and technical degrees, these exclusions represent the largest number dropped from the sample. While it is a serious limitation of the research, this decision contributed to the ease with which the interviews could be arranged and conducted.

Finally, purely tactical considerations required that only civil servants posted within a twenty-five-mile radius of Kuala Lumpur be interviewed. This meant that the sample was skewed toward those holding more responsible posts in the federal capital as opposed to the district officers, whose responsibilities are broad but are cast within the directives issuing from Kuala Lumpur. The men in the federal capital are more likely to hold policy posts,

7. This is true of the 1964 Staff List which was used in this study, but the 1965 Staff List has more posts above M$1400 due to a general augmentation in salaries and the addition of some posts.

while those serving "out station" are apt to have "line" responsibilities. While the effect of this selection method was to exclude, with one exception, those serving as district officers, over half the Malays in the sample had, at one time, been posted as district officers or assistant district officers. Thus there is a good representation of past experience in district work, although only one civil servant actually held such a post at the time of interview.

To summarize, the group from which the sample was selected included Division I male, non-European, nonprofessional civil servants in the Federal Civil Service serving in or near Kuala Lumpur in ministries not responsible for defense, public order, or foreign relations. If all the exclusions are totalled, the universe from which the sample was drawn totaled roughly five hundred individuals.

Below is a brief description of each of the civil servants actually interviewed. All of these men in the course of our long talks confided in me, and in return I guaranteed their anonymity by changing names and posts. Since Malaysia is a small country and Kuala Lumpur a small administrative capital where any high civil servant is very likely to know many other administrators personally, the need for anonymity is all the more apparent. I have tried to be vague about income and place names where they might betray identities, but in all other respects the information and the quotations used throughout the text are accurate. Each of the men whose conversations form the basic evidence for this study are introduced below by the new identities they will assume throughout.

> *Md. Amin bin Yassin:* a Malay approaching middle age, serving in the Postal Service; no post-secondary training.[8]

> *Abdul Karim b. Yussof:* a young Malay in the Malayan Civil Service

8. The term "no post-secondary training" means that the respondent has passed his Senior Cambridge Certificate, High School Certificate, or equivalent examination at the conclusion of his secondary studies. A number of those who passed this stage could have entered a university or other post-secondary institution but elected not to. The academic achievement represented by these examinations is difficult to assess, but among the older respondents the more restricted educational opportunities available made the possession of such a certificate a mark of greater distinction than it represents today. In contrast to times past, the holder of one of these certificates today can no longer count on receiving an exalted post in the bureaucray.

(MCS)[9] now posted to the Department of Social Welfare; no post-secondary training.

Nordin b. Abdullah: a Malay approaching retirement age, serving with the Inland Revenue Department; no post-secondary training.

Hussain b. Jamil: a young Malay in the MCS now posted to the Immigration Department; no post-secondary training.

Ismail b. Ya'acob: a young Malay in the MCS serving with the Federal Establishment Office;[10] university degree.

Zaharuddin b. Md. Nasir: a young Malay in the MCS now posted to the Ministry of Labour; university degree.

Zulkifli b. Ahmad: an elderly Malay nearing retirement in the Postal Service; no post-secondary training.

Abu Bakar b. Md. Said: a Malay near middle age in the MCS and working in the Telecommunications Service; university degree.

Ja'afar b. Musa: a middle-aged Malay serving in the Ministry of Health; post-secondary training abroad.[11]

Mustapha b. Ridzwan: a middle-aged Malay holding a high post in the Ministry of Health; post-secondary training.

B. Sundram: a Tamil approaching retirement employed in the Customs Department; post-secondary training.

R. Jeganathan: a Tamil nearing retirement and posted to the Telecommunications Service; no post-secondary training.

S. Kamalam: a middle-aged Tamil with the Education Service; no post-secondary training.

V. Mahalingam: a Tamil approaching middle age posted to the Ministry of Information; university degree.

Khoo Swee Fah: a Chinese nearing middle age serving in the Audit Department; university degree.

Tay Kuan Teck: a Chinese also nearing middle age who serves in the Education Service; post-secondary training abroad.

Lim Fong Soon: a Chinese close to retirement age posted to Malaysian Railways; no post-secondary training.

9. Cf. p. 20, n. 4.

10. This office might be called "the administration of the administration." It deals with pay scales, General Orders, the posting of administrative generalists, and so forth.

11. "Post-secondary training," as opposed to university degree, indicates special training lasting at least one year for which a certificate was awarded, or one year or more at a university without winning the degree.

TABLE 1: Distribution of Sample
By Communal Origin[12]

Community	Number of Respondents
Malays	10
Tamils	4
Chinese	3

By Age

Age	Number of Respondents
20–30	3
31–40	6
41–50	3
51–60	5

By Educational Level

Education	Number of Respondents
Post-Secondary	9
No Post-Secondary	8

The age and education figures are proportionately similar to the universe from which the sample was drawn, and as usual, those with more education are likely to be younger. Distribution by community is skewed slightly toward Malays, with the Chinese somewhat underrepresented, while among the various Indian communities only the Tamils (the largest group) are present in the sample. Finally, the income distribution among the respondents (ten respondents with an income of between M$700–900 per month and seven between M$900–1400) reflects the distribution in that portion of Division I from which they were selected. With the exceptions just noted, the racial, educational, and age distribution approaches what might have been obtained had the sample been purposely weighed to reflect the distribution of these characteristics in the general population being studied.

Two men originally selected declined to be interviewed, requiring the selection of two more to replace them. The reasons for the refusals became apparent not long afterward, as one left the civil service to join a large commercial firm, while the other was publicly embarrassed by having to declare bankruptcy after being swindled. For obvious reasons, both would have been inter-

12. The multiracial character of the sample provides some unique advantages in interpretation over a sample containing only one ethnic group. These advantages will be treated later in this chaper.

esting subjects. Nevertheless, the loss of two from a sample of seventeen cannot be regarded as a severe limitation. By coincidence, the name of a civil servant who had helped me arrange pilot interviews was drawn in the sample. His prior knowledge of the interview material was sufficient to preclude much spontaneity in the interview situation, so another name was selected as a substitute. Aside from these three special problems, the remainder of the sample agreed to be interviewed.

THE INTERVIEWS

Respondents were first telephoned at their offices by an assistant secretary of the Federal Establishment Office who assisted me. He explained that he was calling in his personal capacity on behalf of a research student and that their participation in the study would be entirely voluntary and unofficial. If they wanted to hear more, and they all did, I then met them individually and explained that I would like to talk with them about their backgrounds and their philosophies of life as a part of my research in developing nations. At this time I told them that their names had come up "by chance" and guaranteed their anonymity—in writing if they requested it.[13] We then arranged the first of many long conversations and thereafter met every week or two until the material in the interview guide had been covered. The interviews often extended over a four-to-five-month period.

The place of the interviews varied according to the preference of whoever was being interviewed. Some were held at my home, some at the subject's house, and still others at government offices on a slow morning or afternoon. For a few respondents the location of our talks mattered; who came to whom said something about our relative status and many, for this reason, preferred that I come to their homes or offices. The uniformity of venue sacrificed as a result was more than offset by having the subject feel that he was, in a sense, in control and could choose a place and time that suited him.

The total length of the interviews with each subject ranged from eight to sixteen hours, averaging approximately eleven hours. A single interview might last an hour or two until weariness set in, and we would then arrange to meet another day. Each session

13. Only one respondent asked for such a letter.

might have been longer but for the fact that I could not use a tape recorder. My original intention was to record each interview, but I quickly discovered, before the first interview, that the mere mention of a tape recorder sends civil servants fleeing. Instead, I took notes and taped them immediately afterwards. With the experience of two full-scale pilot interviews held at the Staff Training Centre, I felt I was able to capture almost all the interview material intact. The transcripts thus produced form the central core of this study.

The content of the interviews was as broad as I could possibly make it. Roughly one third of the interview concerned the civil servant's experience, his opinions of his job, his opinions of other civil servants and of the civil service in general, plus a number of hypothetical decisions which he was asked to discuss.[14] Another third dealt with life history, family, childhood and school experiences, his estimate of his own personality, his attitudes toward friends and money, and his personal values and religious views.[15] The remaining third of the interview guide, which often consumed well over one third of our discussions, was devoted to the respondent's attitudes toward political leaders in general and toward social classes, his conception of the ideal society, his notions of democracy, equality, freedom, and the causes of war and poverty, his political interests and activities, and so on. A more complete account of the interview guide can be found in Appendix A.

The instrument for our conversations was the interview guide I have described. Virtually all the questions were open-ended, permitting a variety of responses from the subject. Quite frequently I departed from the guide in order to probe clichés or to let the respondent continue talking about topics that interested him. The advantages of an interview technique of this sort are multiple: it allows a richer expression of opinion or experience; it permits an examination of attitudes and beliefs in the context of personal experience and personality needs; and it provides a more relaxed, open atmosphere for the interview.

14. A good many of these questions were taken or adapted from the interview schedule used in Morroe Berger, *Bureaucracy and Society in Modern Egypt* (Princeton, Princeton University Press, 1957).

15. Most of this and the following section of the interview guide was patterned after the schedule used by Robert E. Lane in his *Political Ideology* (Glencoe, The Free Press, 1962), pp. 481–93.

I should emphasize here that the interviews differed fundamentally from the classic psychoanalytic situation and more closely approximated a focused interview. While I expressed no opinions of my own, I did agree with the respondents frequently and tried, as much as feasible, to be supportive of their notions and values rather than adopting a neutral stance. The disadvantages of participation and overencouragement inherent in this strategy were outweighed by the confidence subjects felt in expressing beliefs in traditional superstitions and in other non-Western values. Such beliefs are generally not raised with Westerners, since they are expected to be either faintly mocking or openly contemptuous. As the question of rapport is crucial in interviews with someone from another culture, I felt this departure from neutrality a necessary one.

ADDITIONAL SUPPORTING EVIDENCE

After we had finished the last of our conversations, I asked each subject to complete a number of psychological forms. These forms were intended to measure authoritarianism, social trust, dominance, social and neurotic anxiety, and anomie.[16] Initially, I had hoped that the use of these scales, employed also in Robert E. Lane's *Political Ideology*, would afford an interesting comparison between American and Malaysian subjects. But all of these measures were developed in the United States, and their validity in the Malaysian context is open to very serious question. The results from these scales are therefore used sparingly and only when they seem to contribute significantly to the analysis.

As the interviews progressed, I detected a number of belief patterns that seemed important enough to merit testing in a separate, larger group of civil servants in order to confirm their existence and significance. Some of the measures that resulted I invented in the field, some were borrowed from the field work of anthropologists, and still others were drawn from the more familiar regions of political science. Each of these scales was administered to roughly one hundred civil servants enrolled in training courses run by the various ministries in Kuala Lumpur. The results, I believe, offer important support for some of the conclusions of

16. All measures were selected from among the various scales employed by Lane, pp. 494–95.

this study as well as representing independent confirmation of the patterns found in the interview transcripts. In view of the significance of these measures for the analysis, they are reproduced, together with a description of their origins and administration, in Appendix B.

The sources of evidence for an analysis of the ideology of the bureaucratic elite in Malaysia are, then, threefold. The basic evidence is, of course, the transcripts of the extended interviews with a random sample of higher civil servants. But to this evidence are added the psychological measures administered to this sample and the scales developed to test preliminary conclusions on a broader sample of civil servants.

SOME LIMITATIONS

The reader should be under no illusions about the nature of the evidence presented here or about the very real limitations inherent in this form of analysis. To minimize such misunderstandings a few cautionary notes are in order. The decision to focus largely on the homogeneity of political beliefs in the sample represents a choice of some strategic significance. An analysis of variation comparing, for example, the political beliefs of the Chinese in the sample to those of the Malays might well have led to many rich generalizations linking culture to ideology. Valuable information of this nature is, alas, lost in the shuffle when attention is directed to homogeneity rather than to variety. While one approach does not necessarily exclude the other, limitations of time and space in this case make an attack on two fronts impractical. Aside from a discussion of the educational bases of variance in political beliefs in Chapter 9, differences within the sample are strikingly neglected.

Another problem concerns the degree of confidence with which one can generalize from data gathered initially from seventeen civil servants in a single developing nation.[17] Obviously, a rigorous analysis would only permit generalizing to the group of approxi-

17. The size of the sample is small, of course, because of the intensive nature of the interviews. Originally, I intended to interview a minimum of fifteen or a maximum of twenty civil servants. The number seventeen has no magical qualities but merely represents the point at which the interviewer elected to choose no further respondents.

mately five hundred from which the sample was selected. Some attempt is made to test for beliefs found among sample members in the larger bureaucratic community and even in other occupational groups within Malaysia. This procedure creates a bridge allowing statements about Malaysian elites as a whole, but the bridge is admittedly hastily built and provides only tenuous passage to higher ground.

When I speak of elites in other developing nations on the basis of the Malaysian case, I often skip quite shamelessly from one bank to the other, taking advantage of the few empirical stones available when a single leap would seem utterly reckless. In cases where research elsewhere indicates that belief patterns found in Malaysia might be typical of less developed areas, I have proceeded with some assurance, while in other cases, the relative absence of comparable data makes any generalization entirely speculative. Clearly, a decisive confirmation of whether or not elites in new nations hold the beliefs I have attributed to them will depend upon more rigorous comparative efforts than the circumstantial evidence presented here.

As the analysis suggests that certain belief patterns are typical of new nations and distinguishes these states from the wealthy, industrialized nations, there is an analysis of variation at this level Quite often this is supported by comparable data gathered chiefly, but not entirely, in the United States. Even when the data is comparable, however, I am generally contrasting only two nations, whereas a thorough test of these propositions would require comparative studies of many more countries. Social scientists more given to caution and rigor will undoubtedly shudder occasionally at what amounts to speculation based on data of rather slender proportions. My only excuse for this departure from scientific form is simply that, for most non-Western areas, insistence on strict standards of proof means either limiting comparative research to the trivial or abandoning the enterprise altogether.

One last caveat is necessary. A persistent problem in the study of political attitudes and ideology is the relationship between belief and behavior. A belief may be considered a propensity to act in a certain way, but whether or not that propensity is realized depends upon a host of factors, including the emotional loading of the belief, the structure of the environment, social pressures, personal

capacities, and so on. In other words, behavior cannot be successfully predicted from beliefs alone. The behavior of businessmen
might be taken as a case in point here. If it is found that most
managers of commercial concerns in a particular nation are highly
misanthropic, believing that others cannot be trusted when personal gain is involved, it does not immediately follow that joint
ventures among them are doomed to failure. A legal contract enforced by the state may ensure cooperation even in such a hostile
atmosphere, or, as in some developing nations, the fact that
business partners share membership in the same clan or tribal
association may create social sanctions of sufficient strength to
overcome mutual distrust.

For the most part, this study is concerned more with the origin
and maintenance of belief sysems—of ideology—than with behavior. I suggest that certain general beliefs are typical of developing areas and thus constitute a propensity to act in definite ways.
In some areas (e.g. Burma and southern Italy) this propensity
seems realized, and action appears to follow beliefs, but in other
areas (e.g. Malaysia) such continuity seems occasionally absent. In
the latter case one must turn to the historical, environmental, and
structural factors that mediate between beliefs and behavior in
order to explain the discontinuity. A limited analysis of this sort
is attempted for Malaysia at the very end of the study. It must be
realized, however, that even if certain beliefs are shared by elites
in developing nations, they can constitute only a tendency toward
certain forms of behavior.[18] A determination of what behavior
actually occurs depends on a detailed study of intervening variables which this research cannot supply in any systematic fashion.

18. For an excellent survey of the problems of relating beliefs or psychological
predispositions to political behavior, see Fred I. Greenstein, "Personality and Politics: Problems of Evidence, Inference, Conceptualization," *American Behavioral Scientist, 11* (Nov.–Dec. 1967), 38–53.

3

Exploring Personal Ideology in New Nations

ASPECTS OF IDEOLOGY

Ideology as personalized. The choice of the term "ideology" may be an unfortunate one, for the word has meant many things to many people. To confuse matters still more, the way in which I employ the term does not conform to its popular usage. The best known "ideologies" are socialism and communism, each of which refers to a highly organized system of beliefs and values about society as it is and as it should be. Ideology in this sense is apart from individuals and has an independent existence regardless of whether it is accepted in whole or in part by any individual.

The term "personal ideology" is used here because I do not wish to set ideology apart from individuals. Broadly defined, a personal ideology is "an organization of opinions, attitudes and values—a way of thinking about man and society" [1] which is unique to an individual. The relationship between a formal ideology like socialism or communism and a personal ideology is as varied as the diversity of human experience and personality can make it. To say, for example, that socialism is the personal ideology of an individual would be a woefully incomplete statement. One would, at a minimum, have to go farther and discover what aspects of socialism he emphasizes, what personal needs of his are fulfilled by a belief in socialism, and so on. His belief in socialism came about as a result of his unique experiences and personality needs, and each must be seen as part of a whole when one speaks of personal ideology.

It is entirely possible for a personal ideology not to be influenced by any of the available formal ideologies, although life as it is now lived outside purely folk societies makes this state of affairs increasingly rare. Still, I suspect that it is easy to over-

1. T. W. Adorno et al., *The Authoritarian Personality* (New York, Harper Brothers, 1950), p. 2.

emphasize the influence of formal ideology on personal beliefs and neglect the mundane but important impact of personal relations, occupation, and status. Lane has shown that a man's experiences at work and in social life can, because they are generalized, have crucial consequences for his broad economic and political views.[2] A man helps build his personal identity with his personal ideology—it must orient him in space and time; it must hold up certain ends and give him a basis for choosing among means; and it must tell him something about his society and his place in it. In fact, the process of constructing an ideology is, for the individual, virtually the same as constructing a personal identity. If a formal ideology does find a niche in a man's personal ideology, there can be no doubt that it becomes highly personalized in the process.

Ideology as patterned. Not only is an individual's ideology highly personalized, but it is also coherent or patterned at some level. Just as the psychoanalyst can find underlying, latent patterns in the manifest statements of his patients, so too can one find broad themes in a personal ideology that penetrate a great variety of seemingly disparate beliefs. Such underlying patterns may be stylistic in nature. Milton Rokeach, for example, has developed quite convincing measures of dogmatism as a "style," independent of the content of beliefs.[3] Thus, if a person who believes in communism and one who believes in capitalism each strongly reject all differing views and those who hold them, they both are dogmatic with respect to style, even though the content of their beliefs places them at different poles on the subject of the state's role in economic affairs.

Underlying patterns may refer to content, too. The belief that human nature is selfish, for example, may influence attitudes toward leaders and followers alike and affect notions about cooperating with others to realize common goals. Inasmuch as these uniformities of style and content are rarely expressed explicitly but must be sought out as common themes in many disparate beliefs, they are examples of what is called latent ideology. It is this latent ideology among an elite group in Malaysia that I hoped to seek out and describe.

2. Lane, *Political Ideology, passim.*
3. Milton Rokeach, *The Open and Closed Mind* (New York, Basic Books, 1960).

The degree of cohesion in a personal ideology varies greatly from individual to individual and depends to a large extent on whether one set of beliefs is "in touch" with others in the conscious mind. In order to maintain a relatively stable identity, the mind tends to eliminate some of the static caused by dissonant beliefs and to restore some coherence between them by making suitable alterations, by repression, and by other means.[4] How effective the reduction of dissonance is depends not only on the mechanisms available for its reduction and their efficiency, but also on the awareness of dissonance in the first place. Absolute logical coherence of views is never reached, but on the other hand, some reduction of dissonant beliefs is almost always achieved. Were it not for dissonance reduction, it would be more difficult to talk of the underlying themes in a person's ideology.

Some coherence is also created between the cognitive and the emotive or evaluative aspects of a personal ideology. The cognitive portion of an ideology is a notion of what reality looks like —the properties of objects and of people—while the evaluative aspect casts blame and praise, tells what is good and what is bad, and provides sentiment and passion. To distinguish between the cognitive and emotive aspects of a personal ideology is, of course, a purely analytical exercise, as the distinction is seldom if ever made by its possessor. The two are mutually interdependent because a personal ideology tends to achieve and maintain some degree of cohesion, as cognitive dissonance theory has shown. A cognitive belief that other people are helpful and friendly will, for instance, usually be found together with the evaluative belief that one should cooperate and love one's fellowman. Sorensen has expressed the connection between the cognitive and evaluative aspects of a person's ideology in this way: "A stable positive affect toward a certain object will be accompanied by beliefs or knowledge about its potentialities for being an instrument of an end in the realization of desired goals."[5] To put Sorensen's statement in more concrete form, positive affect toward other

4. For a discussion of the theory of cognitive dissonance and the mechanisms for reducing dissonance, see L. Festinger, *A Theory of Cognitive Dissonance* (Stanford, Stanford University Press, 1957), and Jack W. Brehm and Arthur R. Cohen, *Explorations in Cognitive Dissonance* (New York, Wiley, 1962).

5. Alma Don Sorensen, "Toward a Theory of Ideology in Political Life" (unpublished Ph.D. dissertation, University of Illinois, 1965), p. 55.

people, often called "faith-in-people," will generally be accompanied by a belief that they will actually help one achieve desired goals. The fact that a measure of coherence is achieved between the cognitive and evaluative elements of a person's ideology is important for this analysis, particularly because it sheds light on our next concern, the relationship of political ideology to a total belief system.

Ideology as politicized. A person's political ideology can be seen as a more specific sub-ideology together with his religious ideology, economic ideology, ideology of social relations, and so on. His political ideology is simply that system of beliefs, ideas, values, and feelings that constitutes his orientation toward the world of politics. The relationships among different sub-ideologies vary greatly from person to person and often within the same person over a period of time. For a religious zealot, religious ideology may virtually crowd out political ideology, as he casts political conflicts solely in terms of the struggle of the faithful against the heathen. It is not that his political ideology does not exist, far from it, but rather that for him political and religious life are identical. For another, more secular individual, political and religious ideology may maintain more nearly separate existences, although a complete compartmentalization of spheres of belief would probably never be found.

The strength of relationship between sub-ideologies such as the religious and the political may vary greatly from individual to individual, but the relationship between a person's broad ideology and his more specific political ideology is almost invariably strong. An individual's orientation toward political leaders is apt to form a part of his attitude toward authority figures in general; his feelings about political conflict are, in the same fashion, likely to come under the influence of his reaction to disputes and conflict at the personal level, and so forth. More specifically, in developing nations it might be expected that the prevalent view among traditional people that floods, disease, and other natural disasters cannot be avoided would in turn have some impact on feelings of political efficacy and the degree to which a society can affect its own destiny. This relationship between a person's broad, latent ideology and his specifically political beliefs and values is a crucial one. It clearly indicates that we must often look behind the political to get at the underlying themes that will help to weave the broad fabric of which the political forms but a portion.

Ideology as shared. The discussion, to this point, has been focused on ideology at the personal level. In all societies some elements in a personal ideology will be shared with others in the same culture. If this were not the case, if each individual's ideology were totally unique, this study could reveal nothing about the ideology of elites in new nations and would be reduced to a description of individual idiosyncrasies. What a group or society shares in its general beliefs, values, and practices is a part of that society's or group's culture. What a group shares in its political orientation, values, and symbols is a part of that group's political culture. In fact, it would not be inaccurate to say that the political culture of a group is simply the distribution of individual political ideologies for that group's population.[6]

The basis for shared ideology in new nations. Inasmuch as we focus on the aspects of personal ideology that seem to be shared by some or all of the members of the sample, we are dealing with a segment of political culture. We are concerned with the political culture of an elite—not with any individual exotica but rather with what they share in their personal political ideologies. That this elite will have some elements of political ideology in common is virutally certain, but the extent will depend directly on the degree to which its members share an existential base that provides for some common experiences, whether they look at the world with similar cultural premises, and whether they have other corresponding personal qualities.[7] As interest is concentrated on what the Malaysian sample can reveal about the ideology of elites in new nations, it is natural to emphasize those elements of the existential base and experiences that Malaysia shares with most new nations, rather than those that distinguish Malaysia from other new states.

What do new nations share in terms of an existential base and

6. "Political culture" is a still broader term than "shared political ideology," since the former would include material artifacts relevant to politics as well as practices and behavior per se. The concept of shared political ideology does not contain artifacts and practices per se but it *does* include them as objects of cognition and affect in the minds of members of the society.

7. These terms are borrowed from Lane's "paradigm of ideological change" in *Political Ideology*, pp. 415–16.

common experiences? In a preliminary way they can be said to share

1. Elements of a still traditional culture, however attenuated.
2. Relative poverty.
3. A past of alien rule by Western nations.
4. Rapid social change, at least at the elite level, in the recent past.

This study concentrates largely on these four bases of common experience and the similarities in personal political ideology for which they seem to account. The first two are precolonial in their origin, and the final two are direct and indirect products, respectively, of colonialism. While all four are fairly clear-cut, one might wonder whether "elements of a traditional culture" would constitute something new nations do *not* have in common rather than something shared. Without pausing now to discuss the problems involved here, I would suggest that traditional cultures have enough in common in a broad sense to speak of "traditionality" as something shared by new nations.

Furthermore, the nature of the present study contains a unique advantage in that we may in some respects control for the differences in traditional societies. The sample includes three culturally distinct groups—Chinese, Malays, and Tamils. If there are similar elements in their political ideologies, it follows that these arise either from shared cultural premises or from other common experiences, such as education or colonialism. But if these similarities seem to be of the sort that originate in early childhood, then they are most probably culturally determined. Thus if the Chinese, Malays, and Tamils in the sample share culturally determined elements in their ideologies, it is reasonable to say that the traditional cultures of the three societies appear to have some common traits. The tri-racial nature of the sample, then, allows for the discovery of cross-cultural similarities rather than requiring assumptions about their existence.

Malaysia is, in one sense, an amalgam of its Chinese, Indian, and Malay subcultures, and this fact affords many of the advantages of cross-national comparative research that embraces countries of diverse cultural patterns. Common elements in the ideology of members of all three groups are more likely to be found in other new nations than would common elements found in the ideology of a single cultural group. This study is, in some measure then, an examination of three cases rather than of a single case that would be more affected by unique cultural variables.

The four characteristics that all new nations share form the broad basis for whatever similarities in political ideology might be found among their elites. For this reason I stress these characteristics when dealing with Malaysian civil servants and attempt to show what they contribute to the shared ideology of a Malaysian elite and, by example, what they must also contribute to ideology among the elites of other new nations.

LEVELS OF IDEOLOGY IN NEW NATIONS

The Concept of Levels

A discussion of personal ideology must take care to distinguish what level of ideology is being treated. Obviously, a belief that the government should extend the fishing season is in a real sense a more peripheral or shallow belief than a conviction that all power holders are self-seekers. Some conception of level is thus a prerequisite for separating the relatively trivial from the more significant or deep. Milton Rokeach has developed a terminology for characterizing these levels of ideology.[8] He organizes beliefs along a "central—intermediate—peripheral dimension." In the central region are those "primitive beliefs about the nature of the physical world, the self, and generalized others." Two examples of central beliefs discussed later are whether human nature is basically good or bad and whether the environment is supportive or hostile.

Some central beliefs are strictly cognitive—for example, the belief that the sky is blue. As such, they are confirmed only by the observations and agreement of others. A fear of heights, on the other hand, is a belief that cannot be confirmed or denied by outside authority, since it refers to an inner state. Validation is a more complex problem for beliefs that fall between the two just mentioned. Is a belief that people are generally trustworthy as

8. Rokeach, pp. 39–51. Rokeach's typology is similar to the distinction between "dominant" and "variant" value orientations made by Florence Kluckhohn and Fred Strodtbeck in their *Variations in Value Orientations* (Evanston, Ill., Row, Peterson and Co., 1961), pp. 3–4.

testable as the blueness of the sky, or is it more like acrophobia? Actually, it is not entirely analogous to either because of the problem of false validation. Although trustworthiness in others refers to patterns of behavior that are observable, the quality being measured is so ambiguous that the data can often be distorted for a long period to serve personal needs. Those who have studied the psychology of racial prejudice are well acquainted with this problem of false validation when a conviction of the inferiority of another people is involved. Thus, some central beliefs are amenable to validation via the agreement of others and via external authority, while some remain intractable regardless of the evidence. But many more central beliefs, including those of chief concern here, are recalcitrant but not totally impervious to the accumulation of evidence that would contradict them.

The other two levels of a belief system are, according to Rokeach, the "intermediate" and the "peripheral." By intermediate beliefs he means all beliefs about the "nature of positive and negative authorities, personal or impersonal, to be relied upon for information and opinions which we cannot or will not gather and develop ourselves." [9] Reliance on such authority may be total or partial, but knowledge of these positive and negative authorities —the intermediate region of beliefs—will reveal much of the content of the peripheral region. What is left over after the central and intermediate beliefs is the peripheral region, which includes nonprimitive beliefs arising from positive and negative authorities.

The material used to analyze the latent ideology of Malaysian civil servants is composed largely of peripheral beliefs. Beliefs in the central and intermediate region of an ideology are seldom explicitly stated but rather must be inferred from the interview material. The feelings on the part of a civil servant that his father was overly strict, that his boss is "out to get him," and that political and religious leaders are rapacious or menacing are all peripheral beliefs. But taken together they may well indicate a central belief that other people, particularly authority figures, are threatening and exploitive. Inductive procedures of this sort are

9. Rokeach, pp. 42–44. Who can be relied upon for the "right" information and values and who can be expected to hold the "wrong" information and values form a crucial portion of any personal ideology.

the tools employed to reconstruct a person's central and intermediate beliefs.

Discontinuity of Ideology Among Postcolonial Elites

Working back inductively from peripheral beliefs to central and
intermediate beliefs also involves working back through the history
of an individual. The evidence is persuasive that the central strata
of beliefs are laid down at an earlier age than the intermediate,
and the intermediate strata earlier than most of the peripheral.
Many important central beliefs are learned during childhood, in
the primary socialization process within the family. Among these
central beliefs are many that may well have a marked influence
on specifically political beliefs: notions about how authority figures
behave, whether nature can be controlled, and whether others can
generally be trusted in time of need are examples of such central
beliefs.

Because central beliefs and values are learned early, they tend
to persist and to be resistant to change. Students of cultural change
are widely agreed, for example, that a society's early-socialized
values and beliefs are likely to endure long after less central notions have been transformed by contact with another culture.
After reviewing many studies that bear on this point, one anthropologist goes so far as to suggest the universality of this "early
learning hypothesis" to account for the tenacity of central beliefs
in every cultural context.[10] Leonard Doob, a psychologist interested in cultural change, also recognizes the relative persistence
of central beliefs that are learned early. Using a different formulation, he argues that those aspects of a traditional culture which
"serve continuing needs" are likely to be most resistant to change
and that "Traditional beliefs and values that have been learned at
an early age, other things being equal, are more likely to appear
to serve a continuing need than those learned later in life.[11]

The primary socialization of central beliefs is the key process

10. Edward M. Bruner, "Cultural Transmission and Cultural Change," South-
western Journal of Anthropology, 12 (1956), pp. 191–990, reprinted in Neil J. and
William T. Smelser, eds., Personality and Social Systems (New York, Wiley, 1963),
pp. 481–87.

11. Leonard W. Doob, Becoming More Civilized: A Psychological Exploration
(New Haven, Yale University Press, 1960), pp. 150–56.

for maintaining the identity of a culture over time. What Linton has called the "core culture" is transmitted from parents to their children as an integral part of growing up.[12] Successful socialization of this core culture permits the central beliefs and values of a society to persist more or less intact from generation to generation. In a relatively stable, isolated society the intermediate and peripheral beliefs added on layer by layer tend to be congruent with, and to amplify, the basic orientations transmitted by early socialization. To be sure, not even the most stable and isolated societies are without their own particular strains and inconsistencies, but they nevertheless maintain a high order of continuity.

Such continuity was characteristic of most underdeveloped areas before colonialism. With the advent of Western rule, however, it was broken, as colonized societies found themselves in an era of cultural change imposed from outside. The fact that the change originated from without provided the source of discontinuity, while the forceful, imposed nature of colonialism allowed for little of the selective adaptation that often characterizes trade contacts between cultures. These societies had been selecting beliefs and values from outside sources before colonialism, but the choice was usually their own; they could retain or discard what they pleased. Colonial rulers, on the other hand, introduced certain practices that they insisted be followed and exacted penalties for noncompliance. The imperial nations tried in a systematic way to transmit their own beliefs and values to sections of the indigenous population through education and also through the administrative machinery. Much the same could be said of any regime originating in alien conquest. But the Western colonizers were more thorough and systematic in their attempts to change people, while other conquerors were often willing to settle for outward deference and tribute.

Colonial rule created great discontinuities in ideology, especially among the local elite, who were educated and trained under it. Secondary socialization in the schools taught British, French, and Dutch beliefs and values inconsistent with many of the central beliefs of the local culture. The Western insistence on contract relationships and private ownership of land, for example, con-

12. The term comes from Ralph Linton, *The Study of Man* (New York, Appleton-Century-Crofts, 1936), p. 360.

flicted with more archaic networks of obligation and with traditional land tenure patterns. Labor became a commodity in a money market rather than the subject of traditional kin and community obligations. Court justice according to common law replaced what seemed to Westerners to be more diffuse and unjust methods of settling disputes.[13] In short, a whole host of new beliefs and values that did not flow from, and often contradicted, the central beliefs of the colonized people were propagated and enforced by alien rulers.

This gap between central and peripheral beliefs, between primary and secondary socialization, has created a great discontinuity in ideology, the effects of which are everywhere apparent in new nations. The dilemma a civil servant confronts in deciding whether to let his daughter make her own match or to select a suitable mate for her is a microcosm of this conflict. So too is the choice between spending the money he has saved on a feast for his friends and relatives or on his son's education. So is the choice of whether to wear Western or traditional dress at home. The choices to be made are between alternatives of behavior, but each alternative implies a different set of values, and taken together, they imply a way of life. Making a decision is not simple, it is a real dilemma simply because the civil servant simultaneously holds different values that would predispose him to each alternative. He can seldom appease both values at once, and therefore each choice he makes leaves another set of preferences unsatisfied.[14]

There is a discontinuity in specifically political ideology as well, and it is this discontinuity that is more relevant to our purpose. Early-socialized central beliefs, for example, imply a political system quite different from the existing national system that has been adapted from Western forms. While early training stresses obedience to authority and traditional bases of legitimacy, later school training is likely to emphasize active participation in politics and the doctrine of popular rule. Local political structures are, like the family, autocratic—or oligarchic at best—while the national

13. Even when such a process of change occurs indigenously and over an extended time, its consequences are dramatic and often tragic. For a striking account of the process in England, see Karl Polanyi, *The Great Transformation* (London, Farrar and Rhinehard, 1944).

14. I have dramatized the dilemma by dichotomizing the choices, while in real life many such choices are between many alternatives distributed along a continuum.

political system may be democratic and open. One style may be taught for participation as a citizen in the local community and another, different style for participation in the national political arena. The Westernized school system may emphasize the possibility of government contributing to social change and economic development, but at the same time, a central belief in the powerlessness of man before nature, in fatalism, may seriously undermine this orientation.

These are only a few examples of the discontinuity in political ideology that seems to be a general phenomenon among elites in new nations. Discontinuity in political ideology can be viewed as merely a single facet of the cultural dualism to be found in all new states as a result of the coexistence of Western values at the peripheral level, together with more traditional notions in the central region. This dualism more generally characterizes the elite than the masses, as it is particularly the elite that has had prolonged contact with Westernized values and institutions. The basis of the discontinuity the elite experiences resides in the conflict between the norms of dependence, nonparticipation, and compliance with traditional authority, which are internalized early, and the norms of independence, participation, and critical evaluation, to which they are exposed in school and in the modern sector. Often the clash is between one ideological style emphasizing "subject" values and another representing more of a "citizen" orientation.[15]

Two Consequences of Discontinuity in Political Ideology

Two consequences of this discontinuity in political ideology are of special interest for the present study. The first is that there is often a discontinuity between the content of a person's beliefs and the underlying style of his beliefs. For example, someone may simultaneously hold the view that a government must initiate change together with a firm conviction that social and economic conditions are essentially beyond the control of man. An individual may believe in the formation of groups for political ends, but his

15. Gabriel Almond and Sidney Verba stress correctly that the subject and citizen orientations (their terms) are not mutually exclusive—that Western democracies have not substituted the citizen orientation for the subject orientation but have added a citizen component to already developed subject orientation. *The Civic Culture* (Boston, Little, Brown & Co., 1965), pp. 20–26.

strong pessimism about the cooperativeness of human nature may largely preclude acting upon that belief. Or someone who has come to believe in the modern goals of one party may feel nevertheless that his obligations to kin and community constrain him to support another party irrespective of its program. In each case a belief or value learned presumably during secondary socialization is being undercut, or sabotaged, so to speak, by a more central belief internalized earlier. The discontinuity in political ideology permits central orientations that are often a part of the cultural tradition to seep through and affect the style and content of beliefs which are, on the surface, more Western.[16]

A second result of this discontinuity in political ideology relates closely to the point above but requires a distinction between the "range" of beliefs and their "weight." When peripheral beliefs are consonant with intermediate and central beliefs, they are likely to have considerable weight. But when there is discontinuity in political ideology of the kind just described, peripheral beliefs, while they may have the same range, are likely to have less weight. Erich Fromm illustrates exactly what this means:

> Ideas often are consciously accepted by certain groups, which, on account of the peculiarities of their social character, are not really touched by them; such ideas remain a stock of conscious convictions, but people fail to act according to them in a critical hour. An example of this is shown in the German labor movement at the time of the victory of Nazism. The vast majority of German workers before Hitler's coming into power voted for the Socialist or Communist Parties and believed in the ideas of those parties; that is, the *range* of these ideas among the working class was extremely wide. The

16. Almond and Verba might want to differ with me on this point, as they feel that secondary socialization, particularly education, is closer to politics and has much more influence on one's political beliefs than central, early learned beliefs. This is true for much of the manifest content of political beliefs, which is what Almond and Verba's study deals with. But when speaking of the latent content of beliefs and broad differences in style, the compartmentalization Almond and Verba note is more difficult to maintain. In fact, one can with some justice claim that the many efforts to define democracy in new ways in Africa and in Asia is an effort to bring peripheral values more closely into line with central orientations that are a part of the traditional culture—regardless of whether the new interpretations serve the special interests of reigning elites.

weight of these ideas, however, was in no proportion to their range.[17]

The broad ideas associated with Western liberal democracy may have great currency in the new nations but are likely to rest on shaky foundations; there is a facade of democratic beliefs that are often strongly held at the conscious level but are, at the same time, undermined in style and content by quite contrary central beliefs that are often "pre-political" in origin. Finding out how *deep* a belief goes is a hazardous enterprise, but I shall nonetheless attempt to say something not only about the depth of Western political beliefs among the sample examined, but also about other beliefs that tend to strengthen or weaken these Western notions.

ACCOUNTING FOR AN IDEOLOGY

Explaining the origins and maintenance of beliefs that are widespread in a culture is not an easy task and should perhaps be left to the anthropologists, who are better equipped for the endeavor. Ultimately, however, an explanation of the origin of a personal ideology must be related to personal experience within a cultural context. Failure to trace the genesis of an ideology along these lines results in a largely descriptive analysis that lacks any dynamic character. Some conception of how important beliefs are generated and maintained is a prerequisite to an understanding of the process of change in ideologies.

As the study of ideology in developing areas is in its infancy, there are few systematic attempts to account for what has been found and described. Two of the most prominent, however, deserve attention: Lucian Pye's *Politics, Personality, and Nation Building: Burma's Search for Identity*[18] and Edward Banfield's *The Moral Basis of a Backward Society*.[19] These two are not only more or less systematic, but they are also quite divergent in perspective and in the process of change that they imply. While they are not mutually exclusive, each approach has its unique advantages and disadvantages, and a close examination of each should

17. Erich Fromm, *Escape from Freedom* (New York, Rinehart, 1941), p. 280.

18. Lucian W. Pye, *Politics, Personality, and Nation Building: Burma's Search for Identity* (New Haven, Yale University Press, 1962).

19. Edward C. Banfield, *The Moral Basis of a Backward Society* (Glencoe, The Free Press, 1958).

help to set the problem in sharper focus. A comparison between the two approaches is all the more enlightening because both attempt to explain the same phenomenon, namely, why people are unable to join together effectively for common ends.

Pye's Approach: Discontinuity, Identity Diffusion, and Social Mobility

Pye sees "the problem of political development and modernization as essentially the creation of adaptive and purposeful organizations." [20] According to him, Burma has largely failed to create such organizations, and he sets out to discover why. For the most part, Pye seeks his explanation in the theory of discontinuity, which has been sketched in broad terms above. Politicians and administrators in Burma, he shows, have been socialized at an early age to traditional beliefs and norms and then later exposed to Western beliefs and standards. The result of this discontinuity in socialization is that no clear sense of identity develops among these elites and that "there will be related uncertainty in the political culture of the people." [21] A sense of ambiguity about the colonizers, about traditional culture, and about the West characterizes Pye's subjects, as does the feeling that they may have failed when measured against the Western standards they have partially incorporated. Their political ideology, according to Pye, is a product of their identity crisis and is therefore meant to solve problems of personal identity rather than to provide a path toward objective goals. It is no wonder to Pye that the personally insecure Burmese elites lack the self-confidence necessary to cooperate effectively with others without fear, suspicion, and general anxiety. The general tone of Pye's analysis is pessimistic because personal insecurity will inevitably lead to more failures, and those failures will provoke more anxiety as well as increasingly atavistic programs, which in turn will bring failure, and so on in a seemingly endless, vicious circle.[22] Inasmuch as the core dilemma of insecurity about identity

20. Pye, p. 39.

21. Ibid., p. 53.

22. I do not wish to create the impression in this brief summary that Pye neglects the influence of the traditional culture. He does discuss traditional norms dealing with the scope of politics, the use of power, and so on. But the main thrust of his analysis with respect to personal political ideology is clearly focused on the problem of personal insecurity arising from discontinuities in socialization.

is rooted firmly in colonialism—in contact with the West—there seems to be no way out except perhaps after a long series of disasters with false prophets.[23] If Pye is able to find some slender basis for hope, other analysts, such as David Apter, who agree with Pye's diagnosis see no remedy but rather predict an increase in irrational, messianic flights of fancy.[24]

Pye's analysis is pursued as if the situation he describes were something unique to new nations, but it actually seems to belong in the category of research into the consequences of social mobility. The upwardly mobile individual in the West moves from the subculture of one class into the subculture of another, higher class, while mobility in colonial society represents a more traumatic movement from one culture into an entirely new one. The differences in the degree of change are important but should not obscure the similarity in the kind of movement. At the personal level, mobility in both industrial and transitional societies has strikingly similar effects. The resemblance between the following summary of the personal consequences of "marginality" arising from social mobility and Pye's analysis of Burmese elite behavior is impressive:

> They [those who change social status] are shedding major aspects of their personality and adopting new ones. They suffer from a variety of feelings: *guilt,* because they are to a degree renouncing the people (especially their parents) in the status group which nurtured them and set many of the rules for their behavior; *solitude,* because they have severed old ties and not yet established new ones; *conformism,* because they feel they must sedulously adopt the customs of the better status group if they are ever to be accepted by it; and a radical *ambivalence* of the self, as they see themselves from time to time failing the past that nurtured them, failing in their efforts to enter a new status, and failing to measure up to a self-image of virtue in either the Greek or puritanical sense. They feel neither noble nor free of sin.[25]

23. Pye, pp. 287, 301.

24. See David E. Apter, "Political Religion in the New States," in Clifford Geertz, ed., *Old Societies and New States: The Quest for Modernity in Asia and Africa* (New York, The Free Press, 1963).

25. James C. Davies, *Human Nature in Politics: The Dynamics of Political Behavior* (New York, Wiley, 1963), p. 265.

The personal feelings Pye attributes to transitional elites in Burma bear a strong likeness to the characteristics found among those who are socially mobile. That this similarity should exist is not at all surprising, since social mobility is the central process involved in both situations. Many students of new nations have commented on the conformity, often of a ritualistic nature, and the ambivalence about the old and new ways that characterize their elites.[26] These characteristics can be seen as the result of the special form of social mobility that the elites in new nations have experienced. Certainly the behavioral consequences of such feelings may be quite different in new nations from in the West, but it enhances an understanding of the process to see it as a special case of social mobility.

The use of social mobility theory to explain the personality disorders Pye finds among Burmese elites is more plausible in the light of research results comparing socially mobile persons to those whose class status is stable over time. In their inventory of behavioral propositions for which there is supporting data, Berelson and Steiner summarize the findings by saying, "Those moving up in class are more subject to mild or moderate emotional and mental disorder (neuroticism) than those who are stationary, partly because of the clash of class values to which they are subject and partly because of their own make-up at the outset." [27] The "emotional and mental disorder" to which members of a mobile transitional elite are prone is really the focus of Pye's study, and he, too, assigns a central role to the clash of values involved. The degree of neuroticism, however, may well be even greater for the upwardly mobile in a new nation simply because mobility in transitional society entails such a vast leap from indigenous traditional values to alien, Western norms.

Mobility in transitional nations is a very special case of general social mobility, since in the new nations it is also accompanied by rapid widespread social change. The upwardly mobile person in an industrial nation is moving through a relatively more stable

26. See, for example, Edward Shils, "The Intellectual in the Political Development of the New States," in John H. Kautsky, ed., *Political Change in Underdeveloped Countries: Nationalism and Communism* (New York, Wiley, 1962), pp. 195–234.

27. Bernard Berelson and Gary A. Steiner, *Human Behavior: An Inventory of Scientific Findings* (New York, Harcourt, Brace, 1964), p. 489.

system, while the upwardly mobile person in a transitional society is less certain of the class of status into which he is moving. He is uncertain what the relative ranking of that class will be after five years and what behavior he should conform to in order to be accepted, since status rankings and role behavior for each class or subclass are still comparatively unsettled. The example of local administrators who joined the colonial bureaucracy is especially poignant in this respect. For many of them, no sooner had they attained their new status than independence was declared, and they were revealed by the new political elite to be part and parcel of the exploitative, colonial regime—worthy objects of contempt. Changing status in any society carries its uncertainties, but in a transitional society these uncertainties are compounded by change of a more general nature.

Pye's method of accounting for the beliefs and values that prevent the erection of effective organizations in Burma focuses on the discontinuity in socialization and the conflict in beliefs and values that this discontinuity implies. The "broken" pattern of socialization that he describes is common both to those who move up in status and to those who are most affected by cultural contact, such as colonialism. Therefore, the conflicts highlighted in Pye's study are common to both processes, although there is an important difference in degree, since colonialism occasions more striking conflicts in values. If this analysis is correct, Pye's approach, and that of many who share his orientation, emphasizes the impact of rapid social change, the ideological conflict it produces in individuals, and the behavior that results.

Banfield's Approach: Amoral Familism and the Empirical Base

The setting of Banfield's study is a small town in southern Italy, an underdeveloped area but certainly not a new nation. In this new setting Banfield faced the same problem Pye faced in Burma: how to explain why people in this town seem unable to organize effective groups for either economic or political ends. Like Pye, he feels this ability is the crucial skill involved in moving toward modernity. His explanation of why the skill to create effective organizations is lacking must be different from Pye's for the simple reason that the factors Pye relied upon are absent in the Italian context. Colonialism and rapid social change are not a part of the Italian peasant's experience as they are a part of the living memory of Pye's Burmese subjects.

Banfield observed that interpersonal behavior among the townsmen of Montegrano precluded the formation of lasting, vigorous interest groups. He looked for a unifying principle that would render most of their interpersonal behavior comprehensible and would predict behavior not yet observed. Montegranesi, he concluded, acted *as if* they were following this rule: "Maximize the material, short-run advantage of the nuclear family; assume that all others will do likewise." [28]

This principle Banfield calls "amoral familism" to emphasize that when dealing with people outside the family, the interests of one's nuclear family take precedence over other considerations of right and wrong. This simplifying principle appears to explain why residents refuse to join together for community interests, why they are suspicious of the motives of others, why officeholders pursue personal and not organizational goals, why the law is ineffective when there is no fear of punishment, why the weak prefer strong government, why power holders are seen as corrupt and self-seeking, and finally why community gains are favorably evaluated by a family only when it will share substantially in those gains.[29] Many of the patterns that Banfield finds among the citizens of Montegrano are strikingly similar to those Pye observed among Burmese elites. The interpersonal suspicion, the low estimate of power holders, the pursuit of personal goals within organizations, and the preference for strong government all find echoes in Pye's study. But Banfield sees these characteristics as part of a pattern of amoral familism without reference to discontinuities in socialization or fragile personal identity.

If Banfield makes no use of discontinuities in socialization to account for the ethos of Montegrano, how does he explain its existence? The principle of amoral familism might be called a basic part of the latent ideology of the Montegranesi, but it does not

28. Banfield, p. 85.
29. By way of announcement it should be noted here that many of the same phenomena are found among bureaucrats in Malaysia.

account for the origin of this ideology. It is merely a simplifying principle that brings order to a number of specific beliefs and values associated with political activity.

To explain the origins of the ethos of amoral familism, Banfield turns primarily to the poverty—*la miseria*—of the region, to the absence of a supportive extended family, and to the nature of childhood training. Both the size of the family and the nature of primary socialization are, according to Banfield, heavily influenced by the poverty of the land and the fears of injury or death prevalent amidst such privation.[30] Thus, although he does not say so explicitly, Banfield attributes the amoral familism of the Montegranesi to the existential base of poverty—the severe limits imposed on the ideological superstructure by the strictures of the material culture. Banfield's reliance on the existential base, on a variety of economic determinism, contrasts sharply with Pye's dependence upon the personal consequences of discontinuities in socialization, although both are endeavoring to explain substantially the same phenomenon.

Contrasts of Two Explanations

The quite separate ways in which Pye and Banfield account for the origins of the comparable personal ideologies they found among subjects in Burma and Italy highlight some important analytical contrasts. First, Pye discovers the origins of beliefs that impede cooperation in the dualistic nature of the culture—particularly, the ideological uncertainty produced by colonialism—and in rapid social change. Banfield, to whom these two explanations are not available in the Italian context, finds that much the same beliefs are created by the cultural handcuffs of a poverty stricken economy. For Pye, then, the focus is on social and cultural change and its personal consequences, while for Banfield, attention is concentrated on the static nature of a culture of poverty.

The second point is related to the first and is best illustrated by recalling the four characteristics that new nations share in their existential base and common experience—elements of a traditional culture, relative poverty, a past of alien rule by Western nations, and rapid social change. The first two are characteristic of almost

30. Banfield, pp. 147–61.

any underdeveloped nation whether it is a new nation or not. Banfield employs these when he analyzes the effects of poverty on the beliefs and values of the southern Italian peasant. Pye, by contrast, accounts for the unsettled beliefs and values of his Burmese subjects by concentrating on the last two factors, which are more specifically attributes of new nations than of the broader category of underdeveloped countries. In a sense, then, Banfield's explanation is a broader one, as it could conceivably apply to any culture existing at, or near, the subsistence level, while Pye's explanation, relying as it does on the colonial experience, is restricted to nations that have recently won independence from Western rule.

Thirdly, it is possible to distinguish between the levels of socialization that each writer employs to explain the personal ideology he has found. Banfield relies almost exclusively on primary socialization within the family, particularly those aspects of primary socialization most affected by the pervasive poverty of the environment. Early socialization plays an important role in Pye's analysis, too, but only to the extent that it conflicts with secondary socialization. Pye's reliance on the discontinuity in socialization means that he must concentrate on both levels, while the continuity of socialization in Montegrano allos Banfield to focus on the development of central beliefs during early training, which are then confirmed, not contradicted, by later experience. In brief then, Banfield emphasizes stasis, primary socialization, the traditional culture, and poverty, whereas Pye tends to focus on transition, the discontinuity of secondary socialization, colonialism, and social change.

Not only do these two theories rely on quite different independent variables to explain an ideology, but each approach implies a distinct process of ideological change. Both writers are pessimistic about the possibilities of ideological change in the near future, but it seems that the logic of Pye's analysis leaves less cause for optimism. The discontinuities in socialization that he feels create insecurity about identity and values and predispose elites to failures in modernization are here to stay, and there is no reason to believe that they will disappear now that the imperial masters have departed. The cultural dualism Pye describes seems irreversible in the foreseeable future. His subjects suffer from what might be called personality disorders involving an inability to deal with the real world and real dilemmas.

Banfield's subjects, on the other hand, are in some measure dealing with the real world—a world of poverty in which amoral familism makes sense, given the environment. If their behavior is predicated upon a society where scarcity is the rule, it is quite conceivable that conditions of more abundance would change beliefs and values in the long run. Some evidence that this is the case is suggested by the absence of "amoral familistic" responses to Thematic Apperception Tests administered in the more advanced northern area of Italy.[31] It seems unlikely, of course, that given their ideology, the Montegranesi could get together and pull themselves up by their bootstraps. But opportunities introduced from outside might well begin the process of ideological change. Thus Banfield's analysis has very different implications for ideological change from Pye's. A change in the environment is going to make more of a difference to the southern Italians, who are coping with the real world, than to the Burmese, who have turned their backs on reality. Pye's subjects confront a psychic cul de sac, while Banfield's face largely environmental obstacles.

Further insight into the question of how shared personal ideology originates and changes can be gained by focusing on the functions an ideology serves for an individual. Three functions can be distinguished. Personal ideology always serves personal extrarational needs. A man inevitably expresses his unique intrapsychic problems and needs, and he does this by externalization, including projection and displacement, reaction formation, rationalization, fantasy fulfillment, and so forth. These might be called the "calming" functions of an ideology.[32] The second function a personal ideology serves is to place a man among his fellows, defining his location in his family, neighborhood, and community, and in the society as a whole. He identifies with some individuals and groups and dis-identifies with others. Thus, ideology helps a man create a social identity and maintain his self-esteem in interpersonal

31. Ibid., pp. 110–11.
32. M. Brewster Smith, Jerome S. Bruner, and Robert W. White, *Opinions and Personality* (New York, Macmillan & Co., 1956), pp. 39–47.

relations. A third function could be called the "reality" function.[33] In order to live and to work toward his goals, a man must know what things and people are like, how they respond to his behavior, and so on. The reality function sets some limits on a personal ideology, since a man's beliefs must be approximately correct in telling him what is happening around him and to him if he is to operate at all effectively as a member of his society.

Most writers concerned with the ideology of elites in new nations have, like Pye, largely dwelt on the personal, extra-rational functions fulfilled by personal beliefs and values and, to a lesser extent, on their interpersonal functions. For Pye and many others, the obvious discontinuity in socialization in new nations that creates conflicts in values immediately focuses attention on ways of assuaging the intrapsychic needs and tensions that accompany these conflicts. Once having adopted this mode of analysis, Pye sees no way out of the basic dilemma, except perhaps through an eventual abandonment of reality-cheating mechanisms after failure upon failure has somehow forced an agonizing reappraisal of defense mechanisms. Apter, who shares much of Pye's analytical orientation, appears to see no exit whatsoever but forecasts the triumph of "political religion" as a measure of desperation amidst the failure to modernize successfully.[34]

The Importance of the Reality Function

It should be clear by now that the reality function of ideology has been woefully neglected in explaining the pattern of personal ideology among elites in new nations. It is important that political scientists ask themselves whether a set of beliefs and values seems to "make sense" in the environment—both material and nonmaterial—that they are examining. An ideology need not precisely fit a man's experience; but it cannot be too wide of the mark, or it will not survive. As Lane has stated,

> And even the most facile devices for squaring particular experiences with incompatible interpretations . . . must eventually fail to protect men from the abrasions of reality. Know-

33. Ibid., p. 41.
34. Apter, pp. 82–83.

Nothingism, Social Darwinism, the anarchism of the Western Wobblies are eroded, each in turn, by experience with Catholics, with government regulation, with the welfare departments of cities. *Incongruence between ideology and experience extinguishes a social movement.*[35]

A variety of factors may account for the emphasis placed on the calming function of personal ideology in new nations to the virtual exclusion of the reality function. First, a good many of the beliefs and values present in developing areas may seem, to Western eyes at least, irrational. Once they are perceived as irrational, it is natural to turn to explanations that center on pathology rather than to examine the environment in which these beliefs exist and seek clues to their genesis there. A second and more serious reason is simply the failure to recognize the effect of a society's existential base in restricting the range of available beliefs and values to those which are roughly congruent with experience in that society. The limits placed on the nonmaterial culture by the material culture have been studied repeatedly by anthropologists, and while the latitude of beliefs permitted by a given material culture is the subject of dispute, there is no doubt that some limits are imposed. For example, Shapera has shown that the vast differences in the material cultures of the Bushmen, who are gatherers and hunters moving across the landscape in very small bands, and the Bantu, who are agriculturalists and husbandmen living in larger, settled communities, result in quite dissimilar beliefs about how the community should ideally be managed.[36] A good test of the influence of the existential base on ideology is to observe what happens when forces beyond the control of a culture alter its existential base. This is precisely what happened to the people of Tanala, who had depleted all the available land for dry rice cultivation. Kandiner describes what occurred:

> This psychological balance could, however, be maintained only while the economic basis for subsistence was based on communal land ownership. No sooner did the subsistence economy and the social organization for it change than the

35. Lane, p. 426 (my italics).
36. See I. Shapera, *Government and Politics in Tribal Societies* (London, Watts, 1956).

whole psychological structure collapsed. . . . Social changes therefore do not take place in isolated and detached items. The human mind is integrative, and hence systems of ideas and attitudes become involved, not separate items.[37]

In spite of all the evidence for the relationship between the ideology and the existential base of a culture, there is another important reason why it has been neglected as a partial explanation for the genesis and maintenance of beliefs and values. This arises from the fact that a considerable lag often occurs between a change in the existential base and the consequent change in ideology; that is, the ideology and existential base may not be congruent at each point in time. The farmer who moves to the city or the immigrant who arrives in a new country does not immediately change the whole complex of beliefs and values associated with his past way of life. It may actually require more than one generation to restore congruence between the empirical base and ideology. On a larger scale, I have already noted Doob's comments on the tenacity of central, early-socialized beliefs even after much else has changed. Central beliefs will change only after repeated batterings from experience. The process of slow adjustment may even require an entire epoch, as it did in Tanala.

> Some societies, like Tanala, are able to achieve such stability under conditions like an unchanging subsistence economy. Once the latter is destroyed, as was actually the case, the personality, which was geared for cooperation under the old conditions, is completely unsuited for the new conditions. The society is therefore thrown into a disequilibrium which may last for centuries.[38]

This "disequilibrium" stage, as Kandiner describes it, is not an inappropriate characterization of new nations. An examination of the reality functions of ideology may well demonstrate a congruence between central beliefs now current and the empirical base that was destroyed by colonialism. In fact, the possibility that much of the central belief system or latent ideology of elites in new nations is congruent with a past existential base is a central

37. Abram Kandiner, *The Psychological Frontiers of Society* (New York, Columbia University Press, 1947), pp. 420–21.
38. Ibid., pp. 417–18.

proposition of this study. I hope to show that the approach of Banfield in *The Moral Basis of a Backward Society* can shed more light
on the origin and dynamics of ideology than can an exclusive
reliance on the purely personal, intrapsychic functions of a belief
system. To stress the reality functions of an ideology is not to
ignore the contributions of Pye and Apter. The two approaches
are not at all mutually exclusive but are complementary. Focusing
on the congruence between central beliefs and a preexisting existential base as Banfield does may help to account for the origins
of these central beliefs and to show how change could occur, while
an understanding of the ideological effects of colonialism as analyzed by Pye is essential for an appreciation of the conflict between
central and peripheral beliefs. Banfield's reliance on poverty and
the traditional culture (factors common to underdeveloped areas)
to explain ideology in southern Italy indicates their importance
in accounting for ideology in Malaysia. Pye's reliance on colonialism and rapid change (factors common to new nations) to explain
ideology in Burma bears witness to the fact that these two additional factors complicate the picture in new nations and must be
worked into the analysis where appropriate.

Having established an analytical vantage point from which to
view the data, the next task is to explore the central beliefs of the
sample of high civil servants and ask how these beliefs developed.
Chapter 4 explores the sample's estimate of human nature, and
Chapter 5, their conception of man's relation to nature. In each
case the question is asked, "What are the consequences for political ideology of these orientations?" Chapter 6 attempts some generalizations about ideology in transitional society. The *sources* of
support for democratic norms are analyzed in Chapter 7, and
Chapter 8 probes the *nature* of democratic support in the sample.
Chapter 9 is devoted to a discussion of the sources of support for
an administrative or nondemocratic polity. The final chapter is
an attempt to put the diverse threads of this study in some order
and to reach some modest conclusions about ideology in new
states.

II. Basic Value Orientations

4

Human Nature and Politics

Basic Value Orientations

It is obvious that the gap in new nations between central beliefs and primary socialization on the one hand and peripheral beliefs and late socialization on the other is of primary importance. Central beliefs constitute the core of a person's latent ideology. They are likely to be patterned, shared, and most important, tenacious over time. Compared with the relative variability of peripheral beliefs, they are a more stable element in an ideology, as well as a more pervasive one, by virtue of their centrality. Therefore, it is logical to begin an examination of the ideology of elites in a new nation with these central beliefs.

The rigorous treatment of "basic value orientations" undertaken by Florence Kluckhohn and Fred Strodtbeck provides an economical structure for discussing central beliefs.[1] They feel that the basic values of a culture are relatively stable over time and, taken together, constitute the "personality" of that society. Assuming that "there are a limited number of common human problems for which all peoples at all times must find a solution," [2] they single out five basic problems, stated in question form, which they consider most important:

1. What is the character of innate human nature?
2. What is the relation of man to nature (and supernature)?
3. What is the temporal focus of human life?
4. What is the modality of human activity? [being, becoming]
5. What is the modality of man's relationship to other men? [3]

1. Kluckhohn and Strodtbeck, *Variations in Value Orientations*, passim. Although this is not the first study to concern itself with the problem of basic value orientations, it is the first to develop concepts to a point where they could be operationalized and used in cross-cultural research.

2. Ibid., p. 10.

3. Ibid., p. 11.

Every culture solves each of these problems in its own characteristic way, and the sum of its solutions comprises much of its
core culture. Similarly, an individual adopts unspoken answers to
these same questons, and the sum total of his answers constitutes
much of the core of his personal ideology. The extent to which
his orientations are shared by others of his group determines the
extent to which it is possible to speak of common cultural—or
subcultural—orientations. Kluckhohn and Strodtbeck examine
five distinct societies, all living in the same region of Texas, and
using an ingenious method, are able to trace the distinct pattern-
ing of solutions that characterizes each of the five cultures.

The problems of chief concern here are 1, 2, and 5: human nature, man-nature, and man-others, respectively. Important as they
are, the time and activity orientations will be less systematically
treated.

How does one discover, for example, what the temporal focus
of a cultural group is? How can one decide whether the group
tends to be oriented toward the present, the past, or the future?
Since people seldom express their dominant temporal orientation
explicitly, it must be inferred from what they say and do. Behavior such as saving, planning, and talk of times to come might indicate a future orientation, while sleeping in the noonday shade
implicitly places high value on present satisfactions. Any individual exhibits all three orientations toward time, future, present,
and past, but one of the three is usually dominant. In *The Cherry
Orchard,* Chekhov never has his characters say they are oriented
to the past, but the weight of nostalgia is nevertheless painfully
evident. Which orientation is dominant in an individual or group
must be inferred from a wide sample of verbal or nonverbal behavior. The process involved is much like asking oneself, "From
what unspoken assumption about time does this behavior seem to
flow?" When the same question is applied to Malaysian civil servants, the statement that they have such-and-such an orientation
will be understood to mean that they are speaking as if it were
their orientation.

THE NATURE OF HUMAN NATURE

The Selfishness of Man

It would be difficult to overstate the importance of a man's esti-mate of human nature in influencing the construction of his po-litical ideology. Seeing human nature as good, bad, or varied has an effect on how one views the motives of others, whether people are given the benefit of the doubt or whether skepticism prevails, and whether cooperation with others for common ends is consid-ered possible. For example, many of the assumptions behind lib-eral democracy take for granted a certain minimum level of rea-sonableness and concern for others in human nature. Assumptions like these make possible a system in which each man, within rea-sonable limits, may freely pursue his own ends. Democracy is not impossible where low estimates of human nature are the rule, but it is surely more difficult to maintain amidst the partisanship, dis-trust, and suspicion that generally accompany a lack of faith in people.

With almost no exceptions, the civil servants interviewed have a low estimate of human nature. Their skepticism surged to the surface throughout the interviews and permeated more specifically political beliefs. Pessimism about human nature was most appar-ent when the civil servants were asked how important friends are in a person's life. The question in no way suggested comments on the shortcomings of human nature, and yet Jeganathan, an official in the Telecommunications Service, took the occasion to unbur-den himself of this statement:

> If there is to be a friend, he must be a true friend—through thick and thin like marital vows, you see—it's not like—that sort of friend is—if you are sitting in this room and when you leave there is no friendship—he is just a friend because he wanted to get something out of you. That's the kind of friends you have mostly in this world—because I have seen that hap-pen to me—I have been at the bottom and at the top.

For Jeganathan, one's friends are apt to be false friends, ingratiat-ing themselves to gain some personal end. If this were an isolated instance of one angry man, and Jeganathan *was* angry at losing a recent promotion, it would be of little note. But it is merely a more explicit statement of an outlook that is shared widely by others in the sample. Inche' Nordin, an elderly Malay, distinguished between "friends who may be good for everything and others just for money. *Sahabat dalam kedai kopi* [friends in the coffee shop]. We have a lot of that here in Malaya. They are just friends in coffee shops—if you take them to the house they may be dangerous." Mr. Lim, whom we met earlier, echoed Inche' Nordin's sentiments, stating that "nowadays it's very difficult to get a true friend in the sense of the word—The majority of people give you lip service. I may not have been fortunate enough to have met with a sincere friend, but it is very difficult."

Again and again when we discussed friends, the men took this opportunity to emphasize the dangers of insincere, exploiting, and even potentially threatening friends. It is not that sincere, true friends do not exist at all, but rather that they are hard to locate among the multitude of false friends. The accuracy of these opinions is of less importance than the fact that they are strongly held. The older civil servants were somewhat more emphatic on this point and were more likely to characterize the bad faith of friends as a falling away from the grace of the good old days, but the feeling is common among both old and young. What is emphasized is the self-seeking nature of most people. Something seems to be missing, though; there is little of the indignation or moral condemnation of this state of affairs that one might expect. That potential friends are too often self-seeking is regrettable and sad, but nothing which occasions any moral outrage.

If these civil servants see friends as valuing them only for what profit might be gained from the friendship, it becomes relevant to ask what they hope to achieve by friendship. With few exceptions, they themselves see friends in terms of what assistance such people can offer when the need arises. Inche' Mustapha in the Health Service said of friendship, "As I said, it's a part of one's life—you don't use him for some benefit, but he is always there to help you." And Inche' Zaharuddin, a bright young Malay in the Ministry of Labor, felt much the same way: "The degree to which they [friends] are important you can't say—but I think it's important because you can't be alone—there are plenty of occasions when you need help and you ned somebody to turn to for help." Sundram, an elderly Tamil customs official inordinately given to clichés, contented himself with saying, "A friend in need is a friend indeed," and then, scarcely a second later, vent his bitterness over what has happened to friendship in the modern world. "These days they only look to the chair you hold. Once you are out of it, you are no longer of any service to them."

In the same breath used to criticize the exploitation of friendship by others, these administrators made it clear that they looked to the social support and assistance that friends provide. Not all mentioned money, but financial assistance was cited often enough to indicate that it is an important function of friendship for these men. They regard the future with some fear, so that friendship perhaps serves to cushion unexpected blows of fate and provides some measure of social protection. The dividends of comradeship, warmth, and social intercourse are not absent from their concern, but only four of them gave this dimension much prominence—it comes second, after the more important advantages of friendship are assured. Without making any value judgments, it is apparent that the uses of friendship that they condemn in others are uses to which they themselves attach some importance. What they call exploitation by others becomes a natural request for friendly assistance when viewed from their side.

Self-Seeking in Organizations

The blemishes that afflict humans singly are, in the eyes of these civil servants, also at work within organizations. People are seen to exploit organizations in much the same manner as they exploit friends. Kamalam, an affable but firm democrat, belongs to no voluntary organizations and when asked why, replied,

> I do not believe in these organizations because—everyone in these voluntary organizations are becoming members or officers for personal reasons. They want to rub shoulders with V.I.P.'s—and most of them have not the interest of the organization at heart. They say, "I'm the President," "I'm the Secretary."

Inevitably, the problem of self-seeking in organizations is seen as closely linked to the desire for money. Not only do those who join organizations seek recognition and position; they are likely to seek wealth, too. An outspoken Tamil in the Ministry of Information, Mahalingam, put the matter less subtly than most:

> Well, what happens here—there are two kinds of organizations. One is—whatever you do you can't fill your pockets—that's like the . . . . Then you take associations for the blind and crippled. They have a lot of money changing hands—and you find in these associations, you have vested interests taking over, and once they take over, they never like to part with the control—and their membership is supposed to be open, but if you try to join, you find you are very diplomatically discouraged.

Chances are that the situation Mahalingam described is largely a creature of his own imagination, but nevertheless it expresses an orientation he shares with other civil servants. Another notable facet of Mahalingam's belief is that this sort of self-seeking is likely to be found even in the bosom of groups espousing the highest purposes. In fact, it is especially those who parade their noble, unselfish motives that come under the most suspicion, for they are believed to have constructed a righteous facade behind which more prosaic motives are at play. Among Malay peasants the same pattern appears to exist, and Swift has noted that there is usually some suspicion of the pious layman and the religious teacher for this very reason.[4]

Self-seeking and insincerity are thus seen as qualities of human nature that make friendship precarious and difficult. Similarly, when groups are formed they are thought to be run for the sole benefit of their leaders rather than for their expressed purposes. The most disastrous consequence of self-seeking is, of course, war. Inche' Abdul Karim, a young and generally optimistic officer in the Social Welfare Department, spoke for most of the others in the sample when he connected human nature and war. Asked if there will always be war, he answered matter-of-factly, "So long as man stands on this world there's bound to be war." If one were to inquire whether these bureaucrats feel human nature as they see it is mutable or immutable, he could not ask for a more definitive

4. M. G. Swift, *Malay Peasant Society in Jelebu*, No. 29, London School of Economics Monographs on Social Anthropology (London, The Athlone Press, 1965), p. 163.

negative than Inche' Abdul Karim's statement. Perhaps it is because human nature is viewed as immutable that moral indignation over what is wrong with it would serve no purpose.

Comparative Levels of Misanthropy

Some skepticism and even cynicism about human nature are
probably not absent from any culture this side of Utopia and one
might well ask whether the Malaysian sample is not really expressing an attitude that is universal. A measure of skepticism is
no doubt common in every society, but its degree will vary from
culture to culture, as Kluckhohn and Strodtbeck have shown.[5]
The degree of skepticism is crucial, as it determines what is the
predominant orientation toward human nature.

There is some indication that the level of pessimism about human nature found in the sample is relatively high, compared in a
rough way with findings in other nations. At the conclusion of the
last interview, each respondent completed a number of attitudinal
measures, among which was Morris Rosenberg's "Faith-in-People
Scale." [6] Almond and Verba, in their study of political culture in
five nations, administered the same scale. The results for the small
Malaysian elite sample are discussed in relation to the five-nation
survey results, which are displayed in Table 2. The reader should
of course be warned that any comparisons made must be suggestive
at best, as the enormous difference in the size of the sample (seventeen as compared with roughly one thousand for Almond and
Verba's study) render any claim for statistical significance unjusti-
fiable.

With the exception of question 5, Malaysian responses to the
same items are well toward the pessimistic end of the continuum.
The pattern of responses by Malaysian civil servants is, moreover,
as interesting as the overall tendency. Questions 1 and 4 ask
whether one can count on support from others, and a pessimistic
reply implies that one must fend for himself. Thirteen of the seventeen Malaysians (76 percent) chose the distrustful reply to question 1 and all but two (88 percent) responded negatively to question 4. On these two questions, then, the Malaysian civil servants
are exceeded in their pessimism only by the Mexicans in one in-

5. Kluckhohn and Strodtbeck, Ch. 1.
6. Cf. Ch. 2, n. 15.

TABLE 2: Rank Ordering of National Samples by Level of Social Distrust[7]
(1 = greatest frequency of distrustful responses, 5 = least frequency
of distrustful responses; percentage figures in parentheses)

	U.S.	U.K.	Germany	Italy	Mexico
1. "No one is going to care much what happens to you, when you get right down to it."	5 (38)	4 (45)	2 (72)	3 (61)	1 (78)
2. "If you don't watch yourself people will take advantage of you."	5 (68)	3 (75)	2 (81)	4 (73)	1 (94)
3. "Most people can be trusted."	5 (45)	4 (51)	2 (81)	1 (93)	3 (70)
4. "Most people are more inclined to help others than to think of themselves first."	5 (69)	4 (72)	2–3 (85)	1 (95)	2–3 (85)
5. "Human nature is fundamentally cooperative."	3 (20)	5 (16)	2 (42)	1 (45)	4 (18)
N =	970	963	955	995	1007

stance and the Italians in another, and the gap is quite small. On
question 3, all but three of the Malaysians (82 percent) feel that
"most people cannot be trusted." When the question asks not if
people will fail to help you but whether they will actually "take
advantage of you," the Malaysians are unanimous in their agreement that they will, while only the Mexicans (94 percent) begin
to approach this figure. The Malaysian civil servants interviewed
do not only see the human environment as nonsupportive but
agree to a man that it is likely to be actually threatening. Their
concept of human nature does not allow them to count on others
for help; in fact, they feel they can count on others to "take advantage" of them "if they don't watch themselves."

On the basis of the results for the first four questions, the figures
for question 5 seem paradoxical. Mexicans and Malaysian bureaucrats, who chose the most distrustful alternative on the preceding
four questions, are two of the three groups who agree most often
that "human nature is fundamentally cooperative." The clue to

7. Almond and Verba, *The Civic Culture,* p. 213.

the paradox clearly lies in the nature of question 5 as distinguished from the form of the other questions. Each of the other four either refers to "you" or asks about "most people" in a way likely to focus on what personal expectations might be, while simply asking whether "human nature is fundamentally cooperative" allows one to be optimistic without worrying about the personal consequences. This helps to explain the incongruity of responses among Mexicans and Malaysian bureaucrats and also provides an interesting illustration of a type of formalism. In contrast to the British sample, which maintains a fairly high level of social trust on each question, the Malaysians and Mexicans exhibit high trust on a general statement while displaying substantial distrust in replies to more specific, focused statements in which their personal involvement is implied. Later in this study we shall see a similar formalism in regard to support for the freedoms of liberal democracy, a formalism arising from the gap between central and peripheral beliefs.

Misanthrophy in Transitional Nations

One might anticipate on the basis of what has been described that Malaysian civil servants might easily develop a high moralistic tone in condemnation of the present human condition, which could in turn lend a rigid, righteous, ideological cast to political opinions. But the moralizing tendency is absent. Like the Americans whom Lane describes in *Political Ideology*, "a belief in human frailty" replaces "a belief in human weakness." [8] The frailty is, however, seen by Malaysians as more severe and irremediable than it is in Lane's Eastport. Most of the civil servants with whom I spoke find it difficult to imagine anyone with great power not exploiting that power for purely personal ends. People are thought to be governed entirely by their own weakly-restrained wills in the desire for advantage over others. The difference in views of human nature between Eastport and Kuala Lumpur is one of degree, but large enough to constitute a qualitative difference. Malaysia may share this difference with other new nations. Myron Weiner's description of the motives ascribed to others in India, especially

8. Lane, *Political Ideology*, p. 325.

leaders of groups, fits without alteration into the portrait that has
been sketched.[9] A more striking example comes from O. Mannoni's brilliant analysis of the psychological results of colonialism
in Madagascar. Describing Malagasy officialdom, Mannoni says,

> But the Malagasy does not think it reveals a low estimate of
> humanity to say that all human actions are prompted by ego-
> ism; he has not made social prohibitions part of his own con-
> science and, unlike the majority of us, including Gonzalo, he
> hardly ever dreams of a society composed of men of goodwill
> among whom regulations are unnecessary.[10]

Mannoni's statement not only ascribes to the Malagasy the same
estimate of human nature attributed to Malaysians, but also emphasizes the absence of a moralistic tone. He suggests that the
absence of a superego may explain the Malagasy orientation toward human nature. I shall return to this possibility later, but it
is sufficient here to suggest that the Malaysian view of human nature may be equally present in other new nations.

The results from Rosenberg's "Faith-in-People Scale" substan-
tiate the impression gained on the basis of extensive discussions
with Malaysian civil servants. A pessimistic view of human nature
and human motives is pervasive and creates a social atmosphere
overcast with leaden clouds of distrust and skepticism. It remains
to explore the consequences for political ideology of such an estimate of human nature and the suspicion of others which it breeds.

The Political Consequences of an Orientation Toward Human Nature

One might well expect that a pessimistic view of human nature
would spill over into beliefs that relate more specifically to political life. Adorno and his colleagues have suggested that an "inability to identify with humanity takes the political form of national-

---

9. Weiner notes the common distrust of political leaders and feels that the attentive political public believes "that peasants, workers, refugees, and linguistic, religious, caste and tribal committees are organized by politicians, not in the interest
of the organized, but rather to satisfy the power desires of the organizers." Myron
Weiner, *The Politics of Scarcity: Public Pressure and Political Response in India*
(Chicago, University of Chicago Press, 1962), p. 10.

10. O. Mannoni, *Prospero and Caliban: The Psychology of Colonization* (New
York, Frederick A. Praeger, 1964), p. 153.

ism and cynicism about world government and permanent peace." [11] The relationship between pre-political and political beliefs is difficult to establish with any precision, but a contextual analysis of both may reveal strong enough similarities in tone and phrasing to suggest that a consistent pattern is involved. Indeed, the evidence suggests that the qualities attributed to politicians and leaders bear an unmistakable relationship to the conception of human nature described above.

Other consequences for political beliefs have been attributed to a pessimistic view of human nature. Morris Rosenberg has shown that those who score low in "Faith-in-People" are more likely to suspect the motives of public figures, more often find elected officials unresponsive to the needs and desires of the citizenry, and are more inclined to suppress certain political freedoms.[12] If these same beliefs are associated with misanthropy in the Malaysian sample as well as among Americans, it will suggest that misanthropy has an impact on political ideology regardless of the cultural milieu.

Images of Politicans: The Power, the Glory, and the Money

Just as the men interviewed saw others as insincere and potentially exploitive, their view of politicians was couched in almost identical terms. When asked why politicians stand for office only one civil servant, Inche' Abdul Karim, probably the strongest democrat in the group, emphasized the desire to serve the people and to right wrongs. The others stressed selfish motives in general or focused on the political appetite for power, for publicity and social status, and, above all, for money.

There is an abundance of transcript material that illustrates a cynicism about the motives of politicians, but a few examples will provide some appreciation of the tones in which it is expressed. Sundram, an elderly Tamil in the Ministry of Customs, seldom dodges an issue, and when I asked him whether or not Malaysia was getting closer to an ideal society, he replied in staccato fashion, "Further away from it—because—it's more due to aggrandizement and the lust for power. When a man has this lust for power and

11. Adorno et al., *The Authoritarian Personality,* p. 148.
12. Morris Rosenberg, "Misanthropy and Political Ideology," pp. 690–95.

wants to amass everything for himself, it is difficult to see the other man's sufferings." Inche' Mohd. Amin, a middle-aged Malay in the Postal Service, is generally more phlegmatic than Sundram but shares both his animation and outlook when asked why people change their minds in a political discussion. "Most politicians," he said, "are just opportunists, they just want to gain some power; they join any party which could help them up." In contrast, Inche' Ismail, a "young Turk" in the Federal Establishment Office, sees social standing as the primary motive and is willing to grant that politicians may start out initially with good motives. Asked why someone might stand for public office, he answered,

> Social standing. Others are urged or goaded into politics because of the shortcomings of society. They can improve things when they get standing and authority—these are the *genuine* politicians. Even this general intention at the beginning will be polluted when the social standing they desire falls into their hands—and they have ideas about the pursuit of their own interests and the interests of those dear to them.

Regardless of what particular motive is seen as uppermost in the minds of politicians, virtually everyone would agree that politicians are interested above all in "number one." Again, this is not because politicians are the worst in a world filled with bad men, although this feeling is not entirely absent. Rather, politicians are considered to be no weaker or more corruptible than other men, but they are faced with temptations far beyond that of common mortals. Who could really expect them not to succumb in that promised land at the top of society? Inche' Ismail's comment expresses this indirectly, but Jeganathan, whom we have already met, is even more explicit. He does not think Malaysia is getting closer to an ideal society. On the contrary,

> I'm afraid we are drifting further away. [Why?] I mean so long as there is advantage to be gained, no one worries about the means used to gain the advantage. *Opportunity makes a thief.* . . . I have seen absolutely honest people who have been put to temptation where they have succumbed.

It is "opportunity" that corrupts people. The level of human selfishness seems, for these civil servants, to be fixed, and the amount of actual self-seeking which takes place is therefore a function of the level of opportunity. Since the level of selfishness is seen to be fixed at a fairly high level, it does not take much opportunity before the average mortal will succumb. In short, politicians are like everyone else, and it is only because they are constantly tempted by such golden opportunities that they are unable to resist. The word "opportunist" expresses essentially this same notion, and it was used again and again by these men to describe the behavior of politicians. Viewed in these terms, much of the general attitude toward politicians among Malaysian civil servants must be seen as part of their orientation toward human nature.

It is important here to connect evaluations of politicians and evaluations of human nature. Observing similar attitudes toward politicians among Burmese civil servants, Pye concludes that this stance is a result of a feeling of inferiority that arose when these administrators were abandoned by the British in favor of politicians, whom they consider incompetent and only semiliterate.[13] There is no doubt that many of these feelings are real and that they contribute to the prevailing view of politicians. But Pye's explanation focuses attention on the colonial period and the reversal of relationships that independence occasioned. The same attitude, however, can be convincingly attributed to a basic value orientation, namely, the one concerning human nature. The origin of this orientation seems to lie historically deeper than colonialism and independence. If, in fact, the drastic status changes of politicians and administrators were at the root of this evaluation of politicians by civil servants, the attitude should be uniquely directed at politicians; but it is not. Instead it fits clearly into a broader orientation toward human nature. In addition, in Malaysia this attitude is directed by civil servants not only toward politicians but also toward other civil servants. Inche' Abdul Karim talked about self-seeking among the administrative class in precisely the same terms others reserved for politicians, saying that "there are tremendous opportunities and one may succumb. Even if they're well paid and still if there are so many opportunities—probably the sky is the limit."

Most others echoed these sentiments. To attribute the attitudes

13. Pye, *Politics, Personality and Nation Building,* Chs. 15 and 16.

of administrators toward politicians solely to the bitterness and insecurity that characterize a recently déclassé ruling elite seems too narrow an explanation, especially when administrators view leaders of voluntary organizations, and bureaucrats as well, in precisely the same light. It appears that attitudes toward politicians should therefore be seen in the context of a general orientation toward human nature, an orientation whose roots must extend back beyond the recent struggle for independence.

The Need for Control of Human Nature

God and government as controlling agents. Given their orientation toward human nature and the behavior they anticipate of those in positions of power and authority, it is difficult to see how Malaysian civil servants can conceive of a society that successfully regulates its affairs or maintains an acceptable level of cohesion. If everyone acts as if he were motivated exclusively by thought of personal gain regardless of the cost to others, how could society be prevented from degenerating into anarchic self-seeking? How could selfishness be confined to tolerable levels in the interest of preserving the social fabric?

As these men see it, the only limitation to the full play of selfish motives in society is the fear of punishment by some external authority. The agents of this fear of punishment are both sacred and temporal. God (or Allah) keeps man from pursuing his self-interest to the detriment of others by the threat of retribution in the hereafter, while secular authority—strong government—deters him by the threat of swift punishment here and now. It makes sense for these men to talk of their God and their government in the same breath, since each fulfills a similar function for society: each serves to limit the freedom of individuals in the interests of all men. But for their tenuous check on the rapaciousness of man, human affairs would be quite out of control.

The similarity of religious and governmental control, and the implications of both for political ideology, are important enough to merit some elaboration. Mr. Lim, for example, is an excellent illustration of how the basic orientation toward human nature and the views of religion and government fit together. His view of human nature conforms to the pattern already described. Asked if wars are inevitable, he stammered, "You must have—there must be—[Why?] Well—it's a case of—shall we say egoistic ideas—wanting to exert the forces—and also this is one of the laws of nature." When Mr. Lim was asked why religion is important to him, his answer was short and direct, and it represents the substance of all his comments about religion. "For me, it is always some restraining influence against bad actions." We talked about freedom later in the same interview, and the parallels seemed striking. Trying to decide whether there is generally too much freedom or too little freedom, he replied,

> Well—if you give too much freedom—then people are apt to abuse—because they will take too much license on it—you give him too much and he goes out of hand—it tends to be out of hand. There should be some *restraining power*. [How out of hand?] Too free with words, actions, all these things.

Both religion and limitations on freedom are "restraining" influences against the natural law of "egoistic ideas." The idea that the restraints on religion and government are necessary in a world where self-seeking would otherwise predominate is so strong among these men that they cannot give free rein to fantasy and imagine a perfect society where such restraint could be lifted. Speaking of whether government would be needed in an ideal society, Mr. Tay, a young, educated Chinese in the Ministry of Education, said, "Certainly—there must be someone responsible for planning. Even in a perfect society there must be discipline. If there is not, if you let everyone run loose, then there will be chaos."

Discipline is achieved only with a substantial component of fear. Both God and government use fear to curb human beings from the antisocial acts they are inclined to by natural law. The importance of fear can be seen in the comments of Inche' Ismail and Jeganathan: first about fear in religion, and then about fear in politics.

> *Ismail on religion:* [Does religion help a man stay on the right track?] Yes it does, through restraint and also through a certain feeling of *fear of the wrath of Allah.*—It defines a certain etiquette; gives a restraint on one's feelings.

Ismail on politics: [Will there always be wars?] As long as people are not willing to settle things in a round table there will be wars. What prevents war is the fear of what each other will do. Basically people cannot change in this sort of thing—the interests of the individual and the nation stay the same—it is this *fear* which persuades people to talk.

Jeganathan on religion: [Does religion help a man stay on the right track?] Yes, if—you see the king's punishment is then and there but *God's punishment* is slow but sure. And once you have gotten God's punishment there is no chance of redeeming yourself. So if a person considers this—you conduct yourself properly.

Jeganathan on politics: [How do party members in Malaysia measure up to the ideal?] They are ideal to the extent that they—by *fear of party discipline* they conform to party wishes. It is not out of love for any principle or anything—but fear of being chucked out of the party. That goes for the whole world.

There is little indication, then, that any of these men considers self-restraint or social consciousness effective materials with which to construct a viable society without recourse to the threat of temporal or sacral punishment. Only the sort of fear described by Jeganathan and Ismail seems to offer a way out of untrammeled egoism. As Inche' Hussain, a serious, sincere young official in the Immigration Service, sees it, religion is "an upper hand which watches over you, and if you sin you'll be punished in the other world." Similarly, for these top administrators, government seems to be "an upper hand which watches over you, and if you sin you'll be punished in *this* world."

These remarks do not reflect simply a particular religious tradition, for they include statements by a Hindu, a Buddhist, and a Muslim. Nor does this configuration represent some unique cultural heritage, since Malays, Chinese, and Tamils all share the same beliefs on this subject. The causes of this orientation are likely to be found either in the common qualities of the traditional cultures from which they came, or in the existential base and experiences which they share. Before speculating about the origin of these beliefs, however, it is necessary to explore in more detail the consequences for political ideology that they imply.

The need for strong government. If the government's principal role is to keep human passions within acceptable limits, then it must be a strong, firm government. Indeed, with only two exceptions, the civil servants interviewed expressed a preference for strong leadership—strong enough to keep people in line. They are, for the most part, committed to a democratic form of government, but this conviction is vitiated by a feeling that an entirely democratic regime is apt to be a weak structure that could not prevent men from pursuing their natural inclination to exploit others. What they seem to settle on is a combination of strength and fatherly concern, perhaps analogous to what they remember in their families or, more likely, the qualities they would attribute to the "ideal father." Sundram seemed to have this image in mind when he described the ideal government as "some form of control and guidance," as did Mohd. Amin when he described the perfect government: "Government means there must be a leader." This leader would be firm and just." Seldom was strength mentioned alone without coupling it to words like "just" or "guidance." The image was of a strong but benevolent figure—strict but not tyrannical.

The component of strength is central, and there is some feeling that a weak leader will not only fail to inspire respect but will be exploited at every opportunity. Mr. Khoo Swee Fah, an intelligent young Chinese in the Audit Department, made the connection between strength and respect in this way: "Before the War, civil servants were highly respected but not now. We don't rule by the sword. When you treat them as human beings, they have no respect for you. But if you rule with an iron hand, you're very well respected." In and of itself, Mr. Khoo's comment might indicate a straightforward preference for dictatorial rule as the only means to maintain respect for rulers. In a later interview, however, he appeared to advocate the mixed sort of leadership just outlined. Describing what a prime minister should do, he said, "A good prime minister should be a person who will pour oil on troubled waters. The deputy prime minister should be ruling with an iron rod. If both the prime minister and the deputy prime minister rule with an iron rod, then you have a revolution." "Iron" qualities are essential to rule, but unalloyed "iron" would be as productive of chaos as would weakness. With one hand the ruler comforts his subjects, while his other hand holds an "iron rod" in readiness lest things get out of control.

The attractive qualities of firm rule have been noted by H. B. M. Murphy in his study of the mental health of students in Malaysia. He claims that most students looked with favor on the strong rule established in Malaya by the Japanese during World War II. After the initial violence was past, the harsh treatment dealt to lawbreakers by the Japanese authorities was much admired despite the absence of most peacetime freedoms.[14] This desire for the tough leader, for firmness and discipline, is the logical conclusion of a view of human nature in which asocial self-seeking is thought to predominate. And the need for government to restrain selfishness with the threat of swift and sure punishment is a most significant source of antidemocratic strains in the political ideology of this administrative elite.

The limits of freedom. A good indication of the antidemocratic tendency is the degree to which these men are willing to limit freedoms in what they believe to be the interests of society as a whole. When we discussed what freedom meant to them, a majority placed special emphasis on the limits of freedom. Only one respondent failed to mention explicitly the dangers of freedom. For Inche' Nordin, an elderly Malay who is more traditional minded than most, the danger of freedom is the overindulgence of appetites. As he graphically put it,

> It's a great—[danger]. First and foremost is health. [Why?]
> Well, we have more freedom, money, and we take more food
> and you actually drown yourself. If you have a car—accidents.
> Too much freedom is dangerous sometimes. Everybody must
> have freedom, but that freedom must be limited.

Inche' Nordin sees too much freedom as a threat both to oneself and to others, while Sundram, less explicitly, says that when people have too much freedom "they start deteriorating." What Sun-

14. H. B. M. Murphy, "Cultural Factors in the Mental Health of Malayan Students," in *The Student and Mental Health: Conference Proceedings of the 1st International Conference on Student Mental Health* (Princeton, Princeton University Press, 1956), pp. 169–70.

dram and Nordin suspect might happen in an environment of broad freedom persuades them and their colleagues that leaders must be resolutely firm and that freedom must be limited to save people from themselves.

One further aspect of political ideology remains to be examined in this context of controlling human nature—the attitude toward law and its relationship to freedom. Inasmuch as strong government curbs human avarice by passing laws, these men are stout defenders of the law and see it as a central tool for the control a society requires. When they spoke of law they most frequently meant criminal law, since the criminal inclinations of man are viewed as the most dangerous centrifugal forces threatening society. Their attachment to law is over and above the attachment one might expect of a bureaucratic elite that much prefers to run things without politics, as it did during the colonial days. This feeling for law is as much a product of their inability to imagine a society without it as it is a consequence of their positive attachment to it. When Inche' Zukifli was asked whether government would be needed in a perfect society, he answered cryptically, "I don't think so—as long as they conform to government orders." Inche' Zukifli never specified, of course, who was to issue "government orders" in the absence of a government. Much the same view was implied by Mr. Tay when, speaking of the dangers of freedom, he said, "there is not too much danger provided you have a proper system of government—laws and everything—provided people obey and respect the law of the country." To Mr. Tay and others, freedom seems to be what is left over after obeying all the laws and government directives. Put another way, freedom is what remains after the legal structure is strong enough to prevent chaos. Like strong government, the important quality of law, for them, is that of a guide to behavior backed up by the threat of punishment if the guidelines are breached. Their attachment to law often overwhelms their attachment to freedom, since a weakness in law or government might mean nothing less than anarchy, while the loss of some freedom is regrettable but less dangerous.

The government as policeman. The need for strong leadership and limits to freedom is based on assumptions about the fragility of human society, which in turn follow from the assumptions about human nature described. These presuppositions are not entirely the products of lively imaginations. Malaysians have experienced in their own lifetime periods of disorder and violence that have made a deep impression and have reinforced these assumptions. The interval between the defeat of the British and the establishment of an Occupation administration, and again the period between the Japanese surrender and the return of the British, were times of great insecurity and widespread lawlessness. In particular, at the end of World War II, the anti-Japanese guerilla forces, mostly Chinese, settled many real or imagined scores in villages and towns across the nation before order was restored. Coupled with these "times of trouble," the postwar Emergency sabotaged law and order in many areas and exacerbated the communal tensions that are never far below the surface in Malaya. The long shadow of violence has thus contributed to the fear that the stability that now exists is a tenuous achievement—that security and order could easily collapse. After what happened in these times, and given their basic assumptions about human nature, it is not surprising that most of the men expressed a marked preference for strong rulers, for limits on individual freedom, and for obedience to law. Supported by central beliefs and personal experience, their preferences seem durable.

Lane has said that in America the common man sees government as existing to satisfy people and fulfill their wants—"working for the people, not merely restraining them." [15] Government and religion, for the Malaysian administrative elite, exist much less to meet people's needs than to prevent them from meeting the antisocial needs they are presumed to have. The Puritans, perhaps, might have had more in common with these bureaucrats than with their own descendants. Like the ideal traditional leader, the civil servants interviewed see government and God restraining them, preventing them from getting out of hand—a firm master, but benign and paternalistic at the same time, one who instructs when he can and threatens when he must. The police component of government is much more salient to these men than its service component; government is valued less for what it actually does or permits than for what it prevents.

15. Lane, p. 145.

I have tried to show in this section the implications for political ideology of a central belief about human nature. Politicians and others with power and authority are seen as acting in their narrow self-interest regardless of the damage to third parties. They do so because they are cast in the same mold of human nature as others and are in positions where the opportunities for personal aggrandizement are so readily available. It is not that they are any more selfish than other men, but simply that their opportunities are much more numerous and profitable. Thus, the image of politicians held by these civil servants is cut from the same fabric as their basic orientation toward human nature. And it is this conviction of the potential rapaciousness of man which is their rationale for preferring strong leaders, a strict framework of law, and limitations on individual freedom. All these consequences for political ideology follow naturally from a view of human nature which assumes that the freedom and liberty of men must be controlled for their own good—that left to themselves, men will probably serve themselves and harm the community.

Having examined how a basic value orientation casts its long shadow over intermediate and peripheral beliefs and affects the construction of a political ideology, we shall now turn to some speculations about the origin of this basic orientation.

The Development of a Basic Value Orientation

The orientation of the seventeen men toward human nature is broadly characterized by a feeling that "all human actions are prompted by egoism" [16] and can be controlled only by threats emanating from external authorities, whether governmental or supernatural. Suggesting the origin of these central beliefs, however, is a hazardous and speculative enterprise at best, but one which promises to give more than just a static picture of basic orientations. Because central beliefs are likely to persist over time, even when substantial changes in intermediate and peripheral beliefs have already occurred, the place to seek the origin of basic orientations is in the nature of traditional society.

16. Mannoni, p. 153.

Conformity and Dependence Relations
in Traditional Society

Without overemphasizing the homogeneity or rigidity of traditional societies, there can be little doubt that, compared to modern
or even transitional societies, they tend to achieve and maintain a
relatively greater degree of uniformity of behavior and beliefs.
Whether the higher degree of uniformity is a function of material
conditions, such as the restrictions of the physical environment
or the isolation of the society, or of nonmaterial factors, like the
kinship system, is still the subject of much dispute. Doob describes
a number of elements in the environment of traditional society
that contribute to this uniformity of beliefs and behavior.[17] Among
other factors, he emphasizes the slowness of change, the degree to
which conduct is traditionally prescribed, the penalties for non-
conformity, and the relative absence of surprises in interpersonal
relationships. Furthermore, the absence of the large economic
surplus needed to make experimentation less risky and of challenges to custom from outside sources helps to explain the relative
lack of internal critiques that question the correctness of a traditional society's beliefs and values. The conditions in which traditional societies exist, then, produce a social structure that, as
Redfield says, "is a set of limiting conditions within which the
conduct of the individual takes place. It is a system of ethical directives, a set of signposts to the good and virtuous life." [18]

Keeping in mind the relative uniformity of beliefs and values
in a traditional society and their subjective correctness for the
members of that society, there is another, more important quality
shared by traditional societies. This is the phenomenon of dependence relationships. In societies with unilineal (patrilineal or
matrilineal) kinship groups, dependence takes on a more corporate
nature, since kin groups are mutually exclusive and durable over
time; but in societies characterized by bilateral kinship, alliances
are more flexible, and patron-client groups thrive or wither depending on their success in satisfying the goals of their members.

17. Doob, *Becoming More Civilized*, pp. 20–38.
18. Robert Redfield, *The Little Community / Peasant Society and Culture* (Chicago, University of Chicago Press, 1960), p. 46.

Whether permanent or not, the strength of dependence relationships is a pervasive characteristic of traditional societies. Godfrey and Monica Wilson suggest that "in any society, the total degree of dependence on others is the same while the strength of the dependence and the number of persons on whom one is dependent vary, but their product does not vary." [19] What they propose is that in traditional societies one is very dependent on a few people, while in a more modern society one has less intense dependencies but is dependent on a far larger number of people. The idea is not novel, but it highlights an essential distinction between the pattern of life in modern and traditional societies.

Dependency and External Control Agencies

For most situations in a traditional society, custom will do very well, but for the unexpected, one can rely on the patron or the corporate group for shelter. Similarly, the uniformity of beliefs and values that characterizes traditional society is enforced by the social network of dependencies, according to which the crucial test of the rightness of a belief or behavior depends on its being sanctioned by authority—provided it doesn't flout tradition, which is, after all, a kind of dependence on the authority of ancestors. Thus, it is not inaccurate to say that the effect of the strong sex-, age-, and status-based dependencies in traditional society is that much of one's conscience is invested in an authority figure or a "patron." A patron of some men will usually be a client of a more powerful patron, who protects him as he protects his clients, and so on to the apex of the social structure.

The suggestion here is that the observed homogeneity in beliefs and behavior in traditional societies is achieved by a system of strong dependencies, whereby the decision of the superior ordinarily carries with it the weight of moral correctness simply by virtue of the superior's position. In short, the superego is externalized; it is vested in outside authority rather than in the individual. The demands and restrictions of the conscience or superego are not integrated into the ego structure; instead, outside

19. Godfrey and Monica Wilson, *The Analysis of Social Change: Based on Observations in Central Africa* (Cambridge, Cambridge University Press, 1945), pp. 28, 40, cited in Doob, p. 30.

agencies must be relied upon for moral decisions and limits.[20] Mannoni phrases the matter without reference to the superego, but he appears to have the same phenomenon in mind:

> All this would seem to suggest that the ego is wanting in strength, and that is borne out by the fact that hallucinatory disturbances and panic appear the moment the feeling of security is threatened. *The individual is held together by his collective shell, his social mask, much more than by his "moral skeleton." And this, with but slight modifications, must be true of many other "primitive" societies.*[21]

It should be apparent by now that the orientation of the Malaysian sample toward human nature—an orientation that sees men inclined to such a high degree of self-seeking that only the threats and guidance of God and strong leadership can restrain it—bears an unmistakable resemblance to the reliance on outside moral agencies for control that characterizes traditional man. Unable to imagine pure self-restraint and internal controls limiting man's selfishness, traditional man is thrown back to a reliance on the threat of punishment or ridicule by external authority as the only viable means of maintaining social harmony. The very nature of control in traditional society implies a view of man pursuing his own advantage exclusively unless linked to a dependency system —that is, unless controlled by an external authority that sets limits to his behavior in the interest of the group and has sanctions to enforce those limits. There is a marked similarity between the control system for society that the civil servants in the sample see as

20. The absence of an internalized superego is likely to mean that behavior will be motivated by narrowly defined personal goals unless curbed by external authority. In this connection, Pye has noted that almost all those who joined the Malayan Communist Party armed forces during the Emergency joined to realize personal values and had a strong sense of careerism, rather than necessarily having any commitment to the principles of the organization. Political groups, Pye says, were evaluated largely on the basis of their effectiveness in promoting the private interests of their supporters, and when they failed, they were abandoned (*Guerilla Communism in Malaya: Its Social and Political Meaning* [Princeton, Princeton University Press, 1956], pp. 12–73). Similarly, when asked what they liked about the civil service, two-thirds of the sample interviewed mentioned personal goals such as security, pay, and promotions, while only four mentioned anything having to do with the purposes of the organization itself. Moreover, there is no trace of embarrassment when they assert the primacy of their personal goals; it seems natural.

21. Mannoni, p. 41 (my italics).

proper and the control system that actually operates in traditional society. We have only to recall the comments about religion and political leadership to note the congruence between these attitudes and the pattern that characterizes an externalized superego. This congruence is so striking that it seems not unreasonable to suggest that the present attitudes may have originated in traditional circumstances and have been maintained since.

The Externalized Superego and Amoral Familism

The distinction between an internalized and an externalized superego corresponds closely to the distinctions drawn by anthropologists between "guilt cultures" and "shame cultures." [22] In shame cultures behavior that is socially disapproved will be *consciously* suppressed out of fear that others will ridicule or condemn it. The control is external, since shame depends upon witnesses, and generally, if the witnesses are absent, the control of behavior is significantly reduced. A shame culture exhibits "a particularistic or situational ethic as opposed to the more universalistic ethic built around moral absolutes found in Western Christian thought." [23] By contrast, in a guilt culture the automatic reaction of the internalized superego represses the individual's desire to engage in disapproved behavior, usually before it is even perceived, and if not, he feels that sense of sin which is perhaps the hallmark of Western society. The ethic here is internalized and individual rather than externalized and situational, as in the shame culture.

There are two points that should be made about shame cultures. First, since in this kind of culture "much of conscious life is concerned with a system of social sanctions," [24] and since an externalized superego is likely to be the rule, the source of control is located outside the individual, in the authority of patrons and

22. As in most distinctions of this nature, "shame" and "guilt" cultures do not constitute a dichotomy but rather a continuum. Thus, Western Culture, generally described as a "guilt culture," exhibits shame as well, while in Japanese culture, which is generally termed a "shame culture," guilt is not entirely absent. The terms merely refer to the modally preferred means for avoiding disapproved behavior.

23. George De Vos, "The Relation of Guilt Toward Parents to Achievement and Arranged Marriage among the Japanese," in Smelser and Smelser, eds., *Personality and Social Systems*, p. 165 (my italics).

24. Ibid., p. 166.

superiors and in the ridicule and condemnation of peers. If, as Mannoni has suggested, most traditional societies are largely shame cultures, we can expect that the prevalent view of human nature and the system for individual and social control in these societies will match the attitudes found in the elite sample. Putting it the other way around, transitional elites are likely to hold beliefs about human nature and social control that are congruent with the situational-ethic cultures from which they come. A belief in the self-control of man and a preference for a service-oriented leadership would not be congruent with this tradition, but the presumption of man's weakness and a desire for strong, restraining rule are indeed congruent.

The second point about shame cultures, where the superego is externalized, relates to the problem of guilt and sin. De Vos notes that Western missionaries were "perplexed . . . by what they considered a lack of moral feelings in regard to non-familial relationships"[25] among the Japanese. Guilt is not entirely absent, according to De Vos, for

> Whereas the applicability of the more universalistic Western ethic in many aspects may tend to transcend the family, the Japanese traditional ethic is actually an expression of rules of conduct for members of a family, and filial piety has in itself certain moral absolutes that are not completely situationally determined even though they tend to be conceptualized in particularistic terms. *This difference between family-oriented morality and a more universalistic system* is, nevertheless, a source of difficulty in thinking about guilt in the Japanese.[26]

The "family-oriented morality" and the "lack of moral feelings in non-familial relationships" may very well be typical of shame cultures, and more important, it seems almost identical to the amoral familism which Banfield uses to account for the political beliefs and behavior of the southern Italian peasant. While this is frankly speculative, it seems likely that Banfield's amoral familism has essentially the same content as the family-oriented morality that De Vos attributes to the Japanese. The welfare and advantage of the family, whether it be nuclear or extended, are the criteria

25. Ibid., p. 165.
26. Ibid.

against which the correctness of behavior and values is judged. As a result, the orientation toward those outside the family appears to be amoral.

There is a distinct possibility that amoral familism is quite typical in developing nations. It may be a characteristic of cultures with a situational ethic as well as a product of both the strength of primordial attachments and the poverty of the material culture.[27] If family-oriented morality is typical of shame cultures, as De Vos' comments might indicate, then the predominance of shame cultures and situational-ethics outside the West indicates that amoral familism and its social and political consequences may characterize many developing nations. Surely, the family-oriented morality observable in many non-Western and some Western nations goes a long way toward explaining the relative absence of civic consciousness or dedication to abstract principles of justice in these areas.[28] A situational ethic is contextual and is therefore quite incompatible with principles of justice or morality when clothed in their universalistic Western garb.

A NOTE ON OTHER-DIRECTEDNESS

Evidence of Other-Directedness in the Interviews

The concept of an externalized superego implies the operation of some external agency to serve the function of discouraging socially disapproved behavior and beliefs. Aside from supernatural authority, these sanctions operate through people who evaluate and then either sanction or condemn. As appropriate roles for different situations are learned, however, a kind of precensorship takes place, so that sanctioned behavior is normally produced. A person's social antennae sense what others expect, and thus he

27. Aside from the individual himself, the family constitutes the narrowest unit of loyalty. The process of change away from a family-oriented morality most probably entails a broadening of the concept itself, so that one feels a degree of "kinship" with a wider group. Loyalty to the kin group persists, but other loyalties are added. The existence of fictive kin and godfather relationships, which are common in the Philippines and elsewhere, is an effort to draw outsiders into an alliance with a kin group by an artificial kinship arrangement. This creates a broader loyalty group for purposes of cooperation and mutual protection. Cf. James C. Abegglen, *The Japanese Factory* (New York, The Free Press, 1958).

28. One suspects that much of the present "Great Cultural Revolution" in China is aimed precisely at eliminating this family-oriented morality and replacing it with loyalty to the teachings of Chairman Mao.

avoids ridicule and condemnation. This is the "radar" to which David Reisman refers in explaining the concept of "other-directedness." Cultures in which the superego is modally externalized are "other-directed" cultures, since "others" perform the function of the superego.

It is useful to be more specific about the "other" in "other-directed." Presumably, one may be directed toward peers, superiors, or inferiors in terms of their status rankings. Given the paramount importance of hierarchy and the network of dependencies in traditional society, the relevant others are superiors and perhaps peers, but not inferiors since, if anything, inferiors rely on the social judgment of their superiors rather than vice versa.

If traditional societies are characterized by the externalization of the superego and a concern about the favorable evaluation of others, so are the elite administrators in the transition nation we are examining. Already indications of an externalized superego have been prominent in their attitudes about human nature, God, and leadership. The evidence of their other-directedness is equally convincing.

All the administrators were asked, at one point or another, whether they would prefer to be respected for their independent opinions or for their ability to get along with others. The question seems to be a clear-cut choice between other-directedness and inner-directedness. Only four of the seventeen preferred to be respected for their independent stance, while all the rest emphasized the necessity of getting along with others and not appearing antagonistic. Inche' Abu Bakar, a young and somewhat diffident Malay in the Telecoms Service, spoke for most when he explained why he preferred to get along with others: "I mean—independent opinion may not be very attractive to the majority of people." Inche' Ja'afar of the Ministry of Information, whom we met earlier, was more self-conscious in answering this question, but his decision was the same. "One is an ideal—the ideal, I know, would be to be independent. But in my present status I feel the other one is more important. Independent opinions—because, after all, James—what is your opinion—it may not be the right one."

Ja'afar may have taken the humble way out, but in the process he made it clear that too much independence might jeopardize his position.

Early in the interviews each respondent was asked what he would do if he were an economist who was asked to prepare a justification for a policy that was contrary to all he was taught as an economist. The choice between inner-directedness and other-directedness is somewhat muddied here by the problem of bureaucratic discipline, but almost all the administrators said they would prepare the report as requested without questioning its correctness. The most frequent rationalization was that "economists are as fallible as anyone else." [29]

Although these men are well acquainted through their schooling with the entire gallery of British heroes who are honored for their singleness of purpose and independent views, they would themselves prefer to be known for their ability to get along with others, and they said so quite openly, although at the same time making appropriate verbal bows to the ideal. They are, for the most part, clearly other-directed.

The other-directedness of "those who are changing" is attested to by Leonard Doob on the basis of results from projective tests administered cross-culturally: "In comparison with those who remain unchanged or those who have changed, people changing from old to new ways are likely to be generally sensitive to other people." [30]

29. Many students of bureaucracy in new nations have noted what seems to be the absence of professional standards and a tendency to go along with whatever is required by others. The problem is not so much the absence of professional standards per se, but rather the fact that the rewards offered by a quasi-traditional status system are "social relational" rather than "external." In other words, the hallmark of a society still largely traditional is that personal rather than impersonal indications of success are most valued. Unlike the modern entrepreneur who relies on profits, sales, and production—all impersonal indicators of success—the transitional administrator relies on the reassurance of his superiors or the praise of "respect elites" for indications that he is doing a good job. If the superior does not use impersonal indicators to judge his subordinates, the importance of personalistic criteria are reinforced. The high value placed on personal rather than impersonal indicators of success is responsible, I feel, for many of the bureaucratic anomalies observed in developing nations. Cf. Melvin M. Tumin, "Competing Status Systems," pp. 222–33, and David C. McClelland, "The Achievement Motive in Economic Growth," pp. 179–89, in David E. Novack and Robert Lekachman, eds., *Development and Society: The Dynamics of Economic Change* (New York, St. Martin's Press, 1964).

30. Doob, *Becoming More Civilized*, p. 135. Doob's formulation would appear to be at variance with mine, since he ascribes *more* sensitivity to those who are changing than to those who are unchanged. He himself, however, cites studies which

Doob feels that this sensitivity is heightened especially during acculturation, since one is continually testing to see whether his behavior is appropriate to the new group he is entering.

Role-Adaptability Versus Cultural Change

Other-directedness, however, when looked at in a slightly different analytical light, might be called "role-adaptability." The other-directed man is able to adjust to new situations, so that his behavior and beliefs fit in with the new social environment. Many have commented on the apparent role-adaptability of the Indian peasant, who somehow sheds many of the caste rules when he comes to the city and miraculously reassumes the same rules with evident ease when he returns to the village environment.[31] The same applies equally well to the adaptability of the Malay peasant in the city, or for that matter, to the adaptability of the Malaysian civil servant while abroad.

At first glance, other-directedness and role-adaptability seem to be similar to the quality of "empathy" that Daniel Lerner feels is the crucial variable in becoming modern.[32] The ability to adapt to new roles surely entails an ability to place oneself in other people's shoes, to anticipate their reactions and behave accordingly. But it is necessary to distinguish between conformity and the internalization of new norms. The former depends on the pressures of the social milieu, while the latter, presumably, is a more permanent phenomenon which depends less on social support. Conformity that flows from other-directedness tends to evaporate when social support for it disappears; unlike internalzed norms, it is unstable. Although conformity may be the initial step along the road toward new value patterns—because behavior has its own

show that the unchanged American Indian is more sensitive to others than the typical Midwestern, white American. More important, Doob recognizes that traditional people are sensitive to others but that the relevant others do not include outsiders, a caveat that precedes his hypothesis. "A man who remains unchanged may be sensitive only to cues from traditional people and may fail to acquire knowledge of the behavior of outsiders."

31. See Robert O. Tilman, "The Influence of Caste on Indian Economic Development," in Ralph Braibanti and Joseph J. Spengler, eds., *Administration and Economic Development in India* (Durham, N.C., Duke University Press, 1963), p. 216.

32. Daniel Lerner, *The Passing of Traditional Society* (New York, The Free Press, 1958), passim.

influence on beliefs—the two are quite distinct in regard to the stability of beliefs and behavior that they imply.

Other-Directedness, Hierarchy, and Political Beliefs

When the conformity of other-directedness is linked to a strongly hierarchical social structure—when other-directedness is also "upper-directedness," as it is in most transitional societies—it becomes difficult to distinguish information from the source of that information. A communication is evaluated and accepted or rejected by virtue of the position of the communicator, without much reference to the merit of its content by some other impersonal standard. The individual in a hierarchical, other-directed society is so attuned to pressures from the social environment—especially those from above—that it is virtually impossible for information from a disesteemed source to alter his belief system. Exhortations from an esteemed source, on the other hand, can usually secure outward conformity in behavior and even changes in peripheral beliefs. The source of the external pressure for change thus determines what influence that source can exert on one's beliefs and behavior. To this extent an individual's mind is "closed," since what is not fixed by tradition is more responsive to external pressures than to the more rational processes of evaluation.[33]

The influence of other-directedness and hierarchy on the political belief system of Malaysian civil servants cannot be overestimated. First, it means that their peripheral beliefs are often more linked to each other by the authority sources from which they are derived than by any internal logic. It is common, therefore, to find a host of logically incompatible beliefs effectively compartmentalized in an individual's mind, each belief being strongly held by virtue of its origin. For example, a traditional belief that one should not openly criticize leaders coexists quite comfortably with the belief that parliamentary democracy requires an openly critical opposition, since both beliefs come from esteemed sources (i.e. traditional wisdom and Western learning). The welter of conflicting beliefs found among transitional elites becomes less confusing when one realizes that their admission to a belief system

33. Cf. Rokeach, *The Open and Closed Mind*, Ch. 3.

often depends more on the authority from which it emanates than on the logic of its inclusion.[34]

Secondly, hierarchy and other-directedness mean that political beliefs, particularly at the peripheral level, are likely to be quite variable and unstable. Most specific political beliefs are tailored to conform to the social environment, and when for one reason or another that environment changes substantially, changes will occur accordingly in peripheral political beliefs. Given the instability of transitional societies themselves, the sources of external social pressure to conform are subject to rapid and occasionally drastic change. Understanding this variability of political beliefs among transitional elites helps to account for much ideological change by reference to the rise of a new elite and thus to the establishment of a new reference group—a new conformity. More important, though, the instability of these beliefs makes a purely descriptive account of political beliefs in these countries an enterprise of limited usefulness.

The third point about other-directedness and hierarchy as they relate to political beliefs is concerned with how the study of political beliefs among transitional elites should be approached. If peripheral political beliefs are likely to be variable, it becomes more profitable to concentrate on either the broad stylistic characteristics of beliefs and the more stable central values or perhaps on the selective process by which the beliefs transmitted by sources of authority are accommodated.

34. In addition, the fact should not be overlooked that non-Western societies generally may place less emphasis on the logic and consistency of individual beliefs than Western societies. The quotation of proverbs often passes for argument in traditional society, and it is only our particular Western heritage that predisposes us to find such disputation lacking in rigor.

5

Man and Nature: The Struggle for Slices of a Constant Pie

The Man-Nature Orientation

Kluckhohn and Strodtbeck suggest three possible cultural orientations toward nature: "subjugation-to-nature," "harmony-with-nature," and "mastery-over-nature." [1] Unlike the orientation toward human nature, the view of natural forces that prevails in a society seems to depend heavily on the technical and scientific skills of the culture. It is possible for the industrialized West to achieve mastery-over-nature in many respects, whereas simple herding people are in a real sense at the mercy of natural forces. Thus the choice of orientations is, for herders, somewhat circumscribed by the level of their material culture.

Societies whose actual control over their environment is minimal are likely to make some ritual attempts to appease natural forces and to take precautionary measures such as storing water and grain. Even within communities that are subject to nature, certain charismatic figures are thought to possess special powers, however tenuous, to bend natural forces to the will of man. For example, Malinowski has written that the role of magic begins when mastery over nature ends; that is, the part of nature that seems beyond the rational control of a society becomes the province of the magical or religious arts, which attempt to appease and/or to manipulate potentially destructive natural forces.

In contrast to this priestly or sacral manipulation of the environment, the engineering approach typifies societies whose great technical virtuosity allows them to shape nature to their ends, or failing that, to construct havens that are immune to its vagaries. These varied approaches to nature, as categorized by Kluckhohn and Strodtbeck, primarily reflect the degree to which a society

1. Kluckhohn and Strodtbeck, *Variations in Value Orientations*, pp. 12–13.

feels it is in control of its present and future environment. It should be emphasized here that the orientation of a society toward nature depends on how *it* sees its relationship to nature, regardless of the degree of control over the environment that a dispassionate observer judges it to possess. Thus, if a society is objectively prey to nature, but nevertheless feels subjectively that it can control the environment, its subjective mastery is the important cultural orientation. Objective and subjective control are probably strongly associated, but analytically they are distinct.

Whether fatalism or manipulation prevails has a great influence on what is expected of the leaders of a society: whether they are expected to change and improve the environment, or whether their role is simply to preserve a tolerable status quo by means of ritual appeasement of natural forces. A culture's orientation toward nature thus creates distinctive political expectations and demands by which leadership is evaluated. The connection between political ideology and the orientation toward nature is important, as it helps set the parameters of political action.

Before examining the orientation toward nature that characterizes the sample of Malaysian civil servants, two additional points should be made about attitudes toward nature in general. First, although Kluckhohn and Strodtbeck's list of variations seems clearcut and logically exhaustive, it is a far from simple matter to decide how a culture should be classified according to this schema. Taking Japan as an example, the authors state that both historically and at present, Japanese culture emphasizes "harmony-with-nature." Koestler, on the other hand, while not employing the same categories, finds a dominant orientation in Japan that would be more appropriately called "mastery-over-nature." [2] He associates the hostile, volcanic geography of Japan with the attempts in art forms to master nature and reduce it to manageable proportions. The miniaturization of mountain landscapes with stones and sand in trays (*bon-seki*) and the dwarfing and shaping of trees by constant root cutting and by an elaborate system of weights and wires are, he states, only two examples of many symbolic attempts to gain mastery over nature. Koestler finds that in Japanese culture,

2. Arthur Koestler, *The Lotus and the Robot* (New York, Harper & Row, 1966), pp. 189–97.

"Nature is too hostile and threatening to be approached 'in the raw.' To be aesthetically acceptable, it must be stylized, formalized, miniaturized. Uncouth reality must be transformed into civilized artifact." [3] One might even interpret Koestler in another fashion and conclude that the Japanese orientation to nature is one of subjugation. The Japanese art forms he describes might be considered a kind of ritual compensation for a lack of control over natural forces—a symbolic manipulation of nature in art that cannot be achieved in reality.

Which of the three possible categories most appropriately describes the Japanese case is of less concern here than the fact that, as it stands, the typology does not lend itself to unambiguous classification. All societies attempt mastery over the environment by technology and/or magic, and one culture may feel as confident of its shamans as another of its engineers. In addition, each society generally regards some manifestations of nature as manageable by human effort and other natural forces as essentially uncontrollable. Mastery in one sphere may be balanced by subjugation in another. The Japanese example thus alerts us to the fact that characterizing a culture's view of man's relation to nature is a hazardous enterprise at best. For these reasons, it is useful to be more specific about the word "nature." The discussion here will focus largely on the problem of abundance versus scarcity—on nature's provision of the material goods necessary for subsistence.

A second point about orientations toward nature is also suggested by the example of traditional Japan. Presumably, the hostility or benevolence, the scarcity or abundance, of the physical environment in which a society lives will have some effect on that society's orientation toward nature. The influence of the environment's hostility on felt mastery over nature operates in the same manner as the technical level of the society. The higher the society's technical level and the greater the benevolence of the environment, the less likely a society will feel subjugated to nature. Simple societies by definition, however, have a low level of technical skills and live in environments generally characterized by scarcity and by occasional natural disasters such as disease, flood, and fires, over which they exercise little control. In such circum-

3. Ibid., p. 190.

stances, one would expect that a preponderance of simple societies would feel "subject" in large degree to the restrictions and periodic depredations of the physical environment.

As indicated in the previous chapter, the existential base does influence cultural values, particularly in the long run. A society that in fact exists at the subsistence level and is periodically devastated by drought, plague, or locusts is unlikely to sustain forever the belief that it can manipuate natural forces at will. The real gap between its manipulative power and that of a highly industrialized society is so great that it is likely to feel relatively more subject to nature. Within limits, of course, subsistence societies may vary in the degree to which they feel subject to their environments, but the fact that their techniques are so frail and their margins so slim cannot fail to affect their orientations to nature. The common experiences that the existential base provides to a community will be reflected over the long run in that society's basic value orientations.

COMPETITION FOR A CONSTANT PIE: THE POLITICS OF SCARCITY[4]

Focusing on the question of abundance versus scarcity, I hope to show that the orientation of Malaysian civil servants toward nature conforms closely with what one would expect of a society with limited technology, living in conditions of relative scarcity. They have what could be called a *"constant-pie" orientation, an orientation that assumes a fixed scarcity of desired material goods.* The "pie" cannot be enlarged that all might have larger "slices" but rather is constant, so that much of political and economic life is seen as constituting a struggle of one individual, family, group, or nation to expand its slice at the expense of other individuals, families, groups, or nations. Through the words of the civil servants themselves, I shall attempt to delineate their orientation toward nature, at the same time noting the consequences of such an orientation for political ideology.

Not Enough to Go Around

Each of the civil servants was asked, at some point, what he thought was the basic cause of wars, both international and

4. The phrase "Politics of Scarcity" is borrowed from Weiner's *The Politics of Scarcity*. My use of the term, however, is quite different from Weiner's.

domestic. The question is a significant one, as it reveals what the respondents feel are the causes of large-scale violence between groups—what people fight about and what is worth fighting over. Almost all respondents mentioned overpopulation as a prominent cause for war. Implicit, and occasionally explicit, in their replies was the feeling that resources are limited, and therefore an increase in population means smaller shares all around unless resources are captured from other groups or nations. This view of resources as a "constant pie" is clearly evident in what affable Kamalam in the Ministry of Education had to say. Asked if wars can be eliminated, he settled back in his chair and began:

> Here I have to introduce my philosophy. We Hindus consider the earth the "mother," and the mother can only bear a certain burden—and as population increases—so she can't bear the burden any longer.—So you have fate, like earthquakes and tidal waves, but now that war has come you don't even need these, since war kills lots of people in the same way.

And later:

> Let's put it this way—if a particular country is unable to support its entire population, and you've got a neighboring state with plenty, he says, "Why should my people be suffering —what shall we do?"—that sows the seed.

For Kamalam, the bounty of nature is limited; it will support so many and not one more. When the limit is exceeded, there are "earthquakes and tidal waves," or their more modern variant, war. Inche' Hussain, the ingenuous young Malay from the Immigration Service, said much the same thing when he was asked whether the causes of war can be eliminated. "I don't think it is possible. Because as the world gets older there will arise more complicated problems, people will become more ambitious and people will multiply, and there will not be enough to eat." Although Inche' Hussain coupled rising ambition with scarcity, he made it clear that population soon presses on limited resources (and it should be remembered that the nation in which he lives is not plagued by overpopulation according to most standard measures).

Mr. Khoo, a militant Christian in the Audit Department, echoed the sentiments of his Moslem and Hindu colleagues when he said, "There will always be wars—it is predicted in the Bible. It is nature's way of reducing the population." If Mr. Khoo's view of a constant pie of resources was less explicit than those of the men quoted earlier, he nevertheless implied that population must be reduced periodically if it is to stay in line with resources. The view that war is nature's way of reducing the population is, of course, not unknown in the West. But among these men it is more than simply a cliché to be passed off with a smile; it is something quite real. They are in earnest when they state that war occurs when population expands to the point where there is no longer enough to go around.

The inclination of these administrators to view resources as a constant pie was so prominent that it prompted the construction of a number of questions designed to tap this attitude among other civil servants outside the small sample. In all, 107 civil servants were asked whether they "strongly agreed," "agreed," "disagreed," or "strongly disagreed" with the statement, "Even in a rich country, if population grows rapidly, there is great danger that there will soon not be enough wealth to go around." [5] Although the situation was set in a "rich country" to discourage easy agreement, 60 percent of the respondents agreed that there might "soon not be enough wealth to go around." The constant-pie orientation of those interviewed is thus supported by the responses from this larger group.

The function of war for most of those interviewed is to reduce the number of competitors for scarce values. When the number of competitors dividing a constant pie exceeds a certain limit, a war occurs that eliminates enough contestants to make the struggle over the distribution of these scarce values a more manageable and less violent affair. Neo-Malthusians all, they see population growth threatening peace, since men will fight rather than surrender any of their modest share of the nonexpanding pie.

Other civil servants put their argument somewhat differently. Whereas the administrators already cited see war as the inevitable consequence of man's natural desire to preserve his share of the pie, others cast more blame and seemed to imply that if men were

5. Division I, II, and a few Division III civil servants were included in this sample drawn from training courses held by the various ministries in Kuala Lumpur.

less intent upon keeping or enlarging their share of the pie, war might be avoided. Inche' Zukifli, an elderly, vaguely disgruntled Malay in the Postal Service, illustrated this thematic variation when he spoke of the recent *Konfrontasi* launched against Malaysia by Indonesia. "Well, because—for instance this Indonesia—he is something like—not to say greedy—if I express it this way— Indonesia have [sic] been independent since 1948 or about and so far they have no improvement. Jealousy—I think that is the main reason." Jeganathan, who always boils things down to human motives, articulated the causes of war in a similar fashion:

> Basically it is—you see—you want a share in the other man's prosperity. That is what I think it is. A man has a bank balance and you want some of it. So if I want it and you don't give it, then I will rob you. It's because I'm poor that I want it—that I want your money. If I'm equally rich I don't care how rich you are. Take Japan; it was so poverty-stricken, that's why it started the war.

For these two men, the fact that there is only so much to go around must be placed in the context of human jealousy and greed in order to explain why wars occur. While Inche' Zukifli seemed to introduce the possibility of "improvement," he later made it clear that he merely meant reaching the pre-World War II standard of living. Thus, both men appeared to acknowledge the problem of fixed resources, but instead of emphasizing this limitation per se as the cause of war, they pointed to the reaction of human nature to this limitation as the proximate cause. Here, the human nature and man-nature orientations are joined in an explanatory framework. War, for them, resembles robbery, with the "have-nots" taking from the "haves."

The Survival of the Fittest

The struggle over slices of a constant pie is, for these administrators, what sets men at one another's throats. Given this basic orientation, political life resembles a Hobbesian world where all compete against all to preserve or enlarge their share of a fixed pie. An environment in which one man's gain is another man's loss places a premium on strength, for the weak will be lucky just to hold their own. None of these men has ever heard of Charles

Darwin, but their views of political and economic life closely resemble the tenets of Social Darwinism in the late nineteenth century. Shot through their political beliefs is the assumption of unending struggle over the distribution of a constant pie—an assumption that makes the stakes high and allows for no generosity toward other competitors.

Mr. Lim characterized the Hobbesian world of politics this way when he was asked whether we are getting closer to an ideal society in Malaysia: "I don't think we are. [Why?] Well, that is power politics—the big fish eat the small fish and the small fish eat worms." Such a response might have been expected from Mr. Lim, since he scored second highest on the Anomie Scale, but the same tone is characteristic of the most optimistic low scorers as well. When Inche' Nordin, an elderly Malay notable for his bright spirits and confidence in the future, was asked about the usefulness of protective associations for civil servants, he replied,

> I don't know how it is in other countries, but I know Malaya from experience. *Each profession is trying to kill the other. One doctor makes more money and everyone goes to him for one reason, and the others don't have so many people coming to them.* It's better to have your own association to preserve the profession. Even with trade unions, each one is trying to kill the other. They say, "You got, why not I got?"

Inche' Nordin's imagery is vivid, and he seems to see a fixed supply of both patients and money over which doctors and trade unions respectively are "trying to kill the other." The concept of a constant pie is quite explicit here, and the kind of behavior it elicits is equally clear.

Inche' Abdul Karim, another optimist and perhaps the strongest democrat in the entire group, in talking about how people would behave in an ideal society, described what he does not like in the present society. "They should think of one another as fellow human beings—and not to exploit the weaklings. What I mean is the clever ones will not take advantage of the stupid ones." The Hobbesian nature of the present society is what Inche' Abdul Karim would like to change. Only in the ideal society, he feels, could men behave in a way that would allow the least fit, in

Social Darwinistic terms—the weak and dull-witted—to survive along with the strong and clever.

If the weak are likely to lose out in the struggle for the domestic pie, the softhearted and irresolute among nation-states are no more likely to survive in the international arena. Sundram's description of international politics thus bears an unmistakable resemblance to Inche' Abdul Karim's picture of internal exploitation of the weak by the strong. Asked about the inevitability of war, he answered,

> Yes, war is inevitable. Now you have two camps and neutral nations will be eliminated. They must take a stand either in the democratic or communist camp. This will be more or less hitched to ideology—and preservation—the weak must rely on the strong to protect you [sic].

The only way for weak ntaions to survive, according to Sundram, is by joining, or becoming a client of, a strong nation that will act as a patron of its weak ally. This is the formula for survival in a Hobbesian world.

The Hobbesian character of political and economic life is created, as these men see it, by the fact that the size of the pie to be distributed is unchanging. Under such circumstances, it is difficult to establish any ground rules for the competition, and the scope for cooperation is greatly reduced. The weakness of any contestant will be quickly exploited, and unless he can find a strong patron, his only refuge is strength and/or wile. Most of these administrators apply the same reasoning to the international arena as well, where a nation that grants its citizens great freedom may find this a severe handicap in a world where other nations do not allow themselves such luxuries. Inche' Ja'afar expressed the potential danger of freedom in this manner:

> As a nation, we are out to compete with another nation. If we have too much freedom, then it might lessen our ability to compete. But if there is freedom all over—too much freedom may affect the national effort—if the U.S. wants to compete with the Soviet Union, it may have to lose some freedom in order to compete.

Although he is a strong democrat, Inche' Ja'afar feels democracy may be a disadvantage if other countries do not observe the ground rules. The problem is to establish such rules, and if they cannot be set up, a nation is willy-nilly forced to adopt the same methods as the most ruthless of its competitors in order to hold its own.

As already noted, most civil servants are persuaded that the central domestic function of government is to establish strict rules for the competition in order to prevent the struggle from leading to anarchy. Internationally, however, there is no agency to perform this role. Thus it is not surprising that these administrators see great danger in national freedom unless all other competing states are willing to abide by the same rules. Both domestically and internationally, then, the scarcity of desired values and the fact that their supply remains fixed seem to explain the "dog-eat-dog" quality of the competition as it is viewed by Malaysian bureaucrats. When someone can gain only at the expense of another—when economic and political life is a zero-sum game—it is only natural that the struggle should be intense.

To confirm the impression from the interviews, I asked over one hundred civil servants whether or not they agreed with the statement, "Any government that wants to help the poor people will have to take something away from the rich in order to do it." The statement makes the political implications of a constant-pie orientation quite explicit. Roughly two-thirds (65.9 percent) agreed with the statement, and over half of those assenting said they "strongly agreed." [6] These results lend strong support to the more impressionistic analysis of the interview transcripts, which indicated that political competition is viewed as a struggle over the division of a constant pie. The evidence clearly suggests, moreover, that the conflict engendered by this fixed supply of material goods is of central importance in accounting for the conception of both internal and external politics that characterizes the sample.

The belief patterns noted thus far in this chapter have not gone completely unnoticed by other political scientists. Lucian Pye, in his *Guerilla Communism in Malaya,* wrote that surrendered

6. This, despite the well-known fact among civil servants that over half of annual governmental revenue comes from import and export duties rather than from internal taxation.

communist insurgents believed politics consisted of hostility, aggressiveness, and conflict, quite apart from communist teachings.[7] Although he did not elaborate, Pye foreshadowed the present analysis when he remarked that the insurgents he interviewed felt that "from every political development, some groups profited and some suffered." [8] Pye made this observation of a very unique sample, but it seems equally applicable to Malaysian civil servants and may well apply to elites in other underdeveloped nations.

THE RELATION OF THE CONSTANT-PIE ORIENTATION TO OTHER ATTITUDINAL VARIABLES

The prominence of the constant-pie or zero-sum orientation in the interviews and its importance for political beliefs prompted the construction of questionnaire items designed to tap the same attitude in a different manner. A more objective measure of this orientation offers the possibility of replicating the subjective findings and of relating them to other attitudinal variables. The four items constructed for this purpose were as follows:

1. Even in a rich country, if population grows rapidly, there is great danger that there will soon not be enough wealth to go around.
2. Those who get ahead usually get ahead at the expense of others.
3. When an individual or group gains, it usually means that another individual or group loses.
4. Any government that wants to help the poor people will have to take something away from the rich in order to do it.

A central question in research of this nature is whether or not an attitude or orientation unearthed in one setting is really unique to that setting. Inasmuch as we are focusing on patterns of ideology in new nations, it is essential to ask if the constant-pie orientation is typical of new nations or if it is just as likely to be found in the older, more industrialized states. Fortunately, three of the four scale items have been administered in England, and the comparisons these data make possible can provide a partial answer to such a broad question.[9]

7. Pye, p. 168.
8. Ibid., p. 196.
9. I am immensely grateful to Robert Putnam, who administered these items in England as a part of his own research on the comparative political cultures of elite groups in England and Italy. Comparisons with Italian elite groups will be available at a later date as well.

TABLE 3: Responses of British Civil Servants, British Members of Parliament, and Malaysian Civil Servants to Three Constant-Pie Scale Items*

Question 2: Those who get ahead usually get ahead at the expense of others.

	Strongly Agree		Agree		Disagree		Strongly Disagree		Total N
	%	(N)	%	(N)	%	(N)	%	(N)	
British Civil Servants	0	(0)	30	(7)	70	(16)	0	(0)	23
British Members of Parliament	4	(3)	24	(20)	62	(53)	11	(9)	85
Malaysian Civil Servants	21	(17)	40	(33)	27	(22)	12	(10)	82

Question 3: When an individual or group gains, it usually means that another individual or group loses.

	Strongly Agree		Agree		Disagree		Strongly Disagree		Total N
	%	(N)	%	(N)	%	(N)	%	(N)	
British Civil Servants	0	(0)	29	(6)	71	(15)	0	(0)	21
British Members of Parliament	1	(1)	26	(27)	64	(51)	9	(7)	80
Malaysian Civil Servants	16	(13)	32	(26)	46	(38)	6	(5)	82

Question 4: Any government that wants to help the poor people will have to take something away from the rich in order to do it.

	Strongly Agree		Agree		Disagree		Strongly Disagree		Total N
	%	(N)	%	(N)	%	(N)	%	(N)	
British Civil Servants	0	(0)	61	(14)	40	(9)	0	(0)	23
British Members of Parliament	11	(9)	39	(32)	37	(31)	13	(11)	83
Malaysian Civil Servants	36	(29)	28	(22)	24	(19)	13	(10)	80

* Percentages have been rounded to the nearest point.

Items 2, 3, and 4 were given to a small random sample of British higher civil servants and to a larger randomly selected group of members of Parliament. The results from Malaysia and England are tabulated in Table 3.

For questions 2 and 3, which tap the constant-pie orientation in general terms, the Malaysian civil servants view promotion or advancement as a zero-sum affair significantly more often than either their occupational counterparts or elected officials in England. In particular, when Malaysians were asked if "those who get ahead usually get ahead at the expense of others," they agreed more than twice as often as either British group. The differences for the more highly politicized context of question 4 are in the same direction, although they are not as striking. Here the proportion who agreed with the statement is not so much greater among the Malaysians (64 percent) than among British civil servants (61 percent) or members of Parliament (50 percent). Nevertheless, the percentage who "agree strongly" is much higher for Malaysian respondents (36 percent as compared with 0 percent and 11 percent).

These results, important as they are for this argument, do not constitute a decisive test to determine if the constant-pie orientation is more characteristic of elites in new nations than in highly industrialized settings. For that, a comparable scale would have to be administered to comparable elites in quite a few nations. What can be said, however, is that the available evidence tends to sustain this working hypothesis.[10]

In an effort to check whether the constant-pie orientation was unique to bureaucrats as compared with other groups within Malaysia, all items in the scale were administered to twenty-four management trainees from the Malaysian private sector attending a course at the National Productivity Centre. Responses were

10. This data is open to the criticism of "response set," since an affirmative answer is, in each case, indicative of a constant-pie orientation. If, however, the response set were of critical importance, we would not expect the correlation of this scale with other attitudinal variables which are not subject to response set problems. These correlations are explored below. In addition, the evidence of the constant-pie orientation in the interview transcripts as well lends more credence to the results from this scale. In any case, when the scale is used again, controls for response set should be introduced.

scored 5 (strongly agree), 4 (agree), 2 (disagree), 1 (strongly disagree), and the total score for an individual was simply the sum of scores for each item.[11] A comparison between the average scores for the private and public sector respondents allows us to determine whether the orientation is a specifically bureaucratic phenomenon in Malaysia or if it is shared in equal measure by non-civil-servants in the business world. The rigid organization of bureaucratic posts and salaries might lead one to imagine more of a zero-sum orientation among civil servants. On the other hand, firms in the private sector often are victims of the pressure of the competitive environment, and their profits fluctuate according to the vagaries of the market. Following this line of reasoning, one might expect to find more of a zero-sum orientation among managers in the private sector. Different kinds of common sense thus lead in quite opposite directions. In reality, the average score on all the constant-pie items for the private sector respondents was 12.5, and for the public sector, 12.4. The distribution of scores within each group, moreover, was comparable. A difference of .1 is of no significance whatever, and there is thus no reason to suppose that anything peculiar to the experience of civil servants might predispose them to think more in constant-pie terms than other groups. The roots of this orientation must lie elsewhere than in occupational distinctions.

In the context of the interviews it seemed that the constant-pie orientation was related to both a Hobbesian view of the world and a relative absence of social trust. The evidence from the transcripts, persuasive as it seems, is nevertheless somewhat impressionistic. The use of the questionnaire measure, however, permits an exploration of the connection between the constant-pie orientation and other attitudinal variables in a more systematic fashion. These connections serve to put some conceptual "flesh" on the orientation and place it in its proper context among other beliefs and opinions.

The summed scores on the constant-pie items were divided at the median into high and low scorers and correlated with the

---

11. The *median* score for 80 civil servants was 12.35. Actually, more agreement was recorded for items 1 and 4, which place the situation in a more specific context, than for the more general statements represented by items 2 and 3.

scores on other attitudinal variables tapped in the same question-naire.[12] Surprisingly, of the eight other variables tested, the results for five were correlated with constant-pie scores at a statistically significant level (.05 level or better using chi square). Four of these correlations are important enough to merit discussion.

Authoritarianism. Employing the F Scale used by Joseph Elder in India,[13] those who were high scorers in constant-pie thinking were generally high scorers on the authoritarianism scale as well.[14] The association between the two is hardly astonishing, since both orientations share a kind of "over-realism," a belief that conflict rather than cooperation characterizes social relations. Items in the F scale stating that "there will always be wars and conflict," that the division between "the strong and the weak" is the most relevant one in society, and that "evil people" abound clearly approximate the vision of the world one would expect of some-one competing for his share of a fixed pie. That people are pitted constantly against one another is an assumption as common to the man who thinks in constant-pie terms as to the authoritarian man.

Simply because of the widespread misunderstanding of what "authoritarianism" means, I should like to make quite clear what is being said here. One may distinguish between those who, when discussing the dynamics of authoritarianism, concentrate on ego-defensive mechanisms and pathology, and those who focus on cognitive processes. As Greenstein points out,

> The cognitive theory holds that the patterns of expression and behavior that have been characterized as authoritarian are based upon simple learning of the conceptions of reality prevalent in one's culture or sub-culture, and that these patterns also may to some extent be accurate reflections of the actual conditions of adult life faced by some individuals,

12. See Appendix B, Part II, for a complete listing of items and scales used in this questionnaire.

13. See Appendix B, Part II, for this seven item scale. Elder's Scale is subject to response set criticism as well.

14. See Appendix C for correlation table and chi^2. N's for this and the following variables ranged from 35 to 66, thus making chi square an appropriate measure of association.

rather than having the labyrinthine roots in reaction formation suggested by the ego-defensive theory.[15]

The cognitive approach is particularly useful in interpreting
authoritarianism in the non-Western context. Malaysian civil
servants, in particular, manifest some authoritarian traits, while
lacking others. They do exhibit a suspicion and distrust of human
nature, an externalized superego, and conventionalism, but they
are not exclusively power-oriented, nor do they desire unrestrained
leaders (for they do not trust human nature). In this instance, an
externalized superego and a lack of faith in people are probably
cultural norms rather than pathological traits. Moreover, their
constant-pie orientation may well be an accurate reflection of
actual conditions. The cognitive theory of authoritarianism surely
makes more sense than the ego-defensive theory in a cultural
milieu where elements of authoritarian character predominate and
where much of the environment may in fact resemble what the
supposedly pathological person might imagine.

In an environment of this sort, it is difficult to distinguish ego-
defensive strategies from conformity—pathology from acquiescence. There is thus no reason to resort to pathology, as Pye does,
to explain the authoritarian attitudes of Malaysian civil servants.
It is more than likely that the mere assimilation of cultural norms
and adaptation to the environment produce much of the authoritarianism found in Malaysia. The strong affect and reaction formation that characterize the pathological authoritarian are largely
absent, for these men, like Banfield's southern Italian peasants, are
reflecting the cultural norms and existential restraints that are a
part of their experience.

Superiors as vindictive or threatening. Using three items to ascer-
tain whether respondents felt their superiors were vindictive or
threatening, it was found that those who thought more in constant-
pie terms tended to view their superiors in this manner.[16] The
correlation confirms what might have been predicted. If the social
product is viewed as fixed, it is likely that superiors would be expected to seize every advantage and to exploit their subordinates

15. Fred I. Greenstein, "Personality and Political Socialization: The Theories of
Authoritarian and Democratic Character," *The Annals* (September 1965), p. 93.
16. See Appendix B, Part II, for items used and Appendix C for the correlation
table and chi[2].

when the opportunity arose. Although this result was anticipated, the effect of the constant-pie orientation on interpersonal relationships within the bureaucracy is an important one to have established.

Faith-in-People. Rosenberg's Faith-in-People Scale was administered to fifty-four civil servants, but because of the method of scoring, a large number of middle scores had to be discarded in dichotomizing the results into high and low categories.[17] Of the thirty-five remaining individuals, those with a high constant-pie orientation had less faith in people, while those who thought less in constant-pie terms more often evinced a greater faith in people. As noted earlier in this chapter, everyone in a constant-pie world is a potential competitor and is expected to act in a narrowly selfish manner. Surely no one would expect much generalized social trust where the social product is fixed at low levels, and the correlation bears this out.

The link between the constant-pie orientation and a lack of social trust, both in the interviews and in more objective measures, is of some theoretical importance. It connects the view of human nature that was explored in the previous chapter and the belief in a fixed social product. An evaluation of human nature in which a lack of social trust predominates may be the common pattern in any community where the supply of most desired values is seen as severely limited.

For peasant society this connection has been made repeatedly. Foster notes the poor quality of extra-familial interpersonal relations in peasant society and ascribes it to the fact that "each minimal social unit . . . sees itself in perpetual, unrelenting struggle with its fellows for possession of or control over what it considers to be its share of scare values." [18] In addition to the

17. See Appendix B, Part II, for scale items and Appendix C for the correlation table and chi2.

18. George M. Foster, "Peasant Society and the Image of Limited Good," *American Anthropologist, 62* (April 1965), p. 302. Foster also cites a number of anthropologists who have commented on the "mentality of mutual distrust" found in peasant societies. Among others, he mentions Oscar Lewis, *Life in a Mexican Village: Tepoztlan Restudied* (Champaigne-Urbana, University of Illinois Press, 1951); G. Morris Carstairs, *The Twice-Born: A Study of a Community of High-Caste Hindus* (Bloomington, Indiana University Press, 1958); S. L. Dube, *India's Changing Villages: Human Factors in Community Development* (London, Routledge and Kegan Paul, Ltd., 1958); Winifred S. Blackman, *The Fellahin of Upper Egypt*

anthropological evidence for widespread social distrust in peasant societies, including Indian and Chinese peasant communities,[19] Swift has commented on precisely the same pattern among Malay peasants. After describing the lack of social trust within a Malay village, Swift relates it to a constant pie in this passage:

> and when competition moves into the field of power (which I see as a zero-sum concept) it may be said that one man's success can only be achieved at the direct expense of his competitors. Many village leaders are such because they have striven hard to achieve the position, and in the course of their striving have made bitter enemies.[20]

One would be at a loss to describe the great variety of conditions and historical experiences that might provide fertile ground for the growth of social distrust. An event like the French Revolution created cleavages and social distrust that endure to this day, but the form of social distrust that it promoted is quite different from what is found among Malaysian civil servants. The familiar animosities between anti-clerical and pro-clerical groups in France are, for example, highly structured—i.e. social distrust has a relatively clear target. An environment where desired values are seen in zero-sum terms, on the other hand, is more likely to encourage the highly generalized social distrust that has been seen among the seventeen administrators. The suggestion here is merely that the constant-pie orientation may be a sufficient, but not a necessary, condition for widespread interpersonal distrust. The fact that one person's gains must come at the expense of others—or simply the belief that this is true—makes everyone a potential or actual competitor for scarce values, since the progress of one necessarily means the plunder of another. In this sort of atmosphere, it would require a great act of faith to trust others in the absence of firm sanctions to enforce cooperation. Generalized social distrust, in this context, is likely to be the modal orientation, and social trust a deviant one.

(London, George C. Harrap & Co., Ltd., 1927); Hsiao-tung Fei and Chit-I Chang, *Earthbound China: A Study of the Rural Economy in Yunnan* (Chicago, University of Chicago Press, 1945).

19. See n. 31 below.

20. Swift, *Malay Peasant Society in Jelebu,* pp. 156–57.

Control over the future. The degree to which people feel they can successfully plan for the future is an important basic attitude. Two items were included in the questionnaire to tap this feeling, and the correlation between these scores and the constant-pie items was striking. Those who thought in constant-pie terms most often felt they lacked any control over the future, while those who scored low in constant-pie thinking scored high in future control items (N = 57, chi^2 24.10, p < .001).[21]

In a constant-pie environment one must struggle to preserve his share against the depredations of others, while where the pie is expanding, the problem is rather to preserve a rate of advance. In the latter situation, the future is likely to be promising, co-operation and generosity are more possible and more rewarding, and even the weak can participate in gains. An environment of scarcity projected into the future, however, promises danger and uncertainty and makes planning a hazardous enterprise at best. Feelings of fear and helplessness before the future may well characterize those who see the system within which they operate as closed and relatively poor.[22] Fear of the future is, in this context, quite common among more traditional peoples, who actually live in systems of this nature.

CLARIFYING THE CONSTANT-PIE ORIENTATION

An economic view. After I had developed the notion of a constant-pie orientation in the context of the Malaysian research, I came across a discussion of much the same phenomenon in the writings of at least two social scientists. The first, Albert O. Hirschman, an economist, discusses this orientation in his book, *The Strategy of Economic Development,* a work that challenges many of the orthodox theories of economic growth.[23] Hirschman dis-

---

21. See Appendix B, Part II, for scale items and Appendix C for the correlation table.

22. One could reverse the argument and say that a fear of the future will result in a constant-pie orientation. The causal link is, in this case, somewhat more difficult to construct but not entirely implausible. For example, when the economic pie is in fact expanding, a pervasive fear of the future may prevent a person from projecting that expansion into the future and changing his beliefs accordingly. Experience over time with an expanding pie would, however, probably extinguish his fear of the future.

23. Albert O. Hirschman, *The Strategy of Economic Development* (New Haven, Yale University Press, 1958).

tinguishes between tightly knit societies, which are likely to have a "group focused image of change," and more loosely structured societies, which are likely to manifest an "ego-focused image of change." Tightly knit societies, according to this characterization, expect economic development to raise everyone at the same rate, so that relative status rankings are preserved, while loosely structured societies see progress in individual rather than group terms.[24] Hirschman suggests that societies of the latter type tend to stress the "competitive and creative role of entrepreneurs," at the expense of the cooperative abilities needed to ensure the success of any large-scale enterprise. For the Malaysian sample, too, the competitive pattern in politics is likely to be emphasized, and the possibility of cooperative strategies largely discounted. Hirschman feels that this selective emphasis may result from something like the constant-pie orientation. As he puts it,

> When the total social product is believed to be rigidly fixed, the idea that both parties can profit from an agreement is not likely to arise; on the contrary, the more closely one approaches agreement, the more suspicious one becomes about the other fellow's having "put something over." [25]

The belief in a "rigidly fixed social product" is not really different from the constant-pie orientation. Hirschman limits himself to a description of the economic consequences of such a belief, but the consequences for political ideology are similar. The Hobbesian world the respondents see, with its ruthless competition and its many opportunities for exploitation of the weak by the strong, are all analogous to the economic pattern Hirschman finds, and both patterns seem to flow from the same constant-pie orientation.

Hirschman also notes that the "group-focused image of change" can be seen as a "defensive ego-focused strategy"; that is, those who fear that they will be bested in the competition may find it to their advantage to emphasize group-focused change that would enable them to preserve their relative position.[26] Group-focused

24. Ibid., pp. 11–14.
25. Ibid., p. 18.
26. Ibid., p. 13.

change requires strong government that can restrain individuals and groups from acting against the interests of the community at large, and this is exactly the sort of government preferred by Malaysian civil servants, perhaps for the same reason Hirschman outlines. The distinction here is between a conception of reality and a preference: Malaysian administrators feel that ruthless competition characterizes the present situation but desire leaders who will be able to enforce community-serving standards of behavior. Given the loss of status suffered by bureaucrats vis-à-vis politicians after independence and the high level of unrestrained self-seeking they see in society, their preference for strong government may well represent a desire to protect themselves and others who they feel are less fitted for survival in an ego-focused society.

Thus a central belief in a "rigidly fixed social product"—a constant-pie orientation—leads not only to the types of economic behavior Hirschman has described but also helps explain analogous political patterns such as a competitive rather than cooperative view of political life and a desire for strong central government to enforce standards of cooperative behavior.

An anthropological view. The second social scientist who has discussed something akin to the constant-pie orientation is George M. Foster, an anthropologist. Foster contends that "the image of limited good' is a belief that is characteristic of Latin American peasant societies, if not peasant societies, everywhere.[27] His understanding of the term is virtually identical with the concept of a constant pie, although, as the following statement shows, he finds it applicable to a much broader range of phenomena:

> By "Image of Limited Good" I mean that broad areas of peasant behavior are patterned in such fashion as to suggest that peasants view their social, economic, and natural universes—their total environment—as one in which all of the desired things in life such as land, wealth, health, friendship and love, manliness and honor, respect and status, power and influence, security and safety, *exist in finite quantity* and *are always in short supply,* as far as the peasant is concerned. Not only do these and all other "good things" exist in finite

27. Foster, "Peasant Society and the Image of Limited Good," pp. 293–315.

and limited quantities, but in addition, *there is no way directly within peasant power to increase the available quantities.*[28]

Whether or not the image of limited good applies as well to
values like health, love, honor, and so forth, is not of direct concern
here,[29] but Foster does delineate the three essential qualities of a
constant-pie orientation. The size of the pie must be seen as fixed,
it must be seen as small relative to demand, and it must be thought
to remain relatively constant over time. When all three qualities
are present in the minds of community members, they will see
themselves living as part of a "closed system"[30] in which no
appreciable expansion of the social product can occur.

The hallmark of this kind of environment is that no individual,
family, or group can gain unless other individuals, families, or
groups lose. Social life becomes a zero-sum game in which one can
only get ahead at the expense of others. Many of the political views
of civil servants recounted earlier may be viewed as logical in the
light of this basic value orientation. Politics is, for them, imbued
with the Hobbesian qualities that characterize a constant-pie orientation. They would like government to impose sanctions against
this chaos of individualistic self-seeking and to restore order, but
in the meantime, until ground rules and order are created, the
endless struggle for material values continues.

There is good reason to suppose that the constant-pie orientation
is not restricted to peasant societies in Latin America or to Malaysian administrators. Foster himself cites evidence from no less than
thirteen areas[31] in addition to Mexico, where his own firsthand
observations were made, to support his contention that the orientation is characteristic of most, if not all, peasant societies. Since

28. Ibid., p. 296.

29. There is some evidence from the transcripts that the constant-pie orientation
is applicable to values other than just wealth and power. Many respondents exhibit
a good deal of *machismo*—exaggerated toughness and a touchy sense of personal
honor—which Foster thinks flows from this orientation. The men I interviewed
also seem to consider prestige and status difficult to obtain, as this typical quote
from Inche' Ismail illustrates: "But there can't be an ideal man since there can't be
an ideal society. If a man is the ideal of one sector, then another sector will not like
him and even perhaps grow to hate him."

30. Foster, p. 297.

31. Egypt, Uganda, Columbia, Guatemala, Nigeria, Peru, Pakistan, Spain, Greece,
Lebanon, China, India, and Indonesia. See Foster.

most peasant societies are, in fact, societies in which the material pie *is* constant and in which it is often true that one man's gain is another man's loss, the widespread evidence of this orientation is scarcely surprising. Later I shall explain why I feel that the constant-pie orientation is characteristic not only of peasant society but of postcolonial elites as well.

CONSTANT-PIE ORIENTATION AND DISTRIBUTIVE JUSTICE

Evidence for the constant-pie orientation among Malaysian bureaucrats can be found in what they fail to say as well as in what they do say. American workingmen in Lane's Eastport, when they spoke to him of their future, saw an expanding economic pie in which they fully expected to share. Commenting on this, Lane writes, "Many of the men who see themselves as 'better off' in five years think of this in terms of an advancing economy, not individual promotion." [32] Oddly, not one of the Malaysian civil servants interviewed mentioned an advancing economy or a growing civil service as his way to a better life. Those who saw a better future saw it not in terms of a general societal advance but rather as a result of their own promotion through a static system. They not only fail to see total wealth as an expanding quantity; they fail as well to see any future change in the status pyramid. All of them choose to ignore the large expansion of civil service posts in recent years and focus instead on promotion as their superiors retire or die. What seems to be missing is an appreciation of the fact that the total number of positions at each rank is increasing and that there is both an absolute and a relative expansion of the middle and upper class that makes room each year for more and more people. The hours civil servants spend assiduously examining the Federal Establishment List, making notes of retirements, transfers, and promotions, are a reflection of the constant-pie occupational world in which they imagine themselves to be operating. Quite naturally, competition for promotion, suspicion of what others may be doing to get ahead, and disaffection with the distribution of posts are all intensified in this environment. Internal bureaucratic politics are thus but a smaller version of what is assumed to occur in national politics.

32. Lane, *Political Ideology*, p. 18.

When the pie is seen as constant both inside and outside the bureaucracy, concern is focused on whether an individual is getting his share or not. He cannot afford to be generous, since others advance potentially at his expense. An individual or group in this context judges the system largely in terms of its distributive justice, and it is this almost exclusive concern with how justly the slices are parcelled out that characterizes the constant-pie orientation. It is therefore difficult for a group to look with equanimity on the advances of another sector, since that sector's advance leaves a smaller balance to be distributed to the remaining groups. Whether a civil servant groups himself with his racial community, with other civil servants, or simply with his close kin—and all identifications are present in the sample—all of them judge the political system according to how equitable they think their share and that of their group to be. Mere intimation of an advantage about to be conferred on others excites in them a lively sense of personal or group loss and, often, bitterness.[33]

For most of these civil servants, the stuff of politics at present is not the effort to realize common goals, but rather the attempt to mediate and settle disputes over the distribution of scarce values. Ethnic cleavages, coinciding with linguistic, occupational, religious, and urban-rural divisions, exacerbate the disputes and provide a focal point for conflict, but they do not per se produce it. The nature of the cleavages within the society can thus be seen as influencing the structure of the conflict, while the quality or intensity of the conflict will be higher or lower depending upon whether the fund of scarce values is viewed as fixed or not by most members of the society. The ideal politician is thus one who, by appeals, threats, fatherly firmness, and justice, persuades or intimidates individuals and groups to accept less than they would otherwise insist upon. He keeps peace among his children, who are continually at war over the distribution of scarce values.

The desire for a strong government that would promote a group-

33. National politics in Malaysia follows much the same pattern. With the exception of a handful of leaders, party members seem largely concerned with retaining or expanding the privileges their group enjoys rather than with devising policies to enlarge the pie. The competition for these privileges is carried on *as if* the total pie were both small and constant. Similar orientations may be observed in the industrialized West as well; the distinction is one of relative emphasis rather than of an absolute dichotomy.

focused policy can be seen as an effort to eliminate the problem of distribution by freezing the existing distributive pattern. Under this policy, government would in effect guarantee the *relative* financial statuses of all; gains or losses would be evenly distributed throughout the social pyramid, with relative statuses remaining intact. As Hirschman has noted, this is a strategy adopted by those who feel they are potential losers in a period of change. What is required of strong central rule is that it ensure its people against the inherent dangers of a constant-pie society. The same process is involved in the efforts of trade unions to abolish piece-work, which would profit some more than others and divide the group.[34] It is a conservative strategy that values group solidarity over atomized competition.

CONCLUSION

It should be emphasized again that the constant-pie orientation is an ordering principle that unites a variety of beliefs. None of the civil servants ever directly suggested that he viewed the environment in this fashion, and there is therefore no basis for assuming that this central belief is a part of his conscious cognitive orientation. But many of the respondents' political beliefs make sense only if they are interpreted in the light of this ordering principle. The constant-pie orientation does not seem to be contradicted by any of the evidence, and it makes comprehensible and predictable a wide range of political beliefs described.

The quality of politics in a community where the pie is assumed to be constant is fundamentally different from politics in an environment where the pie is thought to be expanding. It is the difference between the politics of scarcity and the politics of affluence. Where the pie is expanding, cooperation and generosity are possible, while where it is constant, one must be callous, since, as Mr. Lim aptly put it, "The big fish eat the small fish and the small fish eat worms." In the one, people can get rich and no one suffers, while in the other, the poor must plunder the rich if they are to advance. In the one, population increase need not mean poverty, but in the other, population growth means smaller shares all around and promotes violence. In the one, groups are fighting to preserve a *rate* of advance in an atmosphere of economic

34. Hirschman, *The Strategy of Economic Development*, p. 13.

growth, while in the other, a group is fighting to preserve its
share of a fixed pie against the assaults of opposing groups. In the
one, compromise comes easily and alliances can endure, while in
the other, the stakes are too high for much compromise, and
alliances are rife with suspicion and distrust. Where the pie is growing, one can afford to give something away occasionally, while
where it is fixed, there is no substitute for strength and ruthlessness. These qualities of a constant-pie world dominate the views
of politics held by Malaysian civil servants. It is not that they
prefer things this way; on the contrary, they would like the government to step in and put an end to the pattern of politics created
by a constant pie.

As already implied in the discussion of misanthropy among
Malaysian civil servants, the constant-pie orientation leaves little
room for the social trust that promotes democratic political styles.
Perhaps this absence of trust lies at the bottom of many of the
political implications of this basic orientation, for Almond and
Verba, among others, have shown that "the role of social trust
and cooperativeness as a component of the civic culture cannot be
overemphasized." [35] As social trust and cooperativeness filter into
political beliefs, they reduce partisanship and fragmentation, facilitate the formation of groups, encourage the use of persuasive
strategies, and make for some level of confidence in the elite and
in the political system.[36] The constant-pie orientation, on the other
hand, discourages social trust and the political dividend that social
trust pays. In the absence of this trust and cooperation, the maintenance of a democratic system becomes vastly more difficult, since
there is great discontinuity between the political culture assumed
by a democratic type of government and the actual political
culture.

Throughout this chapter I have concentrated on demonstrating
the existence of what has been called a constant-pie orientation
and exploring its relationship with other attitudinal variables. In
particular, a view that imparts Hobbesian characteristics to the
environment, a lack of faith in people, a fear of the future, and a
special form of authoritarianism were all significantly associated

35. Almond and Verba, *The Civic Culture,* pp. 356–57.
36. Ibid., pp. 357–60.

with a belief in a fixed social product. These empirical connections place the orientation in a broader context and relate the findings for the orientation toward human nature to the findings for the "man-nature" orientation. Profiting from the insights of other social scientists, I have also attempted to trace some of the political implications of the constant-pie thinking: the concern with distributive justice, the fragility of political cooperation, the desire for government to impose a "group-focused" orientation, and so forth.

In the following chapter, I hope to suggest the origin and development of the constant-pie orientation and, in the process, highlight some essential characteristics of ideological change in transitional societies.

6

The Dynamics of the Constant-Pie Orientation and the Nature of Transitional Society

THE PEASANT'S WORLD AS A CONSTANT-PIE WORLD

The Parameters of Traditional Society

When a peasant assumes that the fund of desired values in his community is both small and constant, he does little violence to the facts. His view is a more or less accurate assessment of his condition and that of his neighbors. Foster is quite explicit on this point: "Peasant economies, as pointed out by many authors, are not productive. In the average village there *is* only a finite amount of wealth produced, and no amount of extra hard work will significantly change the figure." [1]

The social product *is* fixed in peasant society, and it is in this situation that the constant-pie orientation must develop. Not only is the total wealth of a peasant village constant, but the level of technical skills and scientific knowledge is also fixed, making the prospect of greater affluence in the years to come completely unrealistic. Individuals may aspire to more in the future, but not the community as a whole. A peasant society is likely to have only a fixed number of leadership posts as well, and since these posts are less divisible than rice or gold, the potential for inequalities in the distribution of power is particularly great.

In most peasant villages wealth is virtually synonymous with the

1. Foster, "Peasant Society and the Image of Limited Good," p. 297. Foster also makes the distinction between work and the production of wealth.

> In fact, it seems accurate to say that the average peasant sees little or no relationship between work and production techniques on the one hand, and the acquisition of wealth on the other. Rather, wealth is seen by villagers in the same light as land: present, circumscribed by absolute limits, and having no relationship to work. One works to eat, but not to create wealth. Wealth, like land, is something that is inherent in nature. It can be divided up and passed around in various ways, but, within the framework of the villager's traditional world, it does not grow (p. 298).

amount of productive land an individual possesses. While the pattern of "slash-and-burn" agriculture, where there is little population pressure, offers some chance to leave the community and strike out on one's own,[2] the sedentary wet-rice pattern that prevails in most of Southeast Asia more closely resembles a closed system. The labor costs of bringing new land into production—assuming more land is available nearby—are so great they render the total arable land area more or less constant in the foreseeable future. Under the wet-rice pattern, land becomes gradually more scarce as population grows, and as the cultivators become accustomed to this productive technique, it becomes progressively more difficult for an individual to break away and return to slash-and-burn agriculture.

Power, knowledge, skills, land, and wealth are thus all more or less fixed at certain levels in the peasant economy. The progress of one group or individual often does occur only at the expense of a competing group or individual, and the peasant's belief that this is so is no figment of his imagination. The economic system is a closed one, and where some contact with a central government exists, the question is seldom how much will be received from the government, but whether the tax plunder that will surely occur can be minimized. If anything, the net effect of an affiliation with a central government in traditional society is to reduce the quantity of scarce goods to be distributed within the village. That the government will take a share as tax is virtually certain, and only the size of that share is in question, as village authorities plead abject poverty and government officials search for something to squeeze. Thus, the central government itself contributes to the economic scarcity of peasant life.

The constant-pie orientation, then, reflects the inherent limitations of traditional peasant society. More specifically, it reflects the severely limited availability of power, prestige, wealth, land,

2. I do not wish to imply that an individual leaving a slash-and-burn community can look forward to prosperity. On the contrary, he must clear land himself and will, in all probability, only produce a bare subsistence for himself and his family —if he can sustain them until the first harvest. What he gains is simply freedom from dependence on the largesse of relatives in the village. Most anthropologists report that the reason for leaving is usually a desire for independence or a result of factional quarrels in the village, with the weaker party leaving or even being cast out for some serious infraction of village probity, rather than the desire for wealth.

and productive techniques. As a peasant orientation, it is in tune with the realities.

Constant Pie, the Future, and Social Distrust

A belief that the society could to some extent collectively plan its own future might theoretically offer a way out, but the attribution of natural events to supernatural forces and the uncertainty and fear that permeate the peasant view of the future only serve to reinforce the orientation. Nothing in the peasant's attitude toward the future mitigates his belief in the inevitability of scarcity or the permanence of conflict over the distribution of shares.

As has been indicated, the relationship between the constant-pie orientation and the orientation to time is a crucial one. It is particularly relevant to strategies of cooperation, since even in a zero-sum environment, a long-run view might allow one faction to cooperate closely over an extended period to increase its share of scarce values. In other words, a "zero-sum game" (in which the gain of any one player is matched by losses among other players of an equivalent sum) does not per se exclude long-run cooperative strategies, although it may make cooperation somewhat more tenuous, since the potential rewards for switching alliances are comparatively great. But the constant-pie orientation, when coupled with a short-run view of the future as it is in peasant society,[3] drastically reduces the scope for long-term cooperation. When most members join a group to achieve a variety of short-run personal advantages, it becomes impossible for the group as a whole to pursue long-run objectives and still retain its membership. Under these circumstances, groups tend to be short-lived and fragile and to seek only immediate, limited objectives.

This description of the limited nature of cooperation among peasants is at variance with the semi-romanticized image of peasants, which views peasant societies as the very model of collective endeavor. Among such model peasantries, none have been as highly vaunted as the Javanese. The well-known Indonesian term *gotong royong* has come to signify the friendly mutual assistance

---

3. Swift has noted the short-run orientation toward the future among Malay peasants (*Malay Peasant Society in Jelebu*, p. 170), and Foster feels that the general suspicion which inhibits long-run cooperation is a consequence of the "Image of Limited Good" (p. 308).

that is supposed to characterize their behavior. Clifford Geertz, however, warns of the danger of misconstruing the nature of Javanese cooperation:

> What has developed . . . is not so much a general spirit of cooperativeness—Javanese peasants tend, like many peasants, to be rather suspicious of groups larger than the immediate family—but a set of explicit and concrete practices. . . . This sense for the need to support specific, carefully delineated social mechanisms which can mobilize labor, capital, and consumption resources . . . and concentrate them effectively at one point in space and time, is the central characteristic of the much-remarked, but poorly understood, "cooperativeness" of the Javanese peasant. Cooperation is founded on a very lively sense of the mutual value to the participants of such cooperation, not on a general ethic of the unity of all men or an organic view of society which takes the group as primary and the individual as secondary.[4]

Innate peasant suspicion of those outside the family, then, pervades the character of Javanese cooperation and makes it "specific," "carefully delineated," and short-run, and keys it to the personal goals of participants. We would expect that in a society with a fixed social product, cooperation with persons outside the family circle will generally be circumscribed in the manner Geertz describes.

The distrust of those outside the kinship network, which Geertz observed among the Javanese and attributes to peasants as a class, is of course precisely what Banfield has in mind for southern Italian peasants when he characterizes their inability to form durable groups for common purposes as "amoral familism." As a pattern of behavior, amoral familism could not be considered either irrational or pathological in an environment where the struggle for shares of a constant pie is normal and where a short-run time orientation predominates. All three patterns—amoral familism, constant-pie orientation, and limited time horizon—are

4. Clifford Geertz, "The Rotating Credit Association: A Middle-Rung in Development," *Journal of Economic Development and Cultural Change* (April 1962), p. 244, quoted in Foster, p. 312.

typical of peasant society and originate in the material limitations of peasant life everywhere, whether in southern Italy, Latin America, or Southeast Asia.

Extended cooperation with nonfamily members requires a certain level of generalized social trust that is usually absent in peasant society[5] and, as shown earlier, is negatively associated with a constant-pie orientation. In an atmosphere of scarcity compounded by an unknown and recalcitrant future, there is little room for easy, confident social relations. Friends are valued largely for what they can offer in terms of support and protection rather than for their amiable personalities. Because those who befriend another have the same object in mind, it is well to be wary of exploitation.[6] If the material conditions were less constricting, friends might serve sociable rather than survival functions, and there might be greater scope for the easygoing "civic" qualities on which a democracy is supposed by many to depend. But these are luxuries that the competitors for scarce values can hardly afford.[7]

Judging from both the present analysis and from the observations of other social scientists, it is apparent that a belief in a fixed social product, a comparatively high level of social distrust (amoral familism), and a short-run time orientation are all interrelated characteristics of peasant societies. The inherent parameters of wealth and knowledge that typify such communities are responsible for the genesis and maintenance of all three of these qualities.

Scarcity: The Human Condition

The conditions that promote and maintain these orientations have in fact been the common lot of man until the recent past.

---

5. Foster cites a host of studies testifying to the "mentality of mutual distrust" which prevails in peasant communities (p. 302).

6. These are the same attitudes toward friendship found among Malaysian civil servants. They share this orientation with peasants as well as the constant-pie orientation. Later, I shall attempt to demonstrate that a lack of social trust is also a characteristic of both transitional and traditional societies.

7. Presumably, a very strong local government could enforce cooperation in a peasant community, but since, as Foster points out, the locus of power is usually found outside the community and prevents the growth of strong, independent local power centers (p. 301), this situation is unlikely. Nonetheless, a certain degree of local order is generally established in peasant villages, and the nature of this order will be explored later in the chapter.

The arrival of the notion of progress is relatively recent and even now is limited to a small proportion of mankind, while the constant-pie orientation—together with its social and political consequences—continues to be a more or less accurate expression of the traditional condition. Analyzing the writings of Kautlya, minister to the founder of the large Mauryan Empire in India at the end of the fourteenth century, a commentator concludes that he conceived of the politico-economic world as a Hobbesian one. "Above all, he had no vision of a gradually rising level of living; for many if not most, his economy would always be a 'pain economy.' " [8]

To this day the economy of India remains a "pain economy," as do those of virtually all the new nations. If a pain economy is typical of new nations, it is reasonable to suggest that new states also share the orientations that characterize this type of system. Moreover, a fixed social product is not the exclusive property of the non-Western world. Large areas of Italy, Greece, Spain, and Portugal, as well as much of Latin America, constitute peasant enclaves in the West and share a similar material environment, and there is some evidence that they share much the same set of beliefs as well.[9]

Managing the Constant Pie in Traditional Society

The manner in which the constant pie of desired values is managed in traditional society is distinctive and fundamentally different from the pattern in transitional society, and these differences greatly affect the nature of ideology. In traditional society, more specifically peasant village society, a relatively stable system develops whereby limitations are placed on the level of competition for shares of the pie. Certain restrictions also govern the means by which one may try to enlarge his own share or that of his kin group. A variety of social norms, customs, superstitions, dependencies, and other social control mechanisms are established which

8. Joseph J. Spengler, "Arthaśāstra Economics," pp. 224–59, in Braibanti and Spengler, eds., *Administration and Economic Development in India,* p. 259.

9. For Italy, see Banfield, *The Moral Basis of a Backward Society,* especially the differences between the prosperous north and poorer south, which clearly show the effect of the material environment on beliefs and behavior while cultural variables are held mostly constant. For Greece, see Foster, p. 301. For Spain, see Michael Kenny, "Social Values and Health in Spain," *Human Organization, 21,* 280–85.

serve to restrain the fissiparous tendencies inherent in an economy of scarcity. In the relatively static atmosphere of traditional peasant society, these social mechanisms help achieve some community solidarity and a measure of predictability in the distribution of shares within the community. The success of these mechanisms varies, of course, from society to society, but they appear to work tolerably well in maintaining tenuous control over the centrifugal forces generated by a pain economy. The necessity for social control mechanisms is perfectly obvious in a situation where the acquisition of a larger share by one family or group poses a direct threat to the equilibrium of the community as a whole. When behavioral norms are established for the competition, the war of all against all is tempered, and the stability of the community is maintained.

Foster notes that those who fall below a certain level are as much a threat to community solidarity as those who rise too quickly at the expense of their fellows.[10] The very poor threaten village unity by virtue of the resentment, envy, and jeolousy they direct at those who may have gained at their expense. Even in Malay villages, Swift has commented on the important leveling function of envy and jealousy:

> The peasant knows that if he is poor he is regarded with contempt and must be ashamed. But he also knows that to strive for success will arouse envy and resentment. For the ordinary man, sensitive to the feelings of his kin and neighbors, there are strong motives to keep him up to the normal income level, but also important pressures to prevent his making great efforts to rise beyond this point. . . . Thus egalitarian values are not radical, demanding a change in the whole organization of [extra-village] society, but rather conservative, concerned with maintaining existing distinctions and limiting individual mobility.[11]

The importance of jealousy and envy, then, is that they prevent an ambitious person from expressing his ambition by outdistancing his compatriots in the acquisition of material wealth. For this

10. Foster, p. 302.
11. Swift, *Malay Peasant Society in Jelebu*, pp. 153–54.

reason, it is common for members of a peasant community to be sedulously secretive about any relative improvement in wealth and to steadfastly deny that their material status is out of line with community norms. A similar explanation may lie behind the oft-noted reluctance of peasants to seek leadership roles within the community. In the southern Italian town of Montegrano, Banfield says that only state officials concern themselves with public affairs—because they are paid to do so—but that "for a private citizen to take a serious interest in a public problem will be regarded as abnormal or even improper." [12] To seek leadership in a peasant society where the social product is fixed is to open oneself both to the charge that one is attempting to improve his position at the expense of others and to the jealousy and resentment that will follow. This is especially true when, as in most peasant communities, the assumption prevails that people are motivated largely by thought of private gain.

Should an imbalance occur in the distribution of fixed resources within a peasant society, there are a number of sanctioned mechanisms available to redress that imbalance. Loans made by the relatively wealthy of the village to the poor are a prominent example; they are not expected to be repaid but are regarded as part of the normal process of redistribution of wealth within the community. Occasionally the more affluent villagers are expected to sponsor a "blow-out," at which time a large amount of wealth goes up in the smoke of firecrackers, is consumed at community feasts (*makan besar* in Malaya), or is otherwise distributed in goods and services. Encouraged by the villagers to sponsor such events, the wealthy villager signifies to all that he has no intention of hoarding his wealth or using it in a way that might threaten communal solidarity. In effect, the sponsor trades his wealth for prestige, which presumably is felt to be of less danger to village cohesion. Finally, the wealthy are expected, as patrons, to take on an ever larger number of dependents and make larger ritual contributions to the mosque, temple, or church, both of which activities function to redistribute their wealth while adding to their status. The cost for the wealthy family of not availing itself of these sanctioned

12. Banfield, p. 87.

redistributive mechanisms is a loss of status and prestige, as the flood of antagonism, resentment, and envy makes life uncomfortable and operates to eliminate any threat to the community posed by an inordinate concentration of wealth.[13]

Over time, then, traditional society has evolved a variety of social control mechanisms that limit inequalities, set norms for the struggle over scarce resources, and constitute something of a "containment policy" against the centrifugal potential of a constant-pie environment. Mechanisms that permit both a modest "leveling-up" and a "leveling-down" are the defenses of a society in which the gains of one family are the losses of another. The plunder of those outside the community is permitted, even encouraged, because outsiders are not a part of the system, and whatever booty is brought in from outside is in the long run an addition to communal assets, to the pie itself. By the very nature of peasant society, however, such opportunities are so few and far between that they have no appreciable effect on the community ethos.

In addition to the mechanisms described, the small inequalities that fall within accepted limits are generally legitimized by existing beliefs, which anticipate that important families and perhaps teachers or religious leaders will have somewhat higher standards of living. These inequalities will continue to be sanctioned so long as they are of modest proportions and so long as those who profit from such inequalities behave in conformity with community norms governing their conduct.

Thus, within the narrow confines of the peasant village, the Hobbesian struggle for shares of a fixed pie is held to tolerable levels by the practices and beliefs mentioned. Both a zero-sum material environment and the constant-pie orientation that accompanies it are still present. But the social control mechanisms available to traditional society place a limit on gains and losses anyone may suffer and thereby prevent mutual antagonisms from reaching a level that would destroy the community.

13. Swift writes of Malays, "The importance of the rich man is recognized but he is far from popular. Too obvious economic success opens the way for bad relations with kin and neighbors. The newly rising man runs great risk of shame if he blossoms too quickly with the symbols of his new status. Everyone will be watching for his first mistake, and longing for the day when he defaults on his hire-purchase payments and the Chinese comes to take his goods away" (p. 152).

The Survival of the Constant-Pie Orientation

The persistence of a basic value orientation in the long run depends upon the continuance of an existential base which provides experiences compatible with that orientation. It is necessary to use the term "long run," since a central belief that is no longer in line with common experiences is not extinguished or replaced immediately. On the contrary, it may persist long after the circumstances that produced it have disappeared. Even after the orientation itself has changed, it may be still longer before the practices and peripheral beliefs that were stimulated by that orientation finally change. In *The Psychological Frontiers of Society,* Abram Kardiner suggested that beliefs and attitudes suitable to an "unchanging subsistence economy" remained intact long after changes in the nature of the economy made them wholly unsuitable to the new situation.[14]

Inasmuch as the constant-pie orientation—and the political beliefs and practices associated with it—originate in, and are maintained by, continuous experience with a pain economy, they will persist at least as long as this existential base lasts. Before the Industrial Revolution in the West, a pain economy was the normal state of affairs for mankind, and a constant-pie orientation was undoubtedly a common, shared belief. Even in the West the slow growth of civic consciousness and political cooperation, which depend on a relatively high level of interpersonal trust, indicates that there was a substantial lag between a change in the existential base and a change in the orientation itself. One supposes that as people experienced the growth of the social product, the assumption that one person's gain was another's loss gradually faded from one generation to the next and eventually lost most of its significance. The overriding question of survival haunted politics less and less and was slowly replaced by the desire to preserve a rate of material improvement. When the issue becomes the protection of a rate of improvement, there is room for political trust and cooperation, since the stakes involved are less vital in the literal sense of that word.

In the underdeveloped nations of the world, this process has yet to occur. With a few notable exceptions, new nations have ex-

14. Cf. Ch. 3, n. 38.

perienced little if any growth in real per capita income over the
last three or four decades, and some have even witnessed a decline.
Real per capita income is used as the crucial measure because even
an appreciable expansion in the gross national product at constant prices will not be reflected in common experiences if it has
no effect on the per capita figure.[15] Thus, in the underdeveloped
world as a whole, there has not been the economic growth that
would lead one to expect any appreciable weakening of the constant-pie orientation. Existential support for the orientation is the
rule rather than the exception.

The example of Malaysia, whose economic progress has surely
been the most impressive in Southeast Asia, will illustrate this
point. Although real per capita income has grown significantly
over the past twenty years, one economist estimates that it was
only in the late 1950s that the real domestic per capita product
of Malaya attained the level it had reached in 1929.[16] Due to the
effects of the Great Depression, World War II, and the postwar
Emergency, it was almost thirty years before an improvement in
real per capita income occurred. The growth that took place between 1910 and 1929, and again from 1957–58 to the present, is
therefore not perceived as a permanent phenomenon, since within

15. A *short-run* rise in per capita real income can, of course, be achieved by
drawing down foreign reserve balances, incurring large foreign debts, and even
diverting capital allocations to consumption. Under Nkrumah, it seems that Ghana
did precisely this. The short-run nature of this strategy, however, is readily apparent in the austerity program Col. Ankrah presides over at the moment. Another
short-run strategy would be a fundamental redistribution of wealth in a society
with great initial inequalities, which would provide the majority with rising real
incomes in the short run. Something of this nature occurred when U Nu's Burma
created a welfare state before it industrialized and, in effect, redistributed poverty.
Because both are short-run measures, their influence on a constant-pie orientation
is not appreciable, and in the long run they perhaps reinforce the orientation.

16. See forthcoming study of Malaya's economic growth by Van Dorn Ooms in
the Yale Economic Growth Center's series. Even from 1955 to 1964, the growth of
the Malaysian economy is not so impressive as one might anticipate. Per capita
GNP at market prices (more realistic than constant prices, since much of Malaysia's
product is sold on the world market) has risen from M$262 to M$294, or 12.59
percent, in this ten-year period. Pierre R. Crosson, *Economic Growth in Malaysia*
(Jerusalem, U.S. Department of Agriculture, Economic Research Service, 1966), p.
27. See also Douglas S. Paauw, "Economic Progress in Southeast Asia," *Journal of
Asian Studies*, 23 (November 1963), pp. 69–92. Paauw writes, "Most of Southeast
Asia's 215 million people—about 70 percent—appear to share approximately the
same low levels of per capita real income and consumption that was their lot prior
to World War II when the area was predominantly under colonial control" (p. 69).

living memory it has been rolled back. It is one thing to hope for a rising standard of living and another to count upon it. The economic growth of even a relatively exceptional nation like Malaysia is perhaps enough to make men wish for better times, but it is surely not of either the magnitude or duration that would occasion a change in fundamental expectations.[17]

Aside from the West, there are very few areas where extended recent experience with an expanding social product has created and sustained a belief that progress is normal. The rest of the world, including backward areas of the West, continue to live by and large in a zero-sum material environment and to tailor their beliefs accordingly.[18]

THE CONSTANT PIE AND THE NATURE OF TRANSITIONAL SOCIETY

The Breakdown of Social Control

While the constant-pie orientation is characteristic of both traditional and transitional society, the centrifugal tendencies generated by this orientation are, in traditional society, more or less effectively managed by a variety of social control mechanisms. In transitional society, however, these mechanisms, which serve both to prevent the growth of great inequalities and to legitimize some limited differences in incomes, have largely broken down. Particularly in the urban areas of a transitional nation, there are few if any of the traditional customs that temper the competition for

17. I have generally assumed that the belief is the dependent variable and the existential base the independent variable. It is possible, although probably only in the short run, to *create* among a population the expectation that a nation's wealth will improve over time even though no improvement has yet been experienced. This act of faith might characterize the early post-independence period as well as periods when an old social order is overthrown and a new one established with great promise and hope. But unless such faith is buttressed by experience, it is likely to wither, and further efforts to stimulate its growth in the absence of concrete results are certainly foredoomed.

18. In the rest of Southeast Asia, Indonesia and Burma have probably suffered declines in real per capita income in the past few years, while Thailand and the Philippines have enjoyed some progress, but not as much as Malaysia. Vietnam is, of course, a special case. Where growth has occurred outside the West—and Latin America's record is more impressive than Southeast Asia's—it has come about comparatively recently; it has been sporadic rather than continual; and its distribution has often left the living standards of the broad masses untouched.

shares of a fixed pie. No longer are there clear rules governing the competition, no longer are individuals as susceptible to the social pressures of traditional society, and no longer are the criteria for the distribution of wealth, power, or prestige as clearly defined as they were before.

Rapid change in transitional society not only impedes the effectiveness of social control mechanisms but also heightens status anxiety. In traditional settings, the stability of the social structure and of community norms enables an individual to predict what his status and income will be over the short run. The multiple status systems of transitional society, on the other hand, make it difficult to forecast one's own position within a status pyramid that is in constant flux. Thus, while the constant-pie orientation characterizes both types of society, the world appears more Hobbesian to transitional man simply because the corrective pressures and stability that provide traditional man with a measure of security are no longer operative.

In this context, many of the comments by civil servants cited in the previous chapter imply that change and confusion have replaced stability and that unrestrained competition has replaced cooperation. Inche' Nordin, who spoke of unions and professional associations "trying to kill each other," clearly felt that somehow things were better long ago. The fact that his already grown children are constantly at his door demanding large amounts of cash represents for him a measure of the breakdown of social controls. He often dreams of buying a winning national lottery ticket, which would allow him to give a house and a stand of rubber to each and to wash his hands of them once and for all. Taken alone, his opinion might be considered the normal prophecy of moral collapse made by the elder generation in times of rapid change. Inche' Nordin's comments about trade unions and professional associations, however, indicate that his distress with his children is bound up with a broader view of what is happening to young and old alike.

Others, younger than Inche' Nordin, see a breakdown in social controls, too, although they express it in diverse ways and find it hard to explain. Inche' Ismail, himself an individualist, sees the growth of individualism destroying community solidarity. When asked whether Malaysia was moving closer to the ideal society, he replied, "We are getting further and further away from that. The most responsible for that is the development of character and individuality. The development of character has gone too far—there's too much individuality—and concern for the progress of one's position." For Inche' Ismail, the development of character is synonymous with the growth of self-seeking. His image of the ideal society is one in which generosity and a concern for the conditions of others prevail over personal goals, but he is pessimistic about the chances of such values being realized under present conditions:

> Every person in society is drifting away from this ideal. He is drifting away in proportion to the degredation of society—disintegration of society itself. Our society nowadays is all the while trying to fall apart with the coming of new ideas—different sectors in opposition—conflicts of interest groups. The only thing that holds it together—that is the political factor.

Clearly, the "political factor" is the only available instrument to replace the breakdown of social control mechanisms, which, in Inche' Ismail's eyes, have failed with "the coming of new ideas." The vision of increasing competitiveness and self-seeking is the spectre that occasions the need for some new form of social control. Strong, firm government is increasingly necessary in an environment where the more traditional forms of solidarity and community feeling have all but disappeared.

Few civil servants expressed themselves as lucidly as Inche' Ismail, but almost all exhibited some concern over the speed of change and the lack of control over its direction. Asked about the usefulness of professional protective associations, Inche' Mohd. Amin replied, "In a changing world when anything could happen—everyone is striving for better—trade unions have their own organization—only by these means can we get our share." The chances of falling behind "in a changing world" are much greater than under more traditional circumstances, and Mohd. Amin is painfully aware of the dangers of being bested in the competition. Others feel they have already been bested and imply that the controls that held some groups closer to the common level are now inoperative. As Mr. Lim noted disapprovingly, "Those

who suddenly become rich—they have a big say in things now
—everyone tends to give them respect." The emphasis is on
"suddenly" becoming rich, and Mr. Lim feels that the rate of
status change in an ideal society should be more modest and
that personal wealth should more frequently be used on behalf of the community.

Virtually all the civil servants have a more or less vague feeling that important social bonds have been broken and that no
comparable controls have replaced them. The kinds of social
bonds to which they implicitly refer are those that govern the
distribution of material wealth within the community. In the absence of established norms governing the distribution of wealth
and status, the competition becomes more anarchic, and uncertainty about one's present and future position creates great anxiety.
The need for a strong government that will reimpose community
solidarity is even more apparent to men who live in an atmosphere
where the traditional boundaries to self-seeking have collapsed.

Social Control Mechanisms and Modernization

Most theories of modernization compare the content and style
of behavior and beliefs in traditional society with behavior and
beliefs in modern, industrial society and then place transitional
societies somewhere along the imaginary continuum between
these two states. Some theorists recognize the mixed quality of
modern political systems; for example, Almond, using the Parsonian pattern variable schema, shows that the family is still important as a political structure in modern societies, but that in
comparison with traditional systems, its importance has been
diluted by the growth of a host of secondary associations. But
even these investigators still tend to place transitional nations
midway between modern and traditional societies along most
dimensions they discuss. The expression of political demands thus
tends to be manifest in modern state, latent in traditional states,
and a mixture of both in transitional states. Similarly, recruitment to political roles in modern society, according to Almond,
is likely to stress achievement or performance criteria; in traditional society ascriptive criteria are mostly emphasized; and recruitment in transitional systems fluctuates somewhere between

these two modes.[19] Once this basic scheme is accepted, research is likely to focus upon precisely what mixture of the modern and traditional most appropriately describes each facet of the political system in a transitional nation.

This method of analysis has many strengths, but it contains a basic weakness as well: it ignores one essential quality that modern and traditional societies share and that distinguishes them both from transitional societies—the existence of effective, nongovernmental, social control mechanisms. Both traditional and modern societies are characterized by more or less effective social control mechanisms, while in transitional societies these controls are comparatively much weaker.[20]

The three "value features" attributed to industrial society by Wilbert Moore illustrate what this means:[21]

    a. Minimal cognitive consensus.
    b. An acquiescence in, if not positive acceptance of, a normative order.
    c. A minimal consensus on ultimate values.[22]

All three characteristics applicable ceteris paribus to traditional society as well as to industrial society. The cognitive consensus in industrial nations is largely secular and is reinforced by the educational system and by the mass media, while the consensus of traditional society is sacral and receives the sanction of religion and custom. Notwithstanding these differences in the nature of the consensus, both systems achieve a substantial measure of cognitive agreement. Secondly, the "normative orders" in modern and traditional societies are vastly different, but in each case they are accepted passively or actively by most members. This is so despite the fact that the normative order is broader and more

19. Almond, *The Politics of the Developing Areas*, pp. 31–38. Almond's general reliance on the Parsonian pattern variables that distinguish between traditional and modern styles (manifest-vs.-latent, diffuseness-vs.-specificity, ascription-vs.-achievement, and universalism-vs.-particularism) leads to a continuum approach which places transitional society at a more or less "half-way point."

20. The term "social" control mechanisms should be understood here to mean that, in modern society in particular, these controls may have been internalized and no longer depend much on social reinforcement or social sanctions.

21. Wilbert E. Moore, *The Impact of Industry* (Englewood Cliffs, New Jersey, Prentice-Hall, 1965), p. 34.

22. Ibid., p. 35.

variegated in the modern instance. "A minimal consensus," the third value quality, is perhaps more characteristic of traditional structures than of modern, although the politically stable industrial nations have achieved some degree of consensus on standards of equality, justice, and the distribution of such values as wealth and power. All three qualities, then, are more or less attributable to both industrial and traditional systems. Transitional society, on the other hand, lacks all three to a significant extent; there is less cognitive consensus, less agreement on a normative order, and less consensus on ultimate values.

The consensus that is typical of modern and traditional structures adds to the stability and predictability of politics as well as of interpersonal relations. Modern and traditional systems are thus closer to what might warily be called an "equilibrium" situation, even though the equilibrim of the modern society is a more dynamic one in which even change is, to a degree, institutionalized. Fred W. Riggs, comparing what he calls "Agraria" and "Industria," writes:

> The governments of Agraria and Industria both enjoy substantial "authority," which is to say, there is widespread consensus about the political myths, doctrines, and formulas which confer formal legitimacy on the acts of their governments. In this respect, both are political systems in "equilibrium," as distinguished from "transitional" societies in which consensus about myths, doctrines, and formulas is often lacking.[23]

The "consensus" that Riggs describes is largely absent in transitional societies but usually present in both industrial and agrarian communities.

Thus, in respect to consensus and social control, transitional society is not midway between the traditional and the modern but toward one end of the continuum. Both modern and traditional states share a relatively high level of consensus (whether internalized or supported largely by external social sanctions), while transitional society is, virtually by definition, low in consensus.

23. Fred W. Riggs, "Agraria and Industria—Toward a Typology of Comparative Administration," in William J. Siffin, ed., *Toward the Comparative Study of Public Administration* (Bloomington, Indiana University Press, 1957), p. 82.

In transitional states the social control mechanisms that sustained consensus in the traditional milieu have broken down, and no new value consensus has yet emerged. Figure 1 is a rough comparison of the three types of societies and the variables I have been discussing.

FIGURE 1

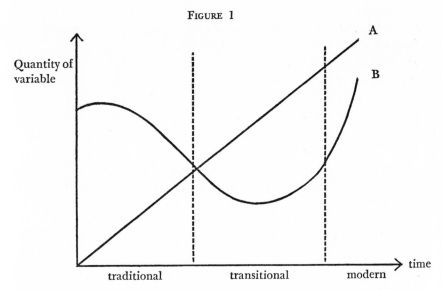

A — Extent of modern variants of Parsonian pattern variables; achievement, manifestness, universalism, specificity.

B — Degree of cognitive consensus, consensus about normative order, and consensus on ultimate values.

The slopes of the lines are intended to be merely suggestive, and if the variables that are lumped together were separated out, the result would be a multiplicity of lines with varying slopes. The consensual qualities represented by line B do not exhibit the roughly unilinear progression from the traditional to the modern as do the Parsonian pattern variables, but rather they distinguish transitional societies on the one hand from traditional and modern societies on the other.

Transitional society is thus characterized not only by the breakdown of social control mechanisms but also by a relative loss of cognitive and normative consensus. It has lost the two factors that served to mediate the potential strains of a fixed social product in its traditional setting. Without either of these defenses, transitional nations face what seems to be a zero-sum environment as well. The effects of a constant-pie orientation are more severe under these circumstances, since the "rules of the game" have broken down. As a result, anxiety about the future and interpersonal suspicion are likely to increase. New structures of competition, new political norms, and a new consensus have not yet begun to reduce the level of uncertainty and the threatening qualities of this situation. Moreover, if the social and political environment seems more Hobbesian to people in this setting, their view is more a reflection of actual conditions than an indication of personal pathology. It is in this atmosphere that a desire grows for strong government—a government that would act in the interests of the community as a whole. This government is expected to reestablish control mechanisms that preserve solidarity in the face of the divisive tendencies of a zero-sum material world and, on the political level, recreate the equilibrium that traditional mechanisms maintained.

Uncertainty

In transitional society, where A's gain is perceived as B's loss and where the traditional means of redistributing wealth and enforcing some limited community-focused behavior are largely absent, uncertainty about one's future wealth and status in the society is intensified. The rapid changes in status and wealth characteristic of transitional societies, particularly at the elite level, only compound the problem of uncertainty. Long-run cooperative strategies, which were tenuous before, become increasingly difficult, since one cannot, in fact, plan effectively for the future. The conditions for success—or even the criteria of success—are uncertain because of competing status systems and the inherent instability of transitional society. The important point here is simply that uncertainty is based on an accurate estimate of reality rather than on personal or collective fantasy. A man functioning in an environment in which the social cues are ambiguous or conflicting is sure to be confused, but it is the confusion of his surroundings that disorients him. His confusion has an existential base.

The other side of conflicting norms, however, is a certain freedom of choice. Among a host of conflicting norms and cues, one can choose those to which he will respond and those that he will ignore. Unlike traditional society, where a single norm or custom generally directs behavior in a specific situation, transitional society permits a person to choose those norms he feels will be most to his advantage and conform to them. In his relations with the civil service, for example, a citizen will insist on legalism when it is to his advantage and on favoritism when that serves his interests.[24] But if the citizen has a choice in this situation, so do all those with whom he deals, so that no dependable expectations about how others will react are possible. The civil servant can switch his behavior, too, depending on which norm is most advantageous to him. The "poly-normativism" of transitional society thus sabotages plans for the future, aggravates the competition for scarce values, and generally intensifies personal insecurity.[25]

The fact that there is more uncertainty (less consensus) about behavioral norms and community goals in transitional society than in either industrial or folk societies has another important consequence. Where the means and goals of politics are more settled, administration occupies an increasingly important place vis-à-vis politics. But where conflict over means and goals still prevails as it does in transitional society, politics achieves primacy. The society that has not yet attained a viable consensus on ultimate goals—which values should be emphasized (equality? freedom? progress?) and how they should be achieved—is the politicized society par excellence. Different political ideologies, whether they be formal and rigorous, or, more likely, syncretic and vague,

24. Fred W. Riggs, "The Sala Model: An Ecological Approach to the Study of Comparative Administration," *Philippine Journal of Public Administration, 6* (January 1962), pp. 3–16.

25. The consequences of other-directedness are also different in transitional society. The other-directed man in traditional society is responding to cues and pressures which usually do not conflict and which reflect the settled norms of the community. Being other-directed in a transitional society, however, means responding to conflicting cues and social pressures. The seeming inconsistencies and changes of behavior often remarked on in transitional society may be largely accounted for by other-directedness in a social setting where different norms coexist and where social pressures are contradictory and/or ambiguous. The Malay who behaves differently at a traditional *makan* from on the golf course is not confused but merely conforming to different social contexts. Cf. Alex Inkeles, "Social Change and Social Character: The Role of Parental Mediation," in Smelser and Smelser, eds., *Personality and Social Systems*, pp. 357–65.

offer alternative solutions to the problem of consensus, and the champions of each potential consensus compete for the allegiance of the masses as a means to power. Lying somewhere between the informal rigidity of folk society and the formal certainty of mod-society,[26] transitional society is more likely to be highly politicized than either. Uncertainty over key values and goals thus provides the basis for the primacy of politics.[27]

The Time Orientation and Risk-Taking

Again and again observers of administration in new nations have commented on the short-run orientation of government administrators and their seeming inability to take risks for long-run gains. The composite picture is one of civil servants who only think, at best, of next week and who will avoid taking chances for any goal beyond that horizon. With few exceptions, this picture accurately describes the administrators who were interviewed in Malaysia as well.

Most Malaysian civil servants are in fact unwilling to take on new ventures that might jeopardize presently adequate arrangements. They prefer, for the most part, to protect their present position and status rather than to take even moderate risks that might propel them higher up the status ladder. Jeganathan's thinking provides a typical illustration of this conservative bent. When asked to talk about the early days of his administrative career, he replied,

> I had an intention of studying medicine and then—while I was halfway in my Senior Cambridge [examination], in July 1928 my father died and I completed my Senior that year. Somehow or other I felt being the eldest—I don't want to put all the gold into one boat and have it sink.

Rather than trying to become a doctor, Jeganathan felt that he

26. Alvin Boskoff, "Postponement of Social Decision in Transitional Society," *Social Forces, 31* (March 1953), pp. 55–72, passim.

27. Even when political contests seem to be between personalities rather than issues, key values are often at stake. The personalities contending may represent different communities—different ways of life—or one may be felt to be more religious and traditional and another more secular and modern. In either case, even though the issues remain unstated, the fundamental choice between values is clearly present.

should enter the lower civil service, where a steady income would be assured. Consistently thoughout his career, even when family security was not in jeopardy, he has been faced with comparable situations and opted for the safer course.

Mr. Lim's ambition as a teen-ager was to become a doctor, too, and he considers himself fortunate not to have pursued it: "My ambition was to be a doctor, but it was a blessing in disguise that I didn't go on to the university, since then if my father died all my deams would have been smashed to the ground." The fear of failure is prominent, and both Mr. Lim and Jeganathan would prefer to abandon voluntarily their own dreams rather than to run the risk of having them "smashed to the ground" by events beyond their control. The desire to cut losses is also apparent in the motives Mayalsian administrators give for having joined the civil service. By a wide margin they focus on the steady pay, security, leave and pension provisions, and comfortable life, rather than on self-advancement or on the exercise of power that the bureaucracy might provide. Quite a few have given some thought to leaving the public service for a higher paying job in the private sector, but the risks have deterred them.

Muneer Ahmad, in a sample survey study of the Pakistani civil service, has arrived at the same conclusion. The most frequent reasons given for joining the bureaucracy were either the prestige and status of office or the security of tenure.[28] In a similar study of the civil bureaucracy in Egypt, Morroe Berger found that most administrators entered government service for its security, high pay, and prestige and were only rarely motivated by the desire to acquire skills or serve the nation. Berger feels that the emphasis on skills and service that characterizes Western professionalism is largely absent in the Egyptian civil service, whereas the self-protective aspect of professionalism is quite strong.[29]

As in Malaysia, administrators in Pakistan and Egypt seem to manifest a sinecure mentality and are only rarely performance or achievement oriented. Uppermost in their minds is the preservation of their status, ample pay, and security, all of which might

28. Muneer Ahmad, *The Civil Servant in Pakistan: A Study of the Background and Attitudes of Public Servants in Lahore* (Karachi, Oxford University Press, 1964), p. 78.
29. Berger, *Bureaucracy and Society in Modern Egypt*, Ch. 3.

be jeopardized if they innovated and took risks. For most, the possession of an administrative post is more important than exploiting the opportunities for performance or service which that post offers. In this context of risk-avoidance, the oft-remarked reliance on routine, regulations, and pat formulas in developing nations can be viewed as a means to avoid new, unsettling problems and to preserve the comfortable, secure, bureaucratic nest.

That civil servants in most developing states are largely inclined to a short-run view and avoid long-term risks is firmly established as a research finding, but the explanations for why this is so are in some dispute. Some claim that, as in the West, bureaucratic self-selection is involved, whereby those who are motivated to seek security are likely to choose bureaucratic careers. This is unlikely to be the case in Malaysia or in other new nations, where the civil service represents even today the most significant occupational alternative for nonprofessionals above a certain educational level. Unlike the industrial nations of the West, the majority of university graduates in these nations can only look forward to a career of government service, and little psychological self-selection is involved in their occupational choice.

Two other quite different explanations have been offered for this risk-avoidance. One stresses discontinuities in socialization and the resulting value conflict, while the other emphasizes qualities in the environment that affect values and behavior. The former thus relies on the personality factors emphasized by Pye, and the latter on those aspects of the existential base employed by Banfield in his study of a southern Italian village.

Hahn-Been Lee is a proponent of the first mode of explanation.[30] According to his analysis, most civil servants in developing nations exhibit a "presentist" or "exploitationist" orientation toward time. This orientation leads to hedonism, the maximization of short-run values, and, lastly, to personalism. As opposed to either the "escapist" or "developmentalist" time orientations, the exploitationist pattern manifests a "ritualistic role pattern, a bureaucratic leadership style, and a consumption-centered pro-

30. Hahn-Been Lee, *Developmentalist Time and Leadership in Developing Countries* (Bloomington, An Occasional Paper of the Comparative Administrative Group of the American Society for Public Administration, 1966).

gram orientation." [31] The growth of the exploitationist orientation occurs when old values are largely abandoned, but new values
have yet to be incorporated. In this situation people are likely
to be ambivalent about change and therefore are likely to fall
back on routine and ritualism, since the wider long-run purposes
of organizational activity have not yet been embraced at the personal level: "This attitude is a *distorted* response to the pressure
and tension of change. Such an attitude tries to maximize short-
run returns through manipulation of existing circumstances." [32]

Ambivalence toward change and being "between-values" are
the crucial factors in Hahn-Been Lee's explanation of the exploitationist time orientation. The new values that civil servants have
yet to internalize are, in large part, values imposed on the bureaucracy while it was colonized, and these same values are still built
into the bureaucratic structure in most new nations. We know from
research findings that imposed goals are likely to be pursued in a
formalistic and routine manner simply because the central, ultimate purposes of the organization have not yet become personal
goals.[33] In the absence of long-run goals, a short-run, exploitationist orientation prevails. Hahn-Been Lee's reliance on discontinuity
in socialization to explain the presentist time orientation is essentially the same as Pye's interpretation of similar political and administrative patterns in Burma.

A second and more appealing explanation of this bureaucratic
pattern focuses on the actual qualities of the environment. A
further virtue of this approach is that it helps account for some
forms of economic and political behavior as well. Many economists
have noted that investment in transitional society is frequently
characterized by short-run commercial transactions and high liquidity. This pattern of investment is largely due to the instability

31. Ibid., p. 13.
32. Ibid., p. 5 (my italics).
33. Berelson's proposition, although it specifies "small groups," is applicable to
the situation described: "If the small group's activities are imposed from outside,
the norms set by the group are likely to be limited in character; if they are determined from within, they are more likely to take on the character of ideal goals,
to be constantly enlarged and striven for." Bernard Berelson and Gary A. Steiner,
Human Behavior: An Inventory of Scientific Findings (New York, Harcourt, Brace,
and World, 1964), p. 336.

of the transitional polity and economy—the unpredictability of important factors beyond the very short run which might, if they were stable, lead to more productive, capital intensive, long-run investment. Moreover, "the investor in transitional society has engaged in short-run speculative activity before and knows that it balances out over a brief period." [34] Given the uncertainties of transitional society, then, short-run commercial transactions which do not tie up capital in fixed plant and machinery for a long period may well be the most rational course for the investor.

The same statement might be made of bureaucratic behavior as well. Long-run commitments to organizational purposes may make little sense when those purposes are subject to frequent redefinition and where those who lead the organization often have to adapt quickly to changes in the organizational environment in order to preserve the group and its members. Since there is no consensus on ultimate goals, or even means, long-run values are difficult if not impossible to realize, and by default, short-run formalistic goals, or attachments to superiors rather than values, are likely to predominate. The almost exclusive concern with wages and conditions that characterizes associations of civil servants in Malaysia betrays this short-run, consumption orientation. The function of these associations seems to be the protection of present status against a capricious environment that generally penalizes the pursuit of more ambitious goals. In an unpredictable environment, unwavering loyalty to one's superior may provide some small measure of security, and Malaysian civil servants are well aware of this. Promotion, in the absence of achievement norms, depends most often on the faithfulness of a subordinate rather than upon more transcendent criteria. Thus, the pursuit of short-run gains, the emphasis on fairly narrow, material, personal goals, and the avoidance of long-term risks are as much a rational strategy, given the environment, as they are the result of ambivalence and confusion. Just as the economic climate does not encourage long-run investment, the bureaucratic climate does not inspire a quest for long-run organizational goals.

If the bureaucratic environment in transitional society penalizes those who seek wider values, so does the political environment. The risks of politics in transitional society are so imposing as to

34. Hirschman, *The Strategy of Economic Development*, pp. 14–20.

discourage long-run strategies. The concern with holding on to one's post at all costs and the generally high level of opportunism in transitional politics illustrates a short-run, exploitationist orientation toward the rewards of politics. The instabilities of the politician's status in new nations may be comparable to the situation of union leaders in the United States, as Lipset has described it:

> political positions in democratic nations are insecure by definition. Politicians in most countries may move from electoral defeat to highly paid positions in private industry or the professions, but union leaders customarily cannot do so. This means, as I have noted elsewhere, that *they are under considerable pressure to find means to protect their source of status.* Thus the greater the gap between the rewards of union leadership and of those jobs from which the leader came and to which he might return on defeat, the greater the pressure to eliminate democratic rights.[35]

The potential downward mobility of politicians in transitional society is analogous to that of the union leader in the United States, and the need for status protection is important to both. It is not surprising that many political leaders in new nations, finding themselves in this situation, attempt to maximize their security of tenure by whatever means are at their disposal and, failing that, eschew long-run commitments and concentrate instead on the short-term material and status rewards of office. The very real fragility and unpredictability of the political world, as of the economic and, to a lesser extent, the bureaucratic environment, lend a quite rational quality to the pursuit of short-run, personal values.[36] These short-run goals are realizable, in contrast to the tremendous risks attendant on long-term enterprises, where the future is unpredictable.

For the society as a whole, the only institution which might, in the short run, change the instability and uncertainty just described

35. Seymour Martin Lipset, *The First New Nation: The United States in Historical and Comparative Perspective* (London, Heinemann, 1963), p. 189 (my italics).

36. Of course, another important reason for the tenacious clinging to political posts is a real fear that a host of divisive religious, ethnic, linguistic, and other factions would destroy the fragile new state if the existing political elite were displaced. This fear is only part rationalization, as these primordial ties are an ever-present threat to the tenuous unity of new nations.

is the government, since the more informal traditional mechanisms are no longer viable. Therefore the call for a strong government to restore firm controls over the society becomes both more frequent and widespread. Until controls are restored, however, the pursuit of short-run goals and the avoidance of most long-term risks by businessmen, bureaucrats, and politicians makes sense. Their orientation represents a realistic pattern in a constant-pie environment where the customs which governed both the rules for, and legitimacy of, the existing distribution of scarce values have weakened or disappeared. They are in tune with the world in which they operate rather than being the disoriented victims of cultural shock who can only respond pathologically to change.[37]

The Constant-Pie Orientation: Poverty and Affluence

In *Politics, Personality, and Nation Building,* Pye attributes the inability of the Burmese to create durable, purposeful organizations to two central factors: an uncertainty about the actions of others stemming from uncertainty about oneself, and a lack of trust in human relationships.[38] Both are ultimately connected to the loss of personal identity, in Pye's analysis, and represent a failure to deal rationally with the environment. By contrast, I have attempted constantly to show how these same factors fit into an environmental context and are congruent with the existential base. As regards the first, I have suggested that uncertainty about the future and instability are facts of life in transitional society and that attempts to realize largely short-term personal goals represent a rational strategy against this background. The second factor— misanthropy—has been connected with the nature of traditional society and, more important, with the constant-pie orientation.

37. One might perhaps distinguish between "individual" and "system" pathology. Transitional society might be an example of system pathology, but the patterns of individuals that have been described represent a more or less rational response to a system in which long run calculations are virtually impossible. It is the environment which is "deviant" or pathological rather than the individual. Given the environment of transitional society, it is the entrepreneur, the long-term investor, the person who seeks broad, nonpersonal values who merits study as a "deviant case"—the entrepreneur in England in the early nineteenth century— rather than those who have been described as seeking short-run personal goals.

38. Pye, *Politics, Personality, and Nation Building,* pp. 54–55.

As the constant-pie orientation is finally dependent upon a fixed social product, that is, upon poverty,[39] misanthropy is also associated with environmental variables.

Poverty and the social disorganization customarily accompanying social transition are powerful influences on belief systems, as can be seen by examining their effects in the Western context. Oscar Lewis, in an article entitled "The Culture of Poverty," describes the similarities he found among urban poor, whether in London, Paris, Harlem, Mexico City, or Glasgow.[40] Many of the patterns he outlines are the same ones associated with the constant-pie orientation. In particular, Lewis cites the distrust and cynicism that permeate interpersonal relations, a presentist or hedonistic orientation that excludes goals not both narrowly personal and realizable within a brief span, and a type of authoritarianism. The variant of authoritarianism Lewis finds expresses itself through a belief in widespread moral decay and a wish that the government would put a stop to it all, using whatever coercion is necessary.

The behavioral and belief patterns Lewis describes are similar if not identical to the misanthropy and desire for strong government found in Malaysia, which I argued were related both to constant-pie thinking and to the presentist time orientation typical of transitional society. What these findings suggest is that poverty may have its own belief culture independent of the cultural context in which it occurs. To be sure, the level of distrust and cynicism and of presentist thinking probably vary directly with the level of social disorganization among the group being examined. The ghettos and islands of poverty in most of the West represent deviant cultures of poverty within nations enjoying a relatively affluent life, but in most transitional nations, these cultures of poverty generally represent normal conditions of life. While the degree of social dislocation produces important differences, poverty nevertheless may involve what must seem to those experiencing it as a struggle against others for scarce, fixed resources. Both the

39. As pointed out above, the orientation is likely to outlive poverty, since central beliefs are likely to endure for a time after the existential base which gave rise to them has disappeared.

40. Oscar Lewis, "The Culture of Poverty," in Novack and Lekachman, *Development and Society*, pp. 252–61.

constant-pie orientation and the beliefs it encourages and maintains may thus be a characteristic of poverty in its traditional, transitional, and modern setting.

If the existence of a limited and small social product (i.e. poverty) has the important consequences for beliefs that have been indicated, then affluence should have the opposite effect. Examining these effects offers an indirect means of testing some of the conclusions reached so far. The best known exponent of the consequences of affluence on political culture is, of course, David Potter, who argues in his *People of Plenty* that "economic abundance" is primarily responsible for the democratic style in America.[41] Potter maintains that the American economy was an expanding pie and that it was therefore easier to compromise on economic questions. Generosity was possible precisely because the gain of the "have-nots" was not the loss of the "haves." The frontier, for example, was an expanding pie of land resources, and the landless could have land at no cost to existing landholders. The poor, for their part, did not need to assault the vaults of the rich because they could count on receiving a portion of the continuing additions to American wealth. As the struggle over wealth was limited to dividing up the surplus and did not threaten absolute positions, a democratic style, Poter feels, came easily to Americans and sapped the lifeblood of potential class revolutions. In short, social trust and political trust were possible in the American atmosphere of abundance, where all groups could move up simultaneously.

In his interviews with the common men of Eastport, Lane finds that abundance exerts a powerful influence over their political beliefs, too. He attributes their lack of political rancor and their easygoing political style to the same economic surplus Potter described.

> The social outlook of Eastport is saturated with the influence of the opportunity (abundance, escalation, advancement) that characterizes life in that city. It makes it possible and desirable to focus on the near future when anticipations will be real-

41. David M. Potter, *People of Plenty: Economic Abundance and the American Character* (Chicago, University of Chicago Press, 1954), passim.

ized; these men do not need to live in the present, as the underprivileged of the London slums are said to do, or in an afterlife, or in a millennial world future. They can afford to be tolerant of political opponents because they are not threatened with extinction; they are confident of provender and shelter no matter what happens. The risks of politics, like its stakes, are diminished; politics becomes less important.[42]

What empirical evidence is there for Potter's thesis? Unfortunately, the relationship between affluence and the constant-pie orientation cannot be explored directly, since it is a new measure, and no cross-cultural or time-series data are available. It is logical to expect, however, that the two are inversely related, so that greater affluence would lead to a diminution of the constant-pie orientation. While no direct test can be made, the relationship can be indirectly examined by making use of the known association of social trust with both constant-pie thinking and affluence. Evidence shows that the level of social trust and constant-pie thinking are inversely related at a statistically significant level (see Chapter 5). Furthermore, data is available for relating social trust to affluence. According to my predictions, this data should show that the more affluent the group or society, the higher the level of social trust; hence, the less constant-pie thinking.

In *The Civic Culture*, Almond and Verba administered Rosenberg's "Faith-in-People" Scale to a cross section of respondents in five nations. The American and British respondents scored significantly higher in social trust than the Mexican and Italian respondents; that is, nations where there is relative abundance are likely to show greater interpersonal trust.[43] Furthermore, within each nation the level of social trust rises as the economic level of the respondents rises, a finding which belies the possibility that only cultural differences have been tapped.[44]

A more impressive test of the relationship between affluence and misanthropy—and, therefore, constant-pie thinking—would be a time-series within the same nation. Lane has done this for the United States by tabulating responses to identical poll questions

42. Lane, *Political Ideology*, p. 220.
43. See Ch. 4, Table 2.
44. Almond and Verba, *The Civil Culture*, p. 214.

over time.[45] His findings, which are summarized below, lend strong
support to my predictions.

TABLE 4: The Incidence of the Following Beliefs and Opinions
Has Increased/Decreased Over Time in the U.S.
as the Economy Has Expanded[46]

	Belief or Opinion	Index
Increase	1. Social trust	("Do you think most people can be trusted?")
Increase	2. Confidence in the future	("Ten years from now, do you believe Americans will be generally happier than they are today?")
Increase	3. Control over future	("When you make plans ahead, do you usually get to carry out things the way you expected, or do things usually come up to make you change your plans?")
Decrease	4. Sense of crisis and of high national, personal, and group stakes in national elections	(Variety of questions asking whether, or to what extent, an election will affect personal, national, or group interests.)
Decrease	5. Political alienation	(Questions tapping civic qualities, honorableness of politics.)

Two variables which in my research were inversely related to
the level of constant-pie thinking—social trust and felt control
over the future—are both found to be increasing along with economic expansion in the United States.[47] Similarly, a feeling that
the stakes of politics are great and a sense of political alienation,
which I suggested are common where the constant-pie orientation
prevails, are less common through time in the American context.

45. See Robert E. Lane, "The Politics of Consensus in an Age of Affluence,"
American Political Science Review (December 1965), pp. 874–95.

46. In the case of "Control over Future," the fact that there are only two comparison dates somewhat weakens confidence in the findings. The others have at
least three comparison dates, and often two of the dates occur near the beginning
and end of World War II, respectively, and show no increase in the variable—
perhaps reflecting the fact that there was no appreciable increase in the pie available
for consumption during this period.

47. The attitudinal effects of affluence relate not only to the high level of income but also to a rate of growth over time—probably a considerable amount of
time—so that people have experiences that justify the feeling that growth is a
permanent feature of the economy. Growth marked by severe periodic depressions
or stagnation would probably not have the effects of stable, continuous growth.

On the basis of the findings by Almond and Verba and those by Lane, then, the case for an association between a fixed social product and the constant-pie orientation, on the one hand, and political alienation, social and political distrust, and lack of control over the future, on the other, is strengthened considerably. Gradually, as the economy expands, as the struggle for scarce values becomes a variable-sum game rather than a zero-sum game, and as expectations of continued growth are created, the politics of a constant-pie society evolve into the politics of affluence, where trust is easier, where one merely wants his share of the surplus created, and where the stakes of politics are less vital. Constant-pie politics do not disappear at once but probably considerably outlive the end of an economy of scarcity. The ideological superstructure only reaches a new accommodation with the changed existential base after some lag. But eventually attitudes appropriate to a society with growing wealth develop. The politics of moderate trust replaces the politics of distrust, allegiance grows where cynicism once flourished, and a more or less Hobbesian style of politics is replaced by the politics of compromise and modest generosity. Amidst growing affluence, democracy is not a foregone conclusion, since there are still important interests at stake in politics. Nevertheless, both the risks and stakes of politics are substantially lower than they were for an economy of scarcity, and thus the obstacles to a democratic style are substantially reduced as well.

III. Democracy and Ideology

7

The Sources of Support for Democracy

Until this point, the analysis has focused on central beliefs—basic value orientations—and their influence on the political beliefs of Malaysian civil servants. I have traced the broad effects of a pessimistic view of human nature, a constant-pie conception of desired values, and a presentist time orientation as they extend their powerful tendrils up into the realm of political beliefs.

In this chapter and the two following, the focus shifts from central to intermediate and peripheral beliefs, from latent to more or less manifest ideology. The center of attention changes in another sense, too. Of the four qualities shared by new nations that provide the basis for a set of common beliefs—elements of a traditional culture, poverty, a past of alien Western rule, and rapid social change—I have already dealt at some length with all except the third, the element of alien Western rule. The theories of liberal democracy are, of course, Western, and any examination of the nature and extent of democratic beliefs must concentrate on the impact of the West in these areas. While colonialism was the cutting edge of Western influence, that influence continues despite the fact that its original agents have now departed from the scene. Newspapers, movies, the widespread use of the colonizers' languages, the institutional legacy, and above all the educational system represent formidable vehicles for increasing both the weight and range of Western beliefs in now independent states.

In fact, Western beliefs have perhaps acquired new influence precisely because they are no longer imposed. The past representatives of modernization, of Westernization, were outside the local culture, whereas now the "conspiracy" is mostly an internal one, led by self-conscious local modernizers who may vilify the West but are nonetheless the bearers of much of its heritage. In this context, the civil servants of Malaysia are perhaps the most significant group of Western cultural agents in their land, and it is important just how much and in what specific manner they have embraced liberal democratic beliefs[1] as their own. We should hardly expect that democratic beliefs will find this new soil completely hospitable, for it is littered with the rocks of conflicting central beliefs about man and nature, and many of the nutrients available in Western soil are absent here. In such an environment the survival of this tender plant will be tenuous and its growth uneven.

A BELIEF OF SLENDER MEANS

One of the striking aspects of Malaysia, and of most other underdeveloped nations for that matter, is the relative absence of either the primary or the secondary socialization which is said to contribute to the growth of democratic personalities and democratic behavioral patterns. By now a host of writers have suggested that there is a strong relationship between patterns of child rearing and secondary socialization, on the one hand, and the creation of adults whose beliefs, sentiments, and attitudes are supportive of a democratic style, on the other.[2] Without becoming involved in a lengthy discussion of this burgeoning literature, I merely wish to note that there is little basis for expecting democratic personalities to emerge from the patterns of primary and early secondary socialization that characterize the Malaysian sample.

Primary Socialization

According to Erik Erikson, one of the child's earliest established attitudes is a basic trust or distrust of the interpersonal environment.[3] When the child finds that his environment responds reliably to his cries for food and to his need for warmth and affection, he develops trust or confidence; if it does not respond, he develops distrust and greater anxiety. Presumably, this trust contributes to

1. By liberal democratic beliefs is meant support for First Amendment freedoms like free speech and freedom of assembly, support for due process against arbitrary state action, and a preference for a representative government elected by popular franchise.

2. Among others, we might include Lucian Pye, Margaret Mead, Harold Lasswell, Robert Lane, Erik Erikson, Gabriel Almond and Sidney Verba, O. Mannoni, and Else Frenkel-Brunswick.

3. Erik Erikson, *Childhood and Society* (New York, W. W. Norton & Co., 1950), pp. 219–22.

ego strength, faith in people, and felt mastery over the environment, all of which are supposed to assist in the growth of a democratic personality. Child rearing in Malaysia, however, is marred by seemingly unpredictable alternations between shows of affection and its withdrawal.[4] Deprived of effective control over his world, the infant soon becomes painfully aware that the affection of even those closest to him may abruptly cease without warning or provocation. This pattern is hardly supportive of ego strength, interpersonal trust, or confidence in managing the environment.

The nature of authority relationship in early childhood is important, too, particularly in the development of ego strength and independence. Encouraging a child's exploration of his environment and praising and rewarding him for his achievements, a pattern often ascribed to the American middle class, reassures him of his worth and bolsters his self-confidence and independence. Ego strength is the basis for independent behavior and allows the adult to make his own judgments and to avoid becoming the passive instrument of others.[5] In Malaysia, however, the emphasis is on punishment for going against the wishes of parents rather than on rewards for achievements. The child soon discovers that it is simple obedience that is required by his parents and not specific accomplishments—agreement and submission, not assertion. The habits of automatic obedience and of submission to the wishes of authority figures, which are the most likely consequences of this pattern, are hardly characteristic of democratic man. Punishment in Malaysia, moreover, reflects the situational ethic rather than universal standards of behavior. Inche' Abdul Karim could recall vividly the consequences of taking mangoes from the neighbor's compound:

> [Why punished?] For stealing the neighbor's mangoes or fruits. Kampong people take it seriously that you don't behave well—and if the neighbors aren't important people or if they

4. This despite the fact that weaning and toilet training are typically later in the Malaysian context than in the Western. The pattern of maternal affection described here is based on H. M. B. Murphy, "Cultural Factors in the Mental Health of Malayan Students," passim; Judith Djamour, *Malay Kinship and Marriage in Singapore,* London School of Economics Monograph on Social Anthropology No. 21 (London, Athlone Press, 1959); and the author's observations.

5. For a discussion of the relationship between ego strength and democratic attitudes, see Robert E. Lane, *Political Ideology,* Ch. 7.

didn't find out that you had taken a mango, then your parents would just tell you not to do it again—but when the neighbor comes—then they must spank and take offense.

Others in the sample remembered similar experiences, when it was the situation rather than the behavior that dictated the punishment.[6] In this context, the growth of a general respect for law per se or a commitment to general ethical standards is severely stunted. Much of what we have come to call "civic-consciousness" depends largely on precisely these qualities, which child training fails to promote in Malaysia.

Two further points should be made about obedience and punishment in the Malaysian setting. First, disobedience is discouraged most often by the use of fear rather than by explanation or moral suasion. Children are told that if they are not obedient dogs will chew them up, spirits will take them away, or, in the case of Malays, that a fierce, bearded Bengali will carry them off. The component of fear and superstition thus introduced into child rearing hardly contributes to the development of more rational determinants of behavior or to personal responsibility, both of which are linked with the democratic style. Secondly, when punishment is administered, it is likely to be severe. Most of the civil servants interviewed could vividly recall occasions when they were sternly disciplined by their fathers. One remembered being repeatedly immersed in a stream for having disobeyed his father; another recollected being tied to a tree for the entire day after refusing to go to school; and so on. The comparatively minor nature of the offense when coupled with the draconian response is not calculated to produce the balanced attitude toward authority figures that some have suggested is appropriate to a democratic system.

By no means do I wish to suggest that the child rearing pattern in Malaysia is pathological in any general sense. In fact, many Western analysts might find it ideal with respect to its permissiveness, its avoidance of traumata, and its nonpuritanical sexual

6. The author personally witnessed the punishment of two sisters who were caught stealing a sarong from a neighbor's clothesline. They were bound together and shorn of their hair while the neighbors gathered to shame them. From the neighbors' comments it became clear that such drastic measures had been taken because they had been caught stealing from a powerful family in the kampong.

mores.[7] The purpose here, however, has been limited to showing that primary socialization in Malaysia does not conform to those patterns which, it is felt, promote the democratic personality. The emphasis on dependence, nonparticipation, uncritical compliance with authority, and fear and the absence of dependable parental responses are at variance with the growth of interpersonal trust, with mastery of the environment, with an independent spirit, and with norms of participation—all of which are related to the "democratic style." If a democratic system does indeed depend on certain early formed attitudes to help nature and sustain it, then Malaysia's democracy labors under severe handicaps. The fact that the practices in Malaysia are roughly in line with the practices of traditional societies elsewhere suggests that child rearing patterns in most new nations offer scant sustenance for the development of a democratic style.

These patterns of early training may be of more than marginal importance in new nations, for there is good reason to believe that primary socialization has more relevance to adult behavior in traditional and transitional societies than in fully industrialized settings. Comparatively, secondary socialization in a modern nation is much more elaborate and lengthy. It thus substantially dilutes primary training with beliefs and behavior learned in school or in any of a host of other secondary associations. Since transitional society provides less of these intervening experiences (and traditional society much less), the effects of early socialization are relatively more influential for adult orientations.

While family experiences are thus less attenuated by later socialization in both the traditional and transitional settings, the latter suffers from a lack of continuity between childhood and adult roles which does not plague the former. In a simple society the headman's role is virtually identical with that of the head of a large family, as both roles are cut from the same integral cultural fabric. But transitional society is marked by an imported Western political system cut from fabric of a vastly different texture—a system that in all likelihood conflicts with the orientations

7. The reader may be surprised that I have not mentioned the substantial differences among Malay, Chinese, and Indian child rearing practices. Important as these differences are, I have focused on the similarities among all three in order to talk of the group as a whole. An excellent discussion of these differences and their consequences is contained in H. M. B. Murphy.

learned in primary socialization. Compared with modern societies, then, early training in transitional states is of special importance, not only because of the relative weakness of secondary socialization, but also because of the potential strains between the more or less traditional family socialization, on the one hand, and the adult roles implied by a political system adopted from a vastly different cultural context, on the other.

If primary socialization does not contribute to the growth of democratic personalities, neither do the basic value orientations that have been described. The orientation toward man is one that stresses his narrow selfishness and lack of internal restraint. The heavy burden of misanthropy and suspicion generated by this orientation leaves little room for the trust and cooperativeness implied by a democratic system. A presentist time orientation inhibits the development of long-run instrumental or cooperative strategies which strengthen a democratic polity. Finally, the belief that most desired values are scarce and their quantity fixed by nature leads these civil servants to conceive of political and economic life as a zero-sum contest. Each of these orientations nurtures political beliefs and values that are scarcely hospitable to a democratic style.

Secondary Socialization

Not much support for democracy can be located in the character of early socialization or among the basic value orientations of the sample. But what about secondary socialization? When the political system is so different from family norms, as it is in transitional society, later experiences can play a crucial role in developing new attitudes appropriate to democratic politics and thus substitute for the lack of congruent early socialization. This is essentially what Almond and Verba have said in focusing on how late socialization can turn "political subjects" into "political participants."

> Family experiences do play a role in the formation of political attitudes, but the role may not be central; the gap between the family and the polity may be so wide that other social experiences, especially in social situations closer in time and in structure to the political system, may play a larger role.[8]

8. Almond and Verba, p. 305.

The special role that secondary socialization may play in counteracting primary influences and preparing people for democratic participation focuses attention on the school system, on voluntary organizations, and on the bureaucratic experiences of the sample. As far as the authority patterns and participation styles of these structures are concerned, there is little in what the civil servants had to say that would lead us to regard them as bastions of democracy. Teachers were typically seen as strict, humorless taskmasters who demanded much rote learning and were not above caning the recalcitrant with a length of *rotan.* There were relatively few extracurricular activities, and those that did exist were closely controlled by schoolteachers. The school picture has, of course, changed a good deal since World War II, but most of the respondents were educated before or immediately after the war.

Voluntary organizations might potentially provide democratic experiences, but fewer than one quarter of these men belong to any group beyond an Old Boys' Association (secondary school alumni), to which they occasionally pay dues. Moreover, as noted in Chapter 4, those few who do belong to voluntary organizations usually view them as facades behind which individuals pursue wealth or status and cynically exploit the group for whatever it is worth.

Bureaucratic experience in this context is mixed. The fact that these men hold responsible posts in the government means they not only have more knowledge of politics than most but also make decisions of some importance. Undoubtedly their greater knowledge and their small niche on the Olympian heights contribute to a feeling of civic competence. Most of them have voted in elections, and some have even given civics lectures to public groups. On the other hand, the internal authority structure of the bureaucracy is hardly democratic. Lines of authority are clear-cut, and the distinctions in rank as indicated by salary and title are impressively elaborate. Modeled along military lines, working life within the Malaysian bureaucracy is not in itself likely to promote a flowering of the democratic spirit.

Even the informal democracy that often develops within a large organization is much weaker in Malaysia than in the West. Acute status consciousness and the upper-directedness described earlier conspire to minimize group decision making, to restrict fraternization with subordinates, and so on. Thus, while their bureaucratic roles enhance the respondents' sense of political efficacy, the authority structure into which these roles are organized does not help sustain norms of internal democracy.

Although this analysis has not by any means involved a systematic treatment of primary or secondary socialization, it is abundantly clear that little support for democracy is to be found here. Anyone casting about for "democratic pathologies" in these areas would be amply rewarded in his quest. Given the effects of early and late socialization, it is far from astonishing that one does not regularly find adults who fit the stereotype of democratic personalities. In fact, on the basis of socialization and central beliefs, it would be surprising if one were to find even a moderate level of commitment to democratic forms and style. Yet it is probably true that the civil servants of Malaysia represent the largest significant group in the nation supportive of liberal democratic norms and Western political values. How does this commitment, imperfect as it is, come about?

Two Sources of Support for Democracy

So far the discussion of socialization in school and in the bureaucracy has dealt largely with the latent socialization provided by authority patterns and other factors. What has been neglected —and what is too often neglected in studies of political socialization—is the manifest political training that takes place in school or at work. When Almond and Verba came up against adult patterns that conflicted with what one might have expected on the basis of latent socialization, they were obliged to conclude,

> The latent political socialization that is involved in, say, experiences with family authority patterns may create certain predispositions toward political attitudes within the individual; his receptivity of certain types of poltical relationships may be increased. But this is obviously an inadequate explanation of his political attitudes, for there are other forms of political socialization. There is, for instance, *manifest political socialization*—the intentional teaching of political attitudes in the family and in school.[9]

9. Ibid., pp. 268–69 (my italics).

It is precisely this manifest political socialization, particularly in school, that seems to account for much of the commitment to democratic values among the men in the sample. During our discussions of democracy and freedom, their comments took on the distinct hue of a classroom recitation. Quotations from Lincoln, Mill, Churchill, and other "heroes of democracy" sprang uncertainly to their lips from the pages of dimly but fondly remembered school texts. It is important to remember that most of them were in school when Malaya was still a colony and received their instruction from teachers who, for the most part, firmly believed in the British system. Their curriculum was the same any English child would have had to tackle, and if in Malaya it did not produce loyalty to Britain, it did prdouce a substantial loyalty to the British system.

The British they came to know through their teachers was, for the older men, the most powerful nation in the world, the most civilized, and the richest; so it stood to reason that this had something to do with her system of government. For the younger men, the light of Britain was somewhat dimed by nationalist onslaughts and initial British losses in World War II, but nonetheless its ideals were the very weapons that were turned against it in the struggle for independence.

Learning about the British system in Malaya was conducted *in abstracto*. While English, French, or American children receive much the same abstracted, ideal picture of their own political system, they also hear the more concrete and often more cynical observations of their parents, and later they can measure the system's ideals and freedoms against their own experience and that of others. At some point they must draw together the threads of experience, compare them to what they have been taught, and emerge with an evaluation of some sort. This opportunity to test political theory against fact in their own lives was not open to Malaysian civil servants.[10] It is almost as if English school children

10. The colonial regime itself might have remedied this situation, but the prevailing criticism was that the British had failed to give the freedoms to their colonies that they extended to their own people. Socialist or communist critiques might have served this function, too, but unlike in some other colonies, they were few and far between in Malaya, and in any case were scarcely reflected in the school system. One has the impression that in French colonies—especially from the prewar Blum government onward—socialist critiques had more influence in colonial schools.

were to be taught about the theory of the Greek city-state by
Greeks who had a vested interest in presenting the system in its
most advantageous light. This is perhaps a slight exaggeration, but
except for those few who managed to spend some time in England,
the picture of the British political system for most civil servants
was portrayed in the most favorable light possible and was un-
sullied by first hand experience. The selective nature of information about Britain taught in Malaya's schools and the conditions
under which it was offered helped generate an abstract commitment, however imperfect, to liberal democracy.

The process of explicit learning about the British system, moreover, did not stop when these men finished secondary school or
the university. Most of them, when they joined the civil service,
were trained by, and often served under, British colonial servants.
While learning the tools of their trade, they were introduced to
the ideals of the British public service:

> that power is a social function and not simply domination;
> that office is a public service and not a fief to be exploited in
> return for personal service to a prince; that people are really
> equal before the law and that their rights, even if unstated
> in constitutions, can exercise a restraint on the power of gov-
> ernment.[11]

Unlike what was taught in school about the British system in
England, these were norms that could be measured against colonial reality. While performance frequently fell short of these high
ideals, many British colonial servants in Malaya did in fact act in
line with their principles. Those who failed to live up to their own
commandments tarnished themselves, not their principles. Thus,
bureaucratic training and experience served for the most part to
reflect favorably on the already esteemed British political order
and to enhance a belief in democratic norms.[12]

Neither instruction in school nor training in the civil service

11. Nadav Safran, *Egypt in Search of Political Community: An Analysis of the
Intellectual and Political Evolution of Egypt, 1804–1952* (Cambridge, Harvard
University Press, 1961), p. 57. This book contains a sensitive analysis of the failure
of the liberal democratic nationalists in Egypt, which is applicable *ceteris paribus*
to many other new nations.

12. In another sense, bureaucratic experience worked against democratic norms,
as will be taken up in the following chapter.

is quite adequate to explain how these men acquired a commitment to democracy. After all, a majority of those elites in new nations who call for nondemocratic solutions to political problems were educated in a similar atmosphere. For many of these elites, knowledge of Western democratic norms has not meant commitment to them but has served rather as a tool to explain why they are not applicable to the local situation.

What may commit these men, more than others, to Western political norms is the simple fact that they have gained much under the democratic system. While the style of neither primary nor secondary socialization contributes to democratic beliefs, their own progress and success under the system does, in fact, generate a degree of loyalty. Almost all of these men are better off than their fathers; they enjoy greater incomes, greater prestige, and greater security. They are not the unattached, *déraciné* intellectuals who have become radicalized because there is no place for them in the society. They are the opposite side of the coin from this dispossessed intelligentsia, who have gravitated to trade unionism, journalism, teaching, and other fields where neither the financial nor the status rewards are as satisfying as those of the upper bureaucracy. The Malaysian respondents, occupying high posts in the civil service, have been integrated into the system and have been given great prestige by it, so it is not surprising that they have a certain stake in its continuance.[13]

This phenomenon has been called the "halo effect," or, more broadly, "stimulus generalization." [14] These men have every reason to be satisfied with the opportunities for education, status, and pay their society has afforded them, and their general satisfaction inevitably colors their evaluation of the political system as well. It makes little difference whether or not their advancement is objectively traceable to the nature of the political system itself; the fact that their achievements have occurred under a particular form of government is enough to generate the halo effect.[15] Manifest po-

13. This would not hold true in those nations where politics has all but replaced administration, and where civil servants have lost status and high pay and have been attacked as a group by politicians.

14. Lane, in *Political Ideology*, found the same phenomenon among working-class Americans in Eastport (pp. 91–92).

15. It might well be argued that these men have the colonial regime more to thank for their position than popular democracy, since their status and power were

litical socialization and a general sense of satisfaction with the
system may seem slender bases for democratic ideology, but in
the absence of more substantial foundations, they play a significant
role.

SOCIALIZATION SUPPORT FOR POLITICAL SYSTEMS IN NEW NATIONS

Among the elite group that has been examined, democracy receives little nourishment from early family training or from the
style of secondary socialization. It depends for support almost exclusively upon the manifest norms that are taught at school,
through the mass media, and in occupational life—depends, that
is, on a kind of indoctrination. Distinguishing along these lines
between the latent characterological and experiential support for
democracy on the one hand, and the manifest, learned support on
the other, it is possible to construct the diagram in Figure 2.

FIGURE 2

VARIETIES OF SUPPORT FOR THE POLITICAL SYSTEM
IN DIFFERENT STATES [16]

	Manifest Socialization	Latent Socialization	
	Taught Norms	Experiential	Character-ological
Democratic New Nation (Malaysia)	+	− (+)	− (+)
Post-Revolutionary Demo-cratic Nation (Mexico—circa 1920? France—circa 1790?)	+	+ (−)	+ (−)
Old Evolutionary Demo-cratic Nation (England)	+	+	+

greater before local politicians assumed power. This point of view, however, overlooks the fact that it was independence and the consequent departure of expatriates
which were responsible for their rapid advancement. It is true, nonetheless, that
under colonialism an administrator made decisions which are now specifically
political, and the effects of this on ideology will be examined in Ch. 9.

16. Plus signs [+] indicate support for democracy, while minus signs [−] indicate nonsupportive or conflicting socialization. Where two signs appear together,
the one above indicates the predominant influence of socialization, the one in
parentheses a minor influence.

The changes in the existential base—type and level of economic activity, urban-rural residence, social stratification, and other demographic variables—which carry the potential for a new ideology are likely to be "accretionary" rather than "avulsionary" by their very nature. These are the same variables that are largely, but not entirely, responsible for the basic cultural changes which in turn affect experience and character over a long period. If, as in an old evolutionary democratic nation like England, the nature of the reigning ideology changes at roughly the same rate as these accretionary factors, it remains more or less congruent with latent socialization and thus helps stabilize the system.[17] Revolutionary changes, because they occur while the old order is still strong enough to put up stiff resistance, are likely to install a somewhat less stable political order, since the existential base is only partly supportive.[18] In this situation, latent socialization contains some elements that sustain the new order and other elements that tend to undermine it.

In a new nation like Malaysia, however, the new order is more exogenous in origin than indigenous. As a result, latent socialization provides relatively little experiential and characterological underpinning for the new democratic regime. The mere fact that, for the most part, resistance to the nationalist revolution for independence in colonial areas has seldom been as violent and uncompromising as the resistance to revolutions in which a new (in most cases, bourgeois) class ousted the traditional ruling class of their own nation means that the new order in an ex-colonial area accedes to power before its bases of latent support are well developed. Some support, of course, does exist as a result of the social and economic changes wrought by the colonial process itself,

17. Of course, political changes are uneven and lag behind or spurt ahead of changes in the existential base, but one can distinguish between situations of relative equilibrium and those of severe disequilibrium.

18. It is important to emphasize here that Figure 2 is concerned exclusively with the character of socialization. Thus the fact that the forces supporting the old order are still strong may make for a structual balance that might in some circumstances contribute to a democratic form of government; in this instance the analysis of socialization leads toward one conclusion, while the analysis of political structure leads toward a quite different assessment.

In terms of socialization alone, if resistance to the new democratic order is quite prolonged, the situation is probably more auspicious, since the accretionary changes have perhaps gone so far that they are more supportive of the democratic order when it finally arrives.

but this support is likely to be more tenuous in the democratic new nation than in the post-revolutionary democracy.[19] The net effect of this situation in democratic new nations is simply that manifest political socialization must bear a greater weight in supporting the political system. Perched, as it were, on one slender foundation pillar, it is less likely to survive the various storms that beset it than is an old, evolutionary democratic nation, which can depend on all three pillars for support. Unstable as it is, the democratic new nation finds that latent socialization, far from buttressing a democratic form of government, constitutes an additional burden it must carry.

To this point I have focused on what might be called "legitimacy." But as indicated above, an important reason why Malaysian civil servants identify with the democratic system is that they have experienced individual and collective satisfactions within it and thus tend to evaluate it favorably. For civil servants, at least, democratic government has been *effective* in meeting their aspirations. What the system lacks in legitimacy it makes up for by its effectiveness. This distinction between legitimacy and effectiveness has been lucidly explained by S. M. Lipset:

> Effectiveness means actual performance, the extent to which the system satisfies the basic functions of government as most of the population and . . . powerful groups . . . see them. Legitimacy involves the capacity of the system to engender and maintain the belief that the existing political institutions are the most appropriate ones for the society. . . . While effectiveness is primarily instrumental, legitimacy is evaluative. Groups regard a political system as legitimate or illegitimate according to the way in which its values fit with theirs.[20]

In the absence of substantial legitimacy—reflected in the style and content of latent and manifest political socialization—effectiveness furnishes only an uncertain, provisional footing for a democratic regime. As Lipset notes, the Austrian and German

19. The post-revolutionary nation suffers from the special problem of social antagonisms and cleavages exacerbated by the revolutionary process itself, but this is a subject for separate analysis.

20. S. M. Lipset, *Political Man: The Social Bases of Politics* (Garden City, N.Y., Doubleday & Co., 1959), pp. 77–96.

regimes in the late 1920s enjoyed little legitimacy but "remained reasonably effective." However, "When the effectiveness of various governments broke down in the 1930's, those societies which were high on the scale of legitimacy remained democratic, while such countries as Germany, Austria, and Spain lost their freedom, and France narrowly escaped a similar fate." [21]

Should the effectiveness of the democratic system in Malaysia and other democratic new nations decline much, they would not have "capital" in the form of legitimacy on which to weather the crisis and, in all likelihood, would not emerge with a democratic form of government. In fact, this is substantially what has occurred in most of those new nations that have already abandoned democracy. It is ironic, too, that democratic new nations, which must rely upon effective government to preserve their political system while it sends down still frail roots of legitimacy, are in most respects poorly equipped to provide effective government by virtue of their lack of capital, technical skills, organizational competence, and so on.

The relative instability of democracy in new nations is thus thrown into sharp relief by the fact that the experiential and characterological sources of legitimacy are weak in the sample. That democracy continues to maintain its uncertain purchase in these circumstances is due in large part to two factors: manifest political socialization and a presently adequate level of governmental effectiveness. Its future would be cast in grave doubt if the level of satisfaction with the system's output were to decline for any reason—especially if the dissatisfaction were concentrated among powerful groups. Even more than the post-revolutionary democracy, the democratic new nation must rely for its survival more on what it does than on what it is.

21. Ibid., pp. 81–82.

8

The Nature of Support for Democracy

THE ORGANIZATION AND FUNCTION OF POLITICAL MATERIAL

Judging by the findings of Lane or Converse, the way in which Malaysian civil servants order facts and beliefs in their minds is not unlike the way the American common man arranges his ideas.[1] First, with perhaps only four exceptions, these bureaucrats seldom "contextualize" political material; rather, they "morselize" it.[2] The political events about which they think tend to remain isolated and are only rarely placed in either the historical or spatial contexts that might invest them with greater meaning. When they speak of Sukarno, for example, he emerges simply as a madman, without reference to either the conditions that produced him or the long-run consequences of his rule. The secession of Singapore from the Malaysian Federation is similarly most often seen as basically an affair of personal pique among leaders, with little reference to the broader ethnic and economic questions involved. Education, of course, is important here, as it provides powerful tools for contextualization, and in fact the level of contextualization is somewhat higher among university graduates. Nonetheless, morselizing is the rule rather than the exception.

Secondly, it is important to note that formal ideologies—socialism, communism, capitalism, and so forth—play an insignificant role in ordering the political beliefs of these seventeen men. There are, of course, notions of what is democratic and what is not, what capitalism and socialism mean, and so on, but even here there is no rigidity. Between what is clearly democratic and what is clearly undemocratic, there are a host of possible situations

---

1. See Lane, *Political Ideology*, pp. 346–63, and Philip E. Converse, "The Nature of Belief Systems in Mass Publics," pp. 206–61, in David E. Apter, ed., *Ideology and Discontent* (Glencoe, The Free Press, 1964).

2. The terms are borrowed from Lane's *Political Ideology*, p. 350.

which, for them, are "more-or-less," not "either-or." The absence
of much formal ideology is surely one reason why political information is morselized, since formal ideologies provide the context within which the barrage of political news can be ordered and
distilled. Without the ordering principles that a formal ideology
offers, then, political beliefs and events are likely to be littered
about, a small group here, another there, with few cognitive paths
connecting them.

One does not have to look far to discover why formal ideologies
have little currency among administrators in Malaysia. There has
never been a social upheaval of major proportions which would,
as the French Revolution did, create the conditions in which the
search for a new symbolic framework to explain what is happening becomes paramount. Social changes have sometimes come suddenly to Malaysia, but they have come in digestible amounts and
usually without the great social disorganization that destroys continuity. Across the Straits of Malacca the intense search for an
explanatory ideology in Indonesia reflects that nation's political
history, as the weakness of formal ideology reflects Malaysian experience.[3]

At least two important ideological consequences follow from
the morselization of political material and the relative absence of
formal ideology among the Malaysian sample. First, the weakness
of contextual thinking often leads to a personalization of political
causes. Thus Sukarno is alone responsible for the orgiastic excesses
of Indonesian policy, Hitler for Germany's crimes against the
Jews, and Churchill for the gallant British war effort. Inasmuch
as an analysis of impersonal causes requires contextualization of a
sort, these men find it easier to attribute most effects to the operation of human will.[4] The problem with this orientation toward
people is, of course, that it focuses on individuals rather than issues, on personalities rather than policies. When things go wrong,
the answer is to throw out the "bad guys" and replace them with
"good guys." In this context, little learning takes place, and an

3. For an excellent discussion of Indonesia's quest for an ideology, see Clifford
Geertz, "Ideology as a Cultural System," in Apter, ed., *Ideology and Discontent*, pp.
47–76.

4. This is less true for the more educated, younger administrators who more
readily perceive impersonal, social forces. This variation is treated more fully in
Ch. 9.

instrumental or means-end approach often fails to guide evaluations of the political world.[5]

If the morselization of political events and the weakness of formal political theories inhibits integrative thinking by these men,
it also produces a kind of openness toward new information.
There is no rigid, predetermined framework into which new information must be fitted or which excludes contradictory material.[6] Since little integrative thinking takes place, the conflict between different pieces of information is often not perceived, but
when it is, the dilemma is faced squarely; there is little evasion. In
fact, one might fairly say that these men avoid judgment and
commitment when they can. By suspending judgment in this way,
they keep open as many ideological options as possible. Mr. Tay is
typical in this regard. When I asked him about the advantages of
democracy, he took care to leave open a line of possible retreat:
"Well, I haven't seen the other systems yet. . . . To be able to
give you the advantages—you must know the other system—unless it's just through readings and books." Like Mr. Tay, most of
the others made clear that their political judgments were of a
provisional character. Not only are they open to new information
that would challenge their tentative notions, but they tend to con-
fine their convictions to what they have directly experienced; they
will not take someone else's word for it.[7]

Much of the political openness of these men is traceable to their
other-directedness. As noted before, most would prefer to be respected for their ability to get along with others rather than for
their independent views. If their minds were already made up,
they would sacrifice much of the flexibility they feel they need in
responding to others and accommodating to the social context. A
majority, in fact, do not enjoy political discussions with others
who may disagree with them. They are all willing to admit that

5. See Lane, *Political Ideology*, p. 308, for a discussion of why personalization is
dysfunctional for democracy.

6. For an example of the accommodation between traditional and modern medicine in Malaya, see Robert J. Wolff, "Modern Medicine and Traditional Culture:
Confrontation on the Malay Peninsula," *Human Organization*, 24 (Winter 1965),
339–45.

7. There is a little of the *machismo* pattern here. These men see themselves as
autonomous and have a certain fear of appearing to be influenced or manipulated
by others.

political argumentation serves to sharpen their own opinions, but to their minds, this small yield does not begin to justify its social disruptiveness. Inche' Mohd. Amin, for example, dislikes talking with those who disagree with him because "I don't want to quarrel over small things—there's no point of disagreeing over small matters." For him, politics is simply not important enough to merit upsetting others. Mr. Khoo sees similar consequences: "It is difficult—you make no headway at all—and they get rather angry, you see." If politics were more salient to them they might feel differently, but it is not.

Coupled with an unwillingness or inability to contextualize, the emphasis on the social function of political discussion tends to focus attention on those political events having the greatest entertainment value. Almost all prefer political discussion with someone who jokes and keeps the conversation from getting too serious rather than with someone who has all the answers. (Kamalam: "We normally don't like people who know too much—because they don't make it very pleasant"; Inche' Mustapha: "this serious discussion shouldn't last too long or it may become a bore —you have to just ask questions.") If political information and discussion are valued for their socializing function, for their ability to bring men together rather than to divide them, attention is diverted away from basic issues toward the trivial or the spectacular. For most of these men, the *New York Daily News* is more in keeping with their information needs than the *New York Times*. Political information, then, does not seem to tie in closely with the political beliefs of these civil servants, either to reinforce their beliefs or contradict them; it is instead judged more for its spectator appeal.[8]

THE CHARACTER OF DEMOCRATIC BELIEFS

An understanding of the organization and function of political material is essential to placing an analysis of the character of democratic beliefs in its proper context. The very process of ordering a discussion of personal political beliefs is likely to create the mis-

8. For evidence that this pattern is also characteristic of the American electorate, see the paragraph entitled "People who know a lot are often unpleasant" and "Knowledge taken seriously leads to controversy" in Lane's *Political Ideology*, p. 366.

taken impression that the beliefs themselves are ordered and coherent and have, as it were, a life of their own. Thus, it is important to begin with a clear conception of the tendency of these men
to morselize and personalize, of the openness of their beliefs, the
inconsequential role that formal ideology plays, and of the social
function that political information performs for them.

Turning to a description of their democratic and nondemocratic beliefs, it is possible to specify at least five criteria that provide a rough measure of the "democraticness" of a man's political
beliefs.[9] These criteria, phrased in their undemocratic variants,
are

1. A scorn for the mass electorate.
2. Distaste for the confusion and delay of parliamentary procedures.
3. A preference for temporary dictatorship in time of threat.
4. Unrelieved cynicism about the democratic procedures in organizations
   they knew.
5. Doubt about the future of democracy.[10]

An investigation of each should make it possible to construct a
serviceable map of the nature of support for liberal democracy
among the Malaysian sample.

Scorn for mass electorate. In response to a question asking
whether everyone "no matter how ignorant and careless should
have an equal vote" all seventeen men agreed—some emphatically,
others a bit reluctantly—that even the least of their fellows must
have access to the ballot. The unanimity of their reaction is indeed impressive, particularly in light of the fact that the electorate
to which they refer is, by the measure of education at least, less
competent to exercise the vote than its Western counterpart. Having at their disposal a situation tailor-made for elitism, they
choose not to make use of it.[11]

Mr. Khoo is typical of those who support the popular vote with
some reluctance but are nevertheless certain about what is required. "It should be each person one vote. In a new nation like

9. This measure is borrowed from Lane, p. 84. As I shall explain later, this
measure is not entirely adequate for the purpose, but it can serve as a first
approximation.

10. Ibid., p. 98.

11. Asked the identical question, three of Lane's fifteen respondents in Eastport, U.S.A., "argued for some kind of screening process to eliminate 'the ignorant
and the careless'" (Lane, p. 84).

us we should—we must have some tolerance because quite a number of them are illiterates." Here the decision is taken with both eyes open, and the principle of "one man, one vote" affirmed in spite of general illiteracy. Khoo is willing to support a democratic norm with full knowledge of its dangers and costs. If Mr. Khoo inclines to paternalism, Mr. Tay is more affirmatively populist: "I think everyone should have an equal vote, subject to age of course—I don't think education or wealth should be any factors at all."

The consensus on this issue is such that most men replied, "Of course, equal vote" or some statement to that effect, and we have only Mr. Tay's long-windedness to thank for a more elaborate reply. One suspects that their unanimity reflects something absorbed from the nationalist movements in the colonial areas. Was it not the British, after all, who claimed that Malaysians, Indians, and Africans were not sufficiently educated—or perhaps were even congenitally incapable—to become mature citizens? The nationalist rejoinder was to demand the same self-determination and popular government that the British people enjoyed and for which Britain had borne such great hardships during World War II. Since denial of popular rule was the most striking hypocrisy of a democratic colonizing nation, it is scarcely surprising that the nationalist revolutions generated widespread and lasting support for the universal franchise. The assertion of national collective worth that characterizes nationalism requires nothing less than equal civic privileges for a people who are as worthy as their foreign rulers.

International fashion may play a role here, too. Elections have become the index par excellence of democracy and self-determination. A host of United Nations reports condemn the denial of the vote to indigenous populations in Angola, Southern Rhodesia, and South West Africa and demand self-determination. As the most apparent manifestation of popular rule, elections have become an absolute requirement for any state that aspires to international respectability.

Distaste for delay and confusion of democratic procedures. The frustrations of democratic procedures are, as these men view them, considerable. Whether they find the delays and confusions sometimes useful or completely destructive, all agree that these problems beset a democracy more than other forms of government. In spite of the procedural burdens of democracy, almost two-thirds (eleven) of the men find enough that is useful in the delays, or in the democratic system itself, to compensate for these frustrations. Only six intimate that the liabilities are perhaps too great and that efficiency and speed may require a change in the system.[12]

Sundram, who supports democracy in full knowledge of its shortcomings, made an explicit comparison between democratic and totalitarian systems. Asked if democracy creates confusion and prevents important things from getting done, he replied, "Well, the process may be slow but you reach the end. The important thing is you reach the end and with the full backing of the population. In a totalitarian system you reach the end much faster but with a lot of discontent." The notion that democracy causes costly delays is not contested by Sundram; rather, he affirms it and states that he values contentment and wide accord more than speed. Inche' Mustapha, adopting his common pose as amateur psychologist, seems to have much the same set of preferences:

> Yes, I think democracy is a very costly thing and it takes so long to do some things. You have to get the majority opinion —it is a very costly thing. . . . It is a waste of time and a waste of money too. But whatever the final conclusion, everybody knows what it is all about. The funny thing is that once a human being has expressed his opinion, whether he is followed or not in the decision is immaterial.

Although the costs of democracy are more vivid here, full consultation is valued over speed. Along with most of the sample, both men feel that a happy ship which reaches port behind schedule is preferable to one which arrives on time carrying a mutinous crew. Implicit in their statements is the view that short cuts may not be efficient over the long run, however attractive their immediate advantages may seem.

The sources of this tolerance for the inconveniences of democracy may perhaps be sought in the dangers these men see in the authoritarian alternatives to democracy. Eliminating the delays and

12. Malaysian civil servants are, as a group, only slightly less tolerant of the confusions and delays of democracy (eleven of seventeen tolerant) than Lane's respondents (eleven of fifteen tolerant).

confusions of democratic procedures would mean allowing some individual or small group to assume undiluted control of the nation's affairs, a prospect these men do not relish—at least in normal times. As stated before, the general expectation is that unrestrained leaders are likely to follow a natural human inclination to self-serving and to exploit their posts for whatever personal gain they may yield. In this context, the function of the democratic system, however imperfect its controls, is to prevent leaders from becoming plunderers by requiring the consent of the governed. These men do not want unrestrained leaders; they are distrustful of what would happen if human motives were given full rein. They feel that the price of speed and efficiency will in all probability be pillage by voracious rulers. This is a price most of them are unwilling to pay.[13] They want strong, masterful leaders, to be sure, but at the same time these leaders should know that they serve at the pleasure of the people, who can replace them if they stray from the path of public service.

About a third of the sample nevertheless finds the costs of democracy too great or, in most cases, perceives the delays and confusion without grasping the function that delay might serve. Inche' Hussain's views are more or less representative of this group. Agreeing that democracy causes confusion and prevents important matters from getting done, he continued,

> Yes, it does . . . it can. [Why?] Because democracy itself is a very expensive thing. You have to take into account the voices of everybody and reduce it to a tiny thing before de-

13. Another, and much more speculative, explanation for the general tolerance of the burdens of democracy might relate back to their childhood training. Most of these men were pushed and ordered about by their fathers, and because they resented it, they want their children to make their own decisions without parental prodding or impositions. Similarly, in politics they do not want to force their views on others—nor do they want a leader who will impose his views on them and reduce them simply to obeying orders. Thus, the fact that these men had authoritarian fathers may contribute to their support for a form of government where people do not get pushed around or are expected to fall automatically in line. The dynamics of this inter-generational psychology are paradoxical, since authoritarianism is generally assumed to be transferred rather than extinguished from one generation to the next. For a related argument which supports this line of reasoning for the Indian intelligentsia, see Edward Shils, "The Intellectual Between Tradition and Modernity: The Indian Situation," in *Comparative Studies in Society and History,* Supplement I (The Hague, Mouton & Co., 1961), pp. 80–81.

cisions can be arrived at. Along the same lines it takes longer
to get things done—you have to consult everyone. Since all
can express themselves there are bound to be contradictions,
so it becomes confusing at times.

Conjuring up a thunderous din of contending voices in which
it becomes impossible to hear or be heard, Inche' Hussain found
the process of democratic consultation a nearly impossible task.
He focused upon the social disruptiveness of political debate, as
mentioned earlier in this chapter. Viewed in this fashion, political
debate destroys group harmony. When it continues for too long a
time and on a large scale, it ultimately leads to violence and permanent division. While those who are more tolerant of the problems of democratic consultation see the process as one which builds
consensus and popular support, Inche' Hussain looks at the same
process and discovers divisiveness and discontent. Among the six
administrators who find the delays and confusion of democracy
severely crippling, then, there is on the one hand a concern with
the divisions created by political quarrels, and on the other, a feeling that many important decisions cannot wait for the public to
make up its mind—a preference for decisiveness.

Preference for dictatorship in crisis. Asking respondents whether
they agree there is need for a dictatorship in a time of crisis is not
unlike asking whether they think democracy creates delay and confusion. What is new is the assumption of a crisis—a situation that
places a premium on decisiveness. The one asks whether the delay
and confusion caused by popular government are serious handicaps in the normal course of events, while the other asks whether
they are tolerable in a crisis. One would expect that some of those
who are willing to endure delay and muddles in ordinary times
would find them dangerous luxuries in a crisis situation.

As might be anticipated, support for democratic procedures
falls off substantially in a hypothetical crisis situation. Only two
of the seventeen men were reluctant to endorse a "crisis dictatorship" or were explicit about provision being made for a return to
democratic norms afterward. The other fifteen acceded readily to
the requirements of the situation as they saw it. Mr. Khoo, representing the majority, echoed the sentiments of Inche' Ja'afar,
quoted earlier, in saying that one must adopt the same methods as

one's competitors in order to survive: "During war there should be a temporary dictatorship. Especially when things were very black in England, Churchill had to become a dictator. It was one dictator against another and the stronger one wins." For Inche' Abu Bakar the conclusion was the same, but the problem of speed was uppermost in his mind: [Dictatorship in crisis?] "Yes!" [Why?] "Because in a time of crisis there is not time for getting the views —because any time lost might endanger the national situation."

For most of the men, then, a crisis situation is compelling enough to resort to personal or committee rule. The situation is far from academic to them, since they all experienced the postwar Emergency, when normal colonial rule was abandoned for military administration, and the more recent "war" with Indonesia, during which certain freedoms were suspended. In fact, from the time of the Japanese occupation, these men have lived in a continual atmosphere of incipient or actual political crisis. There is, furthermore, a clear recognition on their part of the perilous situation of a nation of but nine million beset by communal tensions and facing one hundred million Indonesians to the south and eight hundred million Chinese to the north. Recourse to dictatorship, when set in this context of national fragility, is surely more comprehensible than it might be in a stable, secure democracy. A crisis situation is both more real and more compelling to them than it would seem to Englishmen or Americans.

Over and above the special dangers faced by a small nation in Southeast Asia, there is some reason to suspect that the commitment to democratic procedures is weaker here than in most Western contexts. The commitment is more formalistic in the sense that it tends to weaken quickly when it threatens other values like security, stability, and so forth. Working class respondents in the United States, for example, shied away from endorsing even a temporary dictatorship in the midst of a war "with a threat of atomic bombing." [14] Confronted with the final holocaust, then, American respondents were still reluctant to countenance a dictatorship. It would seem that democratic procedures are very highly placed values in Amercia; they are doggedly held to in circumstances that would prompt their scrapping in Malaysia.

14. Lane, *Political Ideology*, p. 85.

Unrelieved cynicism about democratic procedures in organizations they know. I have already discussed how these Malaysian bureaucrats evaluate the operation of voluntary organizatons with which they are acquainted. More than two-thirds of them are quite cynical. They see individuals exploiting organizations for social recognition and power, and for material rewards as well. In particular, their comments contain sharp criticisms of the small cliques that discourage wider participation so that they might retain their leadership positions, complaints against those who threaten to quit unless they are elected, and a distaste for the motives of those who join and fail to pull their share of the load.

Two quite distinct factors appear to account for the men's cynicism about voluntary organizations. First, their generally pessimistic assumptions about human motives are projected to include individual behavior within an organizational context. This process is particularly apparent among those who have few or no group memberships and who therefore can more easily invoke their imaginations in describing what happens in general. If, however, this were the main wellspring of cynicism, one would expect that those who participate actively in voluntary organizations would be markedly less cynical. But this is not the case; those with more experience in groups of this sort are every bit as cynical as those making judgments from afar. Even Inche' Mustapha, who serves on no less than four school boards and is an official of two charitable organizations, was discouraged.

> And I was once secretary of a nonpolitical youth organization, until I resigned last year when I found that some of the leaders were making use of the organization for their own ends. [And later] I'm losing touch with many groups—because I've withdrawn from so many of them because of the leadership.

Since research findings in the West have indicated that persons with more political experience are generally less cynical about political institutions than nonparticipants, it is curious that those of our administrators who have extensive group experiences should be as cynical about these groups as those who are less active. The answer to this apparent paradox lies in this actual nature of voluntary groups in Malaysia. With some notable exceptions, the majority of them are not the open, democratic forums that would provide their members with the satisfaction of having actively participated and influenced policy. Many of Malaysia's service organizations, not to mention religious groups, are cast in a somewhat traditional mold, where high-status, elderly leadership perpetuates itself and discourages wider membership. Voluntary groups are, as Inche' Mustapha noted, used frequently as personal vehicles, and prominent politicians, relatives of Malay sultans, civil servants, and wealthy Chinese patrons often exercise a tenacious, durable control over their executive bodies and policy directions.

The point is that, for many of these men, cynicism about how private organizations are run is based on concrete experience within groups that are run along less than democratic lines. Their cynicism about these organizations may actually serve to highlight their commitment to the norms of popular control rather than to indicate a lack of such commitment. If most organizations are not open or democratic, a democrat would be justifiably cynical about their mode of operation.

Doubt About the Future of Democracy

A substantial majority of the civil servants (eleven) are pessimistic about the durability of democracy in their nation. Their pessimism focuses either on the willingness of leaders to forsake democracy when it threatens other values such as unity and economic development, or on the fear that communism, by virtue of its strength and organization, might sweep all before it. Inche' Ja'afar serves as an example of both concerns. Asked if the future of democracy in Malaysia is bright, he answered,

> Not bright in the short term because some of these countries think they have something to do in a hurry—and they are willing to sacrifice democracy to do that—like "Guided Democracy" in Indonesia. And again there is another factor in this part of the world—communism and its ability to infiltrate. It tries in the democratic sysem. They may succeed by their subversion in a democratic system and once they get the majority vote they won't get out. So in order to stop communism perhaps you have to sacrifice some democracy—but I suppose that's not a fair academic answer since, if it's really a democracy, then the communists must have a chance too.

Here is Inche' Ja'afar as the agonized democrat first wondering whether one might not have to forsake democratic freedoms to survive against communism and then realizing that without full freedoms democracy is already lost. The threats he sees in the desire of leaders to develop their nations at a gallop and in the efforts of communism to exploit the many strains and discontents of a transitional society are no shadows called up by a fertile imagination; they are the legitimate concerns of any democrat in Southeast Asia.

Kamalam is pessimistic too. He concentrates largely on communism but does not neglect the conditions that might widen its appeal: "Of course I'm purely basing this on what I've read, but I have the feeling that communism is spreading fast, especially in poverty-stricken areas. If a man is very, very poor and communism promises him a square meal, he will accept communism." Like Inche' Ja'afar, Kamalam recognizes that democracy in his country is a frail bloom unlikely to escape the plowshares of poverty, ambition, and communism. His pessimism over the future of democracy is hardly an indication of his own lack of democratic attitudes but rather a more or less judicious appraisal of the situation as it is.

Taking all five criteria of democratic beliefs together, what can then be said about these Malaysian administrators? On the first two criteria their democratic attitudes compare favorably with the Americans of Eastport in support of a universal franchise and in tolerance for the delays and confusion of democratic procedures. That this tolerance fades quickly in the hypothetical crisis presented as the third test reveals a formalistic quality to their democratic beliefs, but it may as much reflect the compelling reality of such crises in the Southeast Asian context.

Cynicism about democratic norms in organizations they know and pessimism about the future of democracy (the last two criteria) are hardly adequate tests of a man's "democraticness" in an environment where most groups are run along oligarchic or authoritarian lines and where the prospect for democracy is in fact bleak. Both of these questions are not asked in a vacuum; they ask for an evaluation of what exists rather than for subjective preferences. While the replies of these men clearly imply that they would prefer democratic organizations and a durable democratic nation, they are too clear-sighted and frank to mask what they observe. Their pessimism about democracy's future and their cynical appraisal of groups in Malaysia are not pathological distortions; they are rational efforts to evaluate things as they are—to approach reality rather than flee from it. Here again is a case where attitudes that would seem pathological in the stable Western context are seen to be rational or expected when the context is radically different. If a constant-pie orientation and a short-run time perspective have an existential base in transitional society, so do pessimism about the future of democracy and cynicism about how organizations are run.

On balance, then—and I must emphasize that I am dealing only with peripheral beliefs here—Malaysian civil servants are for the most part supportive of democratic norms. An interpretation of their statements that takes account of the existential base shows that they measure up fairly well to the limited criteria of "democraticness" used here. While the extent of their democratic attitudes might not compare so favorably with an equivalent—but more secure—U.S. elite group, they do not fall very short of American working class respondents in this regard. A more persuasive test of democrat beliefs, however, would be not only to inquire into their content but also to ask how consistent they are with other beliefs and how deeply they penetrate. Only in this fashion can one estimate how unambiguous these beliefs are and whether they hold up in situations where other important values are at stake.

THE FORMALISM OF DEMOCRATIC BELIEFS

As noted in the previous chapter, democratic beliefs in Malaysia receive scant support from the nature of primary or secondary socialization. Instead, they are tenuously sustained by the content of manifest political socialization as taught in school, through the mass media, and on the job, and by satisfaction with the outputs of a fragile democratic system. When democratic beliefs cannot rely upon any of the deeper sources of characterological support—when they confront enduring central orientations such as social distrust or a predisposition to seek only short-run personal gains

—their lack of substantial ballast is painfully evident. Having no anchor deep within the personality, democratic beliefs of this sort lead a very precarious life indeed.

"Formalism" is a term which, when applied to beliefs, indicates their lack of depth and weight. A person's beliefs are formalistic to the extent they do not penetrate and mold other beliefs or affect behavior. The Soviet Constitution of 1936, for example, was a formalistic instrument because it made provisions for freedoms that were never really granted; it never represented what was really going on—especially in 1936! Similarly, if a set of democratics beliefs represents what is really going on within an individual, they should be powerful enough to influence other beliefs as well as actual behavior. About behavior this study can have little to contribute, but it can ask how far democratic beliefs seem to penetrate the rest of the belief system.

Formalism in the Interviews

Estimating how formalistic a democratic belief is can be a very complicated business. But as a first approximation, it can be said that when a particular democratic belief is stated and then seems clearly to be controverted by more specific comments, that belief is presumably formalistic, since it fails to carry much weight with other beliefs.[15] Evidence of this nature for the formalism of democratic beliefs in the Malaysian sample is abundant in the transcripts. Three examples can illustrate this point.

Inche' Mohd. Amin provides a case where support for democratic norms evaporates quickly when adherence to them might threaten other, more important values. When I asked him what he would lose if his country were not democratically run, he delivered without pause an impressive catalogue of what he would be reduced to: "I would lose the right to elect a leader—the right to vote and choose a leader—the right to voice grievances in a peaceful way. If you lost all this you would have nothing left but to accept orders from the top—good or bad—there would be no means of redress." But shortly after, when we turned to a discussion of keeping Malaysia united in the face of communal tensions,

15. It should be clear that I am not speaking of hypocrisy in any sense. Hypocisy implies conscious deception, while the use of formalism here means only that certain beliefs are less important or influential than others with which they clash.

the values of democracy were suddenly shuffled into second place. "The leader has to use the power vested in him to keep the people under control. This way may not be democratic, but you have to do it." His last sentence is the crucial one. In some situations the leader will "have to" forsake democratic means to assure tranquillity and unity. There is the feeling that in a fissiparous nation like Malaysia, democratic methods are simply not adequate to the primary tasks of unity and control.

Inche' Hussain exhibited much the same pattern when we talked about the freedoms that a democracy protects. Asked what the word "freedom" made him think of, he replied, "Your mind is free—you can do what you like—your independence is not threatened. Freedom of speech—that is very important." Later in the same session, however, when he was pondering whether freedom of speech can "go too far," a new value appeared that seemed to suppress free speech. He answered, "Because if there is too much [freedom of speech] then there would be a tendency to abuse these freedoms and therefore it would be difficult to administer. There would be less respect for government—for the ruling government." As we continued our discussion, Inche' Hussain made it clear that it was the problem of mudslinging that concerned him. The loss of respect for the government that mudslinging entails is, for him, potentially dangerous enough to require some limitation on freedom of speech. In other words, popular respect for the ruling government takes precedence over freedom of expression when a choice must be made. It is not that he places no value on free speech. On the contrary, he believes in it, but not as strongly as he believes in certain other goals. Freedom of expression, having little weight, is shaken loose when it must contend both with Malaysian realities and with more strongly held beliefs.

The third illustration of the formalistic quality of democratic beliefs is Inche' Ismail, who is one of the strongest democrats in the group. His critical mind and literary ambitions seem to contribute to his appreciation of liberal democratic freedoms. For him, democracy means "Equal rights—to live—to pursue one's interests within the sanction of laws and cultural tradition. The freedom to voice opinion and being given the right to have your opinion considered; not just heard, but considered." Not only does he realize the distinction between being allowed to speak and having one's opinions considered, but he is full of scorn for those who structure freedoms to serve their own interests. Of such leaders he said, "A person who has certain powers in his hand—like Sukarno with 'Guided Democracy' and all that nonsense—wants freedom only at certain places and certain times." In this context it is surprising that Inche' Ismail would like to limit freedom, too. His criteria for distinguishing those who merit full freedoms from those whose freedom should be restricted are of course not so crass as he assumes Sukarno's to be, but they are nonetheless criteria for the distribution of freedom.

> If freedom is given to a man who is confident, well-studied, who has grasped the important things in life, then it's okay, but it's not if it's given to one who needs guidance and hasn't grasped the meaning of life in its fullness. If there is too much freedom in politics, every Tom, Dick, and Harry will start mixing in. This would be disastrous to the administrative side and all those sections that deal with the enforcement of law.

If these standards were really to be applied, there would be few left to enjoy full freedoms, although we may be sure that Inche' Ismail would fall within this select group. The freedoms in which he believes would lead to chaos if extended to "every Tom, Dick, and Harry," so they must be reserved for the thinking, mature elite that is capable of exercising them responsibly. Again, the commitment to democratic freedoms finds itself outranked by the need for order and harmony.

Time and time again in our conversations the sincerely held democratic beliefs of these men tended to crumble when besieged by beliefs that seemed more firmly rooted. A belief in democratic norms costs very little when no other cherished objectives are in the balance, and it is only when it is tested against such adversaries that its weight is actually known. If, for example, a man affirms his belief in free speech and later asserts that this or that seditious person should be put behind bars, or if he speaks of his commitment to freedom of assembly and then calls for a certain "subversive" group to be proscribed, it must be concluded that his belief in these freedoms is somewhat formalistic, since it fares badly in competition with other values. This kind of formalism characterizes a good portion of the democratic beliefs held by Malaysian administrators.

The illustrations used here, although not selected for this purpose, tell a great deal about the beliefs against which democratic convictions flounder. For Inche' Mohd. Amin, the need to "keep the people under control" is worth sacrificing some democracy; for Inche' Hussain, it is the preservation of "respect for the ruling government" and the prevention of mudslinging that take precedence over free speech; for Inche' Ismail, the anarchy generated by the ignorant necessitates withholding some freedoms from them. The common element in all these qualifications to freedom centers on harmony or control—a shared feeling that broad freedoms broadly distributed would in all likelihood lead to a level of disorder that would be difficult to administer. In short, the belief in freedom runs into the much stronger basic value orientation outlined in Chapter 4: the belief that men will destroy the social fabric unless a firm discipline imposed from above limits their scope for self-seeking. This central belief—precisely because it is central—is so firmly and deeply anchored that it easily emerges victorious when it clashes with a peripheral belief in liberal democratic freedoms. The democratic commitments of these civil servants operate in the substantial shadow of basic orientations with clear antidemocratic implications, and when they meet, the contest is unequal, for democratic convictions have few allies outside manifest political socialization, while central beliefs can rely on the support of primary socialization, traditional norms, and so forth.

Finally, it must be emphasized that all seventeen men have good reason to fear for the social and political fabric of their nation. Communal riots, racial allegiances, and armed threats from abroad are the realities that form the inescapable background against which their call for order and discipline must be viewed. Westerners are seldom faced with situations where liberal democracy may jeopardize stability, but for Malaysians, the dilemma is real. Their basic value orientations predispose them to expect breakdowns in public order; the Malaysian realities provide enough evidence to convince them they are not mistaken.

Democratic Beliefs and Formalism in
Questionnaire Results

In an effort to gain a firmer and more elaborate picture of the nature of democratic support among Malaysian civil servants, a questionnaire was administered to 116 bureaucrats outside the small sample. The items were selected, and occasionally adapted, from Herbert McClosky's article, "Consensus and Ideology in American Politics." [16] In his research, McClosky argues that we can codify the central canons of liberal democratic thought and present them in a question form to establish the degree of adherence to these norms in a population. To this end he has constructed questions that tap attitudes along the following dimensions:

1. Free Speech and Opinion.
2. Rules of the Game (mostly due process).
3. Specific Applications of Free Speech and Procedural Rights.
4. Political Equality.
5. Economic Equality.
6. Cynicism toward Government and Politics.
7. Political Futility.

Asking the same questions of a Malaysian elite that McClosky administered to a broad sample of Americans provides an opportunity to compare the extent and nature of democratic beliefs within each group.[17] The variety of questions employed also allows us to speak of democratic support in a more selective and discriminating way than has thus far been possible.

Free speech. The comparative results for "Freedom of Speech and Opinion" are presented in Table 5. A comparison of support for free speech and opinion among the groups shows that the Malaysians choose the democratic alternative as often or more often than the American groups in three items and less frequently on four items. Aside from their unwillingness to endorse the rights

16. *American Political Science Review* (June 1964), pp. 361–82. For a complete listing of the items which I have borrowed, see Appendix B.

17. Not all of McClosky's questions were used for the Malaysian sample, since some of them seemed too politically sensitive and others were so redundant as to lengthen the questionnaire unnecessarily. The results of all questions administered to Malaysians, however, are presented here.

of atheists and agnostics, they achieve roughly the level of "democraticness" as the American electorate and do not fall far short of the American "influentials." [18] If we take a minimum of 75 percent, as McClosky does, to indicate a "democratic consensus," the Malaysian administrators qualify, since their overall average of democratic responses is 76 percent.[19]

Rules of the game. Free speech and opinion are perhaps the best known doctrines of liberal democratic ideology, and they appear to have significantly penetrated the belief system of Malaysian administrators. On the other hand, a concern with due process —with the "Rules of the Game"—is as important as freedom of speech but is not nearly as prominent in the popular mind. When democratic beliefs tend to be formalistic, it may be due process that is cast aside before more celebrated freedoms such as free speech. Table 6 gives the comparisons for the items grouped under "Rules of the Game."

The results show, as was anticipated, that support in all three groups for the "Rules of the Game" drops off considerably from the level achieved on statements of free expression. What is notable, however, is that the drop-off is much more pronounced in the Malaysian sample than among either the American influentials or the electorate. The magnitude of difference between the Malaysian and American samples increases roughly threefold over the more modest figures for "Freedom of Speech and Opinion." The average gap between Malaysian administrators and U.S. influentials on items focusing on free speech was 12 percent, but for due process it increases to 35 percent; for the U.S. electorate, the gap widens from 6 to 19 percent. As striking as these margins are, they would rise to 40 and 24 percent, respectively, if we were to eliminate the responses to the first item dealing with

18. Influentials comprise delegates and alternates to the Democratic and Republican conventions of 1956. In view of the lower response rate from Southern subjects, there is some indication that the level of democratic support from influentials is somewhat overstated. If so, the gap between Malaysian civil servants and American influentials is in fact smaller than these results imply.

19. The 75 percent consensus level is an entirely arbitrary figure. Other levels might be chosen, depending upon what research variables are being considered. Since consensus usually means more than 50 percent argreement but less than 100 percent unanimity, I have adopted McClosky's 75 percent figure, which falls midway between the two.

TABLE 5: Free Speech and Opinion

Items	% Choosing Democratic Alternative			Percentage Points Difference† Separating Malaysians and:	
	U.S. Influentials	U.S. Electorate	Malaysian Civil Servants	U.S. Influentials	U.S. Electorate
1. People who hate our way of life should still have a chance to talk and be heard.	86.9	81.8	97	+10	+15
2. Nobody has the right to tell another person what he should and should not read.	81.4	80.7	66	−15	−15
3. Unless there is freedom for many points of view to be presented, there is little chance that the truth can ever be known.	90.6	85.2	91	no diff.	+ 6
4. No matter what a person's political beliefs are, he is entitled to the same legal rights and protections as anyone else.	96.4	94.3	91	− 5	− 3

5.* Freedom of conscience should mean the freedom to not believe in God [Allah] as well as the freedom to worship in the religion of one's choice.	87.8	77.0	37	−51	−40
6. I would not trust any person or group to decide what opinions can be freely expressed and what must be silenced.	79.1	64.6	53	−26	−12
7. You cannot really be sure whether an opinion is true or not unless people are free to argue against it.	94.9	90.8	97	+2	+6
Average	88.2	82.1	76		

Average Difference for All Items   −12   − 6

*The questions given here are those administered to the Malaysian sample. Occasionally, a change—usually inconsequential—was made from McClosky's items to make the question clearer to Malaysian respondents. Altered questions are marked with an asterisk, and the original formulation can be found in Appendix B. In Question 5 of this table, for example, "freedom to not believe in God" was adapted from "freedom to be an atheist."

† "+" if Malaysians more often choose democratic alternative. "−" if Malaysians less often choose democratic alternative.

TABLE 6: Rules of the Game

Items	% Choosing Democratic Alternative			Percentage Points Difference† Separating Malaysians and:	
	U.S. Influentials	U.S. Electorate	Malaysian Civil Servants	U.S. Influentials	U.S. Electorate
1. People ought to be allowed to vote even if they cannot do so intelligently.	65.6	47.6	78	+12	+30
2. I do not mind a politician's methods if he manages to get the right things done.	74.4	57.6	29	−45	−29
3. It's all right to get around the law if you do not actually break it.	78.8	69.8	21	−58	−49
4.* In dealing with subversives, sometimes you cannot always give them all the legal rights which peaceful citizens have, otherwise many will escape the law.	75.3	52.6	20	−55	−33

5.	We might as well make up our minds that in order to make the world better, a lot of innocent people will have to suffer.	72.8	58.4	59	−14	−1
6.*	Very few politicians have clean records, so one should not get excited about the mudslinging that sometimes takes place.	85.2	61.9	21	−64	−41
7.	There are times when it almost seems better for the people to take the law into their own hands rather than wait for the machinery of government to act.	86.7	73.1	58	−29	−15
8.	To bring about great changes for the benefit of mankind requires cruelty and even ruthlessness.	80.6	68.7	54	−27	−15
	Average	77.4	61.2	42.5	−35	−19

Average Difference for All Items

* Indicates alteration from McClosky's original, which can be found in Appendix B.

† "+" if Malaysians more often choose democratic alternative.
"−" if Malaysians less often choose democratic alternative.

commitment to the universal franchise on which, as noted earlier, Malaysians are in wide agreement for special historical reasons.

The comparative results for Tables 5 and 6 represent persuasive evidence for the formalism of democratic beliefs among the Malaysian elite. Democratic ideology has been absorbed in a highly selective fashion, with its more prominent doctrines of free expression penetrating with much greater success than the somewhat more recondite canons of due process. A certain amount of formalism can be observed in both American samples, too, but the degree in both these groups is so much smaller than for the Malaysians that it constitutes a difference in kind as well as degree.

If we again refer to McClosky's 75 percent consensus figure, the absolute levels of democratic responses among Malaysian bureaucrats have ominous implications. Only on the mass electorate issue do they achieve this figure, while for half of the eight items they do not even muster 30 percent support for certain "Rules of the Game." Particularly when the problem centers on the standards of behavior applied to elected officials or to bending the law, very few administrators rally to the defense of democratic norms. Bear in mind, for a moment, that the group being examined is presumably one of the most important carriers of liberal democratic ideology in the underdeveloped world. Surely, if the "Rules of the Game" find so little patronage among these educated, Westernized power holders, we can hardly be sanguine about the resources of democracy in a nation like Malaysia. The responses indicate that the emphasis on getting things done—on effectiveness—all but overwhelms concern for procedural niceties among Malaysians.

Political equality. Table 7 summarizes the comparative results of a series of statements that express skepticism about the civic qualifications of the electorate and imply elitism or authoritarianism as the way out. Here, too, the Malaysians are in each case less inclined to choose the democratic response than either the influentials or the electorate in America. The percentage points by which they fall short are, on the average, greater than for the free speech items but somewhat less than the wide gap on due process statements. Leadership and indoctrination appear to receive more

TABLE 7: Political Equality

Items	% Choosing Democratic Alternative			Percentage Points Difference† Separating Malaysians and:	
	U.S. Influentials	U.S. Electorate	Malaysian Civil Servants	U.S. Influentials	U.S. Electorate
1. The main trouble with democracy is that most people don't really know what's best for them.	59.2	42.0	22	−37	−20
2. It will always be necessary to have a few strong, capable people actually running everything.	51.5	43.8	39	−13	− 5
3. Political "issues" and arguments are beyond the understanding of most of the voters.	62.5	37.7	26	−36	−12
4. Few people really know what is in their own best interest in the long run.	57.4	38.9	32	−25	− 7
Average	56.1	40.6	29.8		
Average Difference for All Items				−27	−11

† "+" if Malaysians more often choose democratic alternative.
"−" if Malaysians less often choose democratic alternative.

emphasis, given their view of the electorate, than does political equality.

Even though the Malaysians are asked here to evaluate their national electorate, which in fact is less sophisticated and literate than most Western voting publics, the low frequency of democratic responses is quite striking. They choose the democratic alternative less than one third of the time on all but one of the four items, and the overall average is less than 30 percent. In the light of these results, their marked support for a universal franchise must be based on sheer attachment to the principle rather than on any faith in their people's capacity for civic duties. More than two thirds of these civil servants appear to have little faith in the wisdom of the electorate to make the choices entrusted to it by popular government. It is some comfort to realize that their pessimism probably has a basis in reality, since it indicates that they have no illusions about the handicaps that a largely illiterate electorate imposes on a democracy. Nonetheless, this does not alter the fact that the Malaysians are more willing to entrust the political system to "a few strong, capable people" than either American group.

Some of the skepticism found here may be related to evaluations of human nature. Items 1 and 4 imply that democracy is crippled by people's penchant to pursue their own short-run interests at the expense of the community, and this is exactly the dominant view of human nature among the seventeen administrators. This orientation may predispose others as well to hold a low opinion of the possibilities for a civic culture in their nation.

Economic equality. While democratic norms show little penetrative power, the socialist norm of economic equality has fared much better (Table 8). On the three items dealing with the responsibility of the state to provide a decent job, a decent house, and an adequate income to its people, the Malaysian respondents are considerably more egalitarian in economic terms than either U.S. influentials or the U.S. electorate. The magnitude of the difference is especially striking in light of Malaysian responses to the items treating political equality, where they fell far below U.S. levels of support. The desire for economic equality seems to find Malaysian soil more hospitable than the desire for political equality.

TABLE 8: Economic Equality

Items	% Choosing Egalitarian Alternative			Percentage Points Difference† Separating Malaysians and:	
	U.S. Influentials	U.S. Electorate	Malaysian Civil Servants	U.S. Influentials	U.S. Electorate
1. The government ought to make sure that everyone has a good standard of living.	34.4	55.9	92	+58	+36
2. I think the government should give a person work if he cannot find another job.	23.5	47.3	66	+42	+19
3. Every person should have a good house, even if the government has to build it for him.	14.9	28.2	58	+43	+30
4.* There will always be poverty, so people might as well get used to the fact.	59.6	40.6	31	−28	−10
Average Difference for All Items				+29	+19

*Indicates alteration from McClosky's original, which can be found in Appendix B.

† "+" if Malaysians more often choose egalitarian alternative. "−" if Malaysians less often choose egalitarian alternative.

The pattern of responses on item 4 is perhaps more revealing than the overall levels of support for economic equality. Here, when Malaysians are asked if "people should get used to the idea that there will always be poverty," they agree substantially more often than either American group. More than two thirds of the Malaysian civil servants are prepared to project an economy of scarcity into the future. It is likely that their assumption of scarcity may incline them to prefer a government that will at least establish a floor beyond which citizens cannot plunge. In any event, since the constant-pie orientation involves the perception of perpetual scarcity, the Malaysian pattern of responses here provides additional evidence for the existence of a zero-sum outlook.

Specific applications of free speech and procedural rights. Table 9 displays the summary findings for a number of statements in which support for free speech and due process are tested against other values. Respondents are asked if they favor the free expression of people who "don't know what they are talking about," whether due process should extend even to "dangerous enemies of the nation," and so on. The construction of these statements allows us to see how universal principles fare when they are taken from a largely rhetorical context and placed in a setting that demands the sacrifice of other valued goals. It is one thing for a man to be an "other things being equal" democrat, but since in the real world democracy does imply that other goals are postponed or foregone, these items are a more realistic test of democratic beliefs.

As on the "Rules of the Game" items, Malaysians fall far below both American groups in their support for free expression and procedural rights. The average frequency with which they elect democratic alternatives is 18 percentage points below that of the American electorate and a full 35 points behind the level of American influentials. Averaging the frequencies of democratic choices over all six questions, Malaysian administrators fall well below the 50 percent level (42 percent).

While the level of democratic support among Malaysians is extremely low here, it would have been even lower if I had eliminated item 1, which has a very different meaning in the Malaysian context. After all, the school system in Malaysia was founded precisely to teach foreign ideas like science, geography, law, and medicine, and this is undoubtedly the reason why the Malaysian replies are comparatively more democratic on this item.[20] To object to foreign ideas in schools in Southeast Asia is tantamount to objecting to the educational system itself.[21] As low as they are, then, the Malaysian figures may have been overstated.[22]

The figures from Table 9 also offer persuasive evidence for formalism of democratic beliefs in free speech and opinion. Items 1, 2, and 6 deal with specific applications of this freedom, and the average frequency of democratic choices is only 48 percent, while for the more rhetorical statements of Table 5, the figure was 76 percent. Fully 28 percent of those who muster tropological support for free speech seem willing to abandon their belief when they are asked to make sacrifices to defend it. Many of democracy's defenders desert when the assault on their position begins.[23]

If the belief in free speech were not formalistic, one would expect some carry-over from rhetoric to application. Those who support the principle of free expression should, if this belief has weight and depth in their ideology, be more supportive of the same principle in difficult circumstances than those who do not seem committed to the principle in the first place. In a rough way, formalism can be tested by comparing the performance of individuals for the items of Table 5 ("Freedom of Speech and

20. Calculating the comparative figures, excluding item 1, leaves the Malaysians 23 percentage points behind the U.S. electorate and 41 points below the U.S. influentials figure.

21. Some of those who elect to disapprove of "foreign ideas" in schools may have in mind the recurring problem of communist influence in Chinese "middle" schools. This is the most obvious reason why some respondents would agree that "foreign" influence in the schools is to be condemned.

22. The Malaysian figures of item 2 may be similarly affected, since an enormously high respect for books per se developed under the colonial regime, where they so often were the symbol of British rule, whether in the form of General Orders or the Bible.

23. Items 3, 4, and 5 concern specific applications of the "Rules of the Game," and the average frequency of democratic responses for these items is 36 percent. This is only 6 percent below the average figure for the due process statements in Table 6. The relatively small difference is due simply to the absence of even much formalistic support for due process, so that the drop-off from rhetoric to application is, of course, small.

TABLE 9: Specific Applications of Free Speech and Procedural Rights

Items	% Choosing Democratic Alternative			Percentage Points Difference† Separating Malaysians and:	
	U.S. Influentials	U.S. Electorate	Malaysian Civil Servants	U.S. Influentials	U.S. Electorate
1. Freedom does not give anyone the right to teach foreign ideas in our schools.	54.5	43.3	48	− 6	+ 5
2. A book that contains wrong political views cannot be a good book and does not deserve to be published.	82.1	49.7	59	−23	+ 9
3.* If a person is convicted of a crime by use of evidence which is not legal, he should be set free and the evidence thrown out of court.	79.6	66.1	63	−17	− 3
4.* In dealing with dangerous enemies of the nation, we can't afford to depend on the courts, laws, and their slow unreliable methods.	92.6	74.5	32	−61	−42

5. When the country is in great danger, we may have to force people to do certain things against their will, even though it violates their rights.	71.5	63.7	14	−57	−50
6. A man ought not to be allowed to speak if he doesn't know what he is talking about.	82.7	63.3	36	−47	−27
Average	77.2	60.1	42.0		
Average without item 1	81.7	63.7	40.8		

	Average Difference for All Items	
	−35	−18
Without item 1	−41	−23

† "+" if Malaysians more often choose democratic alternative.
"−" if Malaysians less often choose democratic alternative.

* Indicates alteration from McClosky's original, which can be found in Appendix B.

Opinion") with their performance on the statements in Table 9 ("Applications of Free Speech and Procedural Rights").[24]

It is obvious from Table 10 that there is no relationship between scores on the first set of items and those on the second.

TABLE 10: Correlation of Scores for Freedom of Speech
and Opinion with Scores for Specific Applications
of Free Speech and Procedural Rights
(Number of respondents is given in parentheses)

		Specific Applications of Free Speech and Procedural Rights	
		Low Scorers	High Scorers
Freedom of Speech and Opinion:	Low Scorers	48.7% *(19)*	51.3% *(20)*
	High Scorers	52.6% *(20)*	47.4% *(18)*

Those who score high on general support for free expression are no more likely to score high on the specific applications than those who score low. There is no evidence whatever that abstract affirmation of free speech means anything in terms of defending these freedoms in difficult circumstances. This is the most persuasive indication thus far that democratic beliefs among Malaysian bureaucrats are formalistic and tend to crumble under pressure.[25]

The formalism of democratic beliefs apparent in my conversations with Malaysian government servants has been independently confirmed and further clarified by the results of the questionnaire administered to other bureaucrats outside this small sample. Not only do even the most celebrated principles of liberal democracy find less support among Malaysian administrators than among the U.S. electorate (not to mention U.S. influentials), but the gap increases dramatically when we move to democratic norms that are equally central although much less prominent in the public mind. Among the American groups, too, there is less sup-

24. The test is not ideal, since Table 9 contains three items dealing with procedural rights rather than free speech. Nevertheless, if there were substantial carryover the relationship should appear in spite of the dilution effects of the three procedural statements.

25. The lack of any correlation for Table 10 does not mean that Malaysians here are never consistent between abstract principles and specific applications. It does mean, however, that as many are inconsistent as are consistent.

port for due process than for free speech, especially among the electorate. The magnitude of the decrease, however, is much more striking among the Malaysians. That democratic notions are largely formalistic is further substantiated by the fact that those who affirm democratic norms in the abstract abandon those beliefs in specific applications just as often as those who lack even an abstract commitment. No bonds unite rhetoric with specific situations. Finally, when it comes to evaluating the capacity of the masses to shoulder their democratic responsibilities, the realities of their nation and their assumptions about human nature appear to lead over two thirds of the Malaysians to discount the ability of the populace to choose wisely.

Manifest civic learning in the classroom or via the mass media is likely to be, by itself, highly formalistic, whether it occurs in the industrialized West or in transitional settings. In stable Western democracies, however, this manifest socialization to democracy can draw on the capital of small group experience, family training, tradition, and even the desire to conform to popular norms. Set in this context, manifest training is merely the visible greenery of a plant which has sent deep taproots into the cultural soil. When, however, as in Malaysia, belief in liberal democratic norms lacks this deep root system, it must instead depend on the tenuous effectiveness of democratic government and manifest political training. Without more substantial resources, democratic beliefs remain peripheral; they do not run deep or strong. Their formalism can be seen in sharp relief whenever they come into conflict with central beliefs or value orientations which are more firmly embedded in both tradition and experience and which imply quite different standards of justice, authority, and freedom.

9

Cynicism: The Tyranny of the Western Model

All the men with whom I spoke had attended schools and universities patterned after the British model, where they followed curricula identical to those in England and learned Anglo-Saxon practices and values. Later they were recruited by Englishmen to serve in a British style administrative system. The standards and goals of this structure were, and still are in large measure, cast in an unmistakably English mold. Both in school and in the civil service their success was gauged by how well they had learned the lessons that England had sought to convey. Small wonder then that all of them came by their Western (British) orientation honestly.[1] They are all the more Western oriented since their English education and high administrative posts are what set them apart from the general population and confer on them their status and prestige. The maintenance of a Western orientation among higher civil servants is further encouraged by a political elite that is itself largely pro-British and committed to liberal democratic ideals. They do not experience the pressure for change that besets bureaucrats in nations which, like Indonesia, have experienced an intense revolutionary nationalism and have abandoned liberal democracy for more syncretic ideologies.

Out of this acculturation to the West has come the feeling that what is Western is superior to what is Asian (Malay, Indian, Chinese).[2] When they speak of the West, a vague tone of deference enters their voices; it is not the deference accorded to the sacred but rather a stance appropriate in the presence of someone of high position or achievement. The importance of Western standards is

1. I am speaking, of course, of a *peripheral* orientation.

2. Research among students in East Africa has provided strong evidence for the proposition that "The more acculturated identify themselves more closely with the representatives of the new culture than do the less acculturated and are more ready to view them as superior or dominant." Leonard H. and Mary B. Ainsworth, "Acculturation in East Africa," *The Journal of Social Psychology*, 57 (1962), 931–35.

especially evident when they speak of the Asians whom they most admire. With few exceptions, the men they cite are the highly Westernized Asians whom the West itself has honored. Sundram, for example, heard Nehru speak in Malaysia and especially admired him "because Nehru could use the English language better than most native Englishmen could use it." Nehru earned Sundram's plaudits for excelling by British standards—for beating the English at their own game, their language. Other civil servants have different heroes, but like Sundram, when they take the measure of a political figure, they judge by the same standards they feel an Englishman would use.

Nowhere is the Western orientation of these seventeen men more apparent than when they talk about their hopes for Malaysia's future. Modernization is irrevocably linked to Westernization in their minds, and indeed they do not distinguish between these two distinct processes. With no detectable psychic hardship, they feel modernization will make their nation more like the West; the civic culture of a stable democracy is perceived to be every bit as modern as the steel mills or armies of technicians and engineers that characterize industrial states.

THE IDEALIZATION OF THE WESTERN POLITICAL MODEL

Malaysian administrators are committed, at the peripheral level, to the Western political model by their training and occupation. But the model they carry around in their minds reflects the conditions under which it was learned. It is an idealized model, both sketchy and incomplete, much like the model of the U.S. political system as it is conveyed to high school youths in America. The philosophical rationale for the system is there, so are the formal provisions for its operation—the great documents—and so, too, are the celebrated sagas of its finest moments. What is lacking is the corrective of experience, which could fill the gaps and put flesh (blemishes, scars, and all) on the statuesque conception of English democracy that they have absorbed.[3] Their abstract and highly idealized understanding of how Western parliamentary de-

3. Of course, they are aware of the "bad" policies Britain has followed from time to time, but this awareness is not the same as an understanding of how British politics actually works.

mocracy actually operates is, to a social scientist's eyes, a Weberian ideal type that no reality has ever approximated.

As admirable as high standards are, they are likely to make real institutions look somewhat shoddy. Having civics textbook notions, particularly about how the British political system works, the Malaysians cannot easily avoid becoming cynics when they look at their own polity. There is thus no place in their scheme of democracy for the organization of communal groups along racial lines that has taken place in Malaysia. It is taken as a great failure of Malaysian democracy that such groups should have arisen, and most of these men feel that venal politicians are to blame. What they fail to recognize, since it clashes with their conception of the principled politics of democracy, is that most politicians in a democracy will appeal to whatever issues and identifications are most salient for their constituents.[4] They are driven to disappointment and cynicism because they had hoped the political elite would encourage broad civic views among the masses rather than the ethnic loyalties, pressure politics, and patronage that they see developing.[5] Such phenomena are not so discordant with the democratic beliefs of Englishmen or Americans, but there is no room for them in Western democracy as Malaysian civil servants conceive it. Political conflict, in their view, should take place exclusively on classical issues such as workers' rights, the defense of freedom, or socialism, as they imagine it does in the West. When they see the traditionally oriented masses organizing with other goals in mind, they fear it signals the death knell of democracy rather than the beginning of the integration of these groups into a democratic framework.

The idealistic conception of Western democracy held by these civil servants is but a part of a broader pattern of selective acculturation to the West. What is learned from any new and dominant culture generally follows a distinguishable sequence. Limited new

4. Myron Weiner says much the same of Indian senior officials in his *Politics of Scarcity*, pp. 67–68.

5. These men have ethnic political loyalties, too, but they are always cast in terms of wider issues, such as economic equality, political rights, and so on. I was aware and sensitive to the possibility that my presence as interviewer might contribute to the deferential manner in which Western political systems were regarded by members of the sample. With the exception of one civil servant, however, this factor did not seem to play a crucial role in these attitudes, as nearly as I could tell from the style and tone of their remarks.

institutional and behavioral forms are likely to be transferred well before the central values that such forms represent.[6] Legal forms, for example, are adopted more easily and quickly than a more general belief in an institutional framework to protect citizens against the arbitrary acts of leaders.[7] For some time, then, constitutions are likely to acquire the properties of an amulet or charm which protects the wearer against bad government, with little appreciation of the social values or structural restraints that make these guarantees effective. Legalism and constitutionalism are valued per se as forms, quite apart from their content.

Much the same pattern can be observed in the prevailing conception of Western technology and science as well. One economist, for example, has commented that non-Western elites often attribute quasi-sacral or magical qualities to Western scientific techniques and expect them to provide solutions for even the most intractable problems.[8] Five-year plans in the non-West are often a case in point, as is the fascination with T.V.A.–like structures that promise holistic solutions to problems that must frequently be attacked in a more selective fashion. Technical recommendations are adopted in toto, and the problem is henceforth considered solved.[9]

The pattern has perhaps been overstated here, but the purpose is merely to show that Western technology and legal forms are subject to precisely the same selective, idealistic distortion as are Western political forms. They are understood formally but not contextually, and thus their formal adoption is expected to confer the same beneficial results which, it is imagined, followed their adoption in the West. When they fail to flourish or work the miracles expected of them, the blame is laid to their new soil as often as to a failure to understand the innovations themselves. Surely the soil is not all it could be, but the potential of the new forms has been grossly overvalued from the start.

6. Doob, *Becoming More Civilized*, p. 166.

7. Most of the seventeen civil servants express a preference for a "government of men rather than a government of laws," since men are "more" flexible" and "more humane" than rigid legal principles, which often fail to place equity in a broader context. Yet they all seem devoted to "legalism" when it is considered by itself.

8. Hirschman, *The Strategy of Economic Development*, Chs. 1–3.

9. For a detailed description of how this has occurred in Burma, see Louis J. Walinsky's *Economic Development in Burma: 1951–60* (New York, 20th Century Fund, 1962).

When a newly acquired piece of machinery fails to live up to expectations, there are at least two options available to the person who acquired it. He can conclude that the machine was no good in the first place—that he made a mistake in ordering it—or that the operators are not competent to make it work. When these administrators look at the operation of democracy in Malaysia, they feel it is not really working and are faced with a similar choice. Either democracy is not quite the magnificent institution they had thought, or else Malaysians are just incapable of making it work.[10] If the first alternative is preferred, it is likely to set off a search for some new political system, either borrowed or syncretic—as in Burma—to replace what has been rejected. Perhaps because they are more firmly committed to Western forms, Malaysian civil servants elect the latter course; they find the problem in the operators, and not in the machinery. The attractiveness of democracy is undiminished for them, and they conclude that its marred success is due to the shortcomings of the Malaysians themselves.

CYNICISM IN THE INTERVIEWS

When I asked those interviewed how Malaysians measure up to democratic ideals, most of them seemed acutely conscious of how poorly their country compares to what they surmise are Western political standards. For some, this is a fact they accept with only mild disappointment, but for many others it evokes a strong cynicism. After he had described the qualities of an ideal member of parliament, Mr. Tay shook his head vigorously when asked how close Malaysian M.P.'s come to this ideal. "Not like England," he said, "they just toe the party line, the majority of them." Of course, most British M.P.'s toe the line as well, but this is just the point. Mr. Tay supposes that the British M.P. represents the interests of his constituents at all times and goes against party policy whenever his conscience commands. The average Malaysian M.P. appears by contrast to be a spineless follower only because Mr. Tay imagines that politics in England are conducted by men who act on behalf of principles regardless of the cost.

Inche' Abu Bakar was somewhat more realistic about how elected officials should ideally behave, but his evaluation of Malaysian politicians was no less unfavorable. He thought an M.P.

10. Some combination of each is, of course, equally possible.

should "try to reconciliate [sic] between what his electorate requires and the party interests." Malaysia only reaches the "fifty-
fifty" level by this criterion, since "Here they are interested more in
staying in power than in a reconciliation between the two." I do
not think it is reading too much into his statement to suggest
that when he said "here," he was implying that elsewhere M.P.'s
may think more of principles and less of staying in power. Undoubtedly, "elsewhere" means the West.

Others were more explicit than Inche' Abu Bakar. For example,
Mr. Khoo estimated whether Malaysian citizens approach the ideal
by comparing them with what he assumes to be the Western standard. Defining the good citizen as a patriot, he said,

> Among the newer nations they don't come up to the 50 per-
> cent level. They think of themselves first. In England and
> America they think more of the country—it takes the older
> nation to get the right person. [How about politicians?] Most
> of them never reach the 50 percent line. You wonder why
> they should run for a post at all—they are hypocrites.

Much of what Mr. Khoo says has some basis in fact, but he may
well overestimate the gap between his nation and America or
England because of the selective nature of his information about
the West. He also proposes a theory that the age of a nation is what
produces "citizen-patriots." Having a notion like this saves him
from too much cynicism, since he has traced a route by which
Malaysia can eventually achieve what he considers Western standards of citizenship.

Like Mr. Khoo, Inche' Mustapha has a theory to explain why
Malaysians do not meet Western political norms, but his theory
is more elaborate. His ideal citizen is one who fights for principle
and accedes gracefully when he finds himself in the minority.
Asked how Malaysians measure up to this ideal, he replied,

> I think this sort of ideals [sic] are quite prevalent in developed
> countries—but in countries such as ours it will take time.
> There may be one or two such people now—it will take time
> since democracy is new in this part of the world. [later] Not
> many [principled party members] in our country yet—because
> they don't have that real foundation of being independent.

> Once you have that spiritual and financial independence, then you can have principles

Here the cynicism has all but disappeared, since Inche' Mustapha feels he understands why Malaysians are inept at democracy now and how they might improve over time. His cognitive grasp of the situation wards off cynicism, but unfortunately, his perspective is comparatively rare in the sample.

Lacking Inche' Mustapha's perspective or optimism, most of the others are disheartened and/or cynical about the outlook for democracy in Malaysia. Mahalingam made it clear that his countrymen are at fault rather than the democratic system:

> In this country, you know, we don't consider this country a democracy in the true sense. If the Tengku [the Prime Minister] puts up anyone, he will be elected. It would be very rare for him not to be elected. Where people are not ripe for it, there is no such thing as a democratic country. I always say we have ourselves to blame—Britain did a brilliant job—that's where maturity counts.

Mahalingam's program to reform Malaysia is much more radical than any of the others would be willing to countenance. From his secure armchair he calls for the destruction of the traditions and religious superstitions that burden his nation—but this is only the posturing of a fertile imagination. Kamalam, less given to fantasy, seems to regard the situation as irremediable and fears Malaysia will never approach Western standards.

> [Ideal citizen?] The first thing is to—don't break any laws of the country. This is the question of a law-abiding citizen first, and if you can do any good, for heavens sake do it—and don't do any wrong. That state will never come about, but I would love to see it happen. [How close do Malaysians come?] I doubt whether we'll ever reach that stage—but I believe Switzerland is quite a peaceful state.

Finally, when these men measure Malaysia against the West, there is often the feeling that the West is watching. They are quick to admit the shortcomings for which they suspect the West ridicules them. Inche' Zukifli is acutely embarrassed for his nation when

Malay M.P.'s shout "Go to hell!" to a prominent Chinese opposition figure. "What's the use—the whole world can see us and what we do in our Parliament. It's better just to walk off." The Western orientation is so strong that there is a tendency to view their own country's politics as they suppose the West views it.[11] Such goings on could not possibly occur in the London of graciousness and fair play about which they have learned, and it is taken as a mark of Malaysia's backwardness that they should have occurred in Kuala Lumpur.

For most, then, there is little or no expectation of substantial improvement, and they are driven to a certain cynicism about the operation of democracy in their nation. Their cynicism is certainly based to some extent on an appreciation of real differences; for example, Malaysians are less inclined to accept political defeat with equanimity than Englishmen. In spite of these real differences, however, the ways in which they have learned about the West have so distorted and idealized Western practices that the gap they perceive is all out of proportion to the real differences. Consequently, their cynicism is also greater than what the actual differences would merit and must therefore be traced to the perceptual distortion engendered by colonialism.

Cynicism in Questionnaire Results

A rough estimate can be made of the level of political cynicism among Malaysian civil servants by comparing their responses to those of Americans on a series of questions designed to tap this attitude. Table 11 summarizes the results. On all six items Malaysian administrators chose the more cynical reply more frequently than either American group, and on the average their "cynical response rate" is well above the 50 percent level. This high level of cynicism is all the more significant since they are an elite who, under other circumstances, would be expected to constitute one of the most allegiant groups in society. Instead, they seem to have little faith in those who have been chosen to represent the people and almost no expectation of a wider distribution

11. By far the most impressive discussion of the psychological effects of colonialism which lie behind this attitude is O. Mannoni, *Prospero and Caliban*. As interviewer, I made a great effort not to stimulate these comments, but they were frequent, anyway.

TABLE 11: Cynicism Toward Government and Politics

Items	% Choosing Non-Cynical Alternative			Percentage Points Difference† Separating Malaysians and:	
	U.S. Influentials	U.S. Electorate	Malaysian Civil Servants	U.S. Influentials	U.S. Electorate
1. There is practically no connection between what a politician says and what he will do once he gets elected.	78.6	46.0	44	+35	+ 2
2. I usually have confidence that the government will do what is right.	81.6	89.6	78	+ 4	+12
3. To me, most politicians don't seem to really mean what they say.	75.3	44.9	31	+44	+14
4. Most politicians are looking out for themselves above all else.	63.7	45.7	34	+30	+12
5. No matter what people think, a few people will always run things anyway.	70.0	46.2	17	+53	+12
6. Most politicians can be trusted to do what they think is best for the country.	77.1	58.9	51	+26	+29
Average	74.4	55.2	42.5	+26	+ 8
				Average Difference for All Items	
				+32	+13

†"+" if Malaysians more often choose cynical alternative. "–" if Malaysians less often choose cynical alternative.

of political power (item 5). Their pattern of responses thus supports the conclusion that they trace the weakness of Malaysia's political system to the quality of its managers rather than to flaws in the machinery itself.

The belief that the politicians are not capable of making democracy work in Malaysia is closely connected with the conviction that the people as a whole are unsuited to the burdens democracy places on their shoulders. This connection is strikingly borne out by the correlation between scores on "Political Equality" items (items which, for the most part, focus on the capacity of the people to understand issues and choose wisely) and scores on "Political Cynicism" (see Table 12).

TABLE 12: Correlation of Scores for "Political Equality" with
Scores for Cynicism Toward Government and Politics
(Number of respondents is given in parentheses)

		Political Cynicism	
		High in Cynicism	Low in Cynicism
	Low Support for Political Equality	76.3% (29)	23.7% (9)
Political Equality			
	High Support for Political Equality	20.9% (9)	79.1% (34)

Chi^2 = 47.52 with ldf $p < .001$

The link between these two variables is quite a strong one. Cynicism about politicians and government is associated closely with cynicism about the capacity of the people for democratic self-rule. I am not arguing that there is a causal sequence between the two but simply that both are part of a broader pessimism concerning the operation of democracy in Malaysia. The commitment to democratic forms endures, but the hope that Malaysians can now, or even in the future, make a success of the system is largely absent.

A certain pessimism about how well democracy works in new nations is probably common to most Westernized postcolonial elites. This pessimism has at least three distinguishable sources.

First, the prevailing assumptions about human nature and the environment do not lead these men to expect the civic, tolerant, compromising citizens who contribute to a democratic polity. Second, their pessimism is also based on experiential factors. The widespread illiteracy, primordial ties, and social distrust that characterize most new nations have in fact impeded the growth of a civic culture, and all of the men are painfully aware of these handicaps. Finally, the overidealization of the Western democratic model, particularly among Westernized elites, has vastly intensified the painfulness of these shortcomings and thus contributed to the widespread growth of cynicism about the democratic potential of both leaders and masses.

The cumulative product of all three factors is a kind of political alienation. Alienation has generally referred to the feeling that the government is run unfairly for others and by others. A person is alienated from the polity when he says, "I am the object of political life . . . 'they' do not care about me . . . the rules of the game are unfair, loaded, illegitimate." [12] But the alienation in Malaysia is of a different variety. It is based partly on utopian expectations about the operation of liberal democracy, which are in turn created by the process of selective learning inherent in the colonial situation. This is the tyranny of the idealized Western model, which regards much of the ordinary cut and thrust of politics as illegitimate and unworthy, which admits only politicians who carry their consciences on their sleeves, and which expects the masses to organize around the banners of great principles. The pursuit of such a visionary chimera as this is bound to produce cynicism when it runs against democratic politics in the real world.

On the one hand, these government servants are committed to a set of democratic norms, however distorted, and on the other hand, they believe that the people and politicians of Malaysia are incapable of making the system work as they think it should. Supporting a form of government that one feels is not functioning well seems an unstable situation in the long run, since it creates cognitive dissonance. Such dissonance is almost certainly the central dilemma of most democrats in new nations.

This dilemma could be resolved in a number of ways: democ-

12. Lane, *Political Ideology*, p. 162.

racy could be redefined so that it coincides with what is actually happening in Malaysia, or what is actually happening could be distorted so that it approximates their conception of democracy. It will become clear in the following chapter that the solution of Malaysian administrators combines some of both alternatives.

10

Sources of Support
for an Administrative State

Analyzing the administrative life of the seventeen civil servants requires narrowing the focus somewhat from the broader phenomena considered earlier. Unlike basic value orientations, which form part of a broad cultural pattern, or even educational patterns, which are at least shared by the entire Westernized elite, the occupational experience of these men is characteristic of only one sector of the Westernized elite. A narrower focus removes some of the capacity to generalize findings to groups outside the administrative cadre, but in spite of this stricture, the civil service experience does have limited applicability to Westernized politicians in Malaysia. Many now prominent politicians began their careers as civil servants and left only on the eve of independence. In 1963, for example, 50 percent of the Alliance Party's Cabinet were onetime members of the administrative corps.[1] This situation is also typical of much of the elite in nations such as India which have acceded to independence without revolutionary upheavals. The bureaucratic experiences to be described are thus part of the heritage of the political elite as well as the bureaucratic elite in a good many new nations.

If the nature of colonial education contributed to a certain distortion of the Western political model, the nature of colonial administration introduced peculiar distortions of its own. It gave rise to a preference for paternalistic, administrative rule, which was then reinforced both by the actual gap between the Westernized elite and the masses and by the virtual bureaucratic monopoly of knowledge and skills.

1. Robert O. Tilman, "Policy Formulation, Policy Execution, and the Political Elite Structure of Contemporary Malaysia," in Wang Gung wu, ed., *Malaysia: A Survey* (New York, Praeger, 1964), p. 350.

THE IMPACT OF COLONIAL ADMINISTRATION

The Colony as an Administrative State

To speak of the administrative experience of these men is to speak of the colonial administration, for with few exceptions, they were trained by and served under the colonial regime. Like the more celebrated Indian Civil Service, the Malayan Civil Service (MCS) was the elite corps of administrators that ruled its portion of the vast Empire encumbered only by occasional intervention from the Colonial Office. Much like the Jesuits in Paraguay, the MCS saw itself as a philosopher-king entrusted with the instruction and elevation of the colonial peoples. Initially, the MCS was inspired by the dynamic and revolutionary creed of imperialism, but later the creed perished under the blows of World War I, colonial scandals, and, most important, the loss of faith in Britain's natural right to rule. With some notable exceptions, from 1900 on, racial barriers grew apace, and the motives of financial reward and social mobility largely replaced the missionary fervor of the Victorian era.[2] By the time the first of the sample joined the colonial administrative elite in 1926, it was already an entrenched conservative ruling class, more concerned with protecting its status and privileges than with transforming the colony. Emphasis on law and order and the prerequisites of power rather than on development or sense of mission thus dominated the atmosphere of twentieth century colonialism into which these men were incorporated.

Two other aspects of colonial administration are important in assessing its influence on political ideology. First, the bureaucracy itself embodied not only the executive functions of the state but many of the legislative and judicial functions as well. The bureaucratization of the regime tended to routinize political decisions—to divert what would have otherwise been political clashes into questions of legal authority and the interpretation of regulations. This is not to say that politics was eliminated, for there were im-

2. Allen, "The MCS: Fact and Fiction." Allen perceptively traces the growth of "the new class"—the *apparatchiki*—who gradually replace revolutionary imperialism with bureaucratic colonialism.

portant decisions to be made. But since the colonial regime rested ultimately on force and not popularity, appeals to popular passions were unnecessary, and politics became an integral part of bureaucratic infighting. The point is simply that politics was confined almost exclusively to the administrative apparatus of an essentially authoritarian state. In this context, the question of what the people wanted was superseded by the question of what was best for them as determined by their rulers.

The absence of normal political life in the colony was, of course, justified by the belief that an enlightened administration could rule more in the people's ultimate interests than could a fully indigenous regime. The agent par excellence of this enlightened rule was the all-powerful district officer. Aubrey Menen was not entirely facetious when, in his novel *The Prevalence of Witches,* he had Catallus remark after being posted as a district officer in North India, "I came up to Limbo because I had always wanted to possess a country of my own." [3]

The district officer was indeed a virtual sovereign in the often substantial territory under his jurisdiction, and to the colonized population at least, he was the very symbol of British rule. He was responsible for collecting taxes, settling disputes, providing land titles, promoting the welfare of his district, and, most important, preserving law and order. The high status and great satisfactions afforded this representative of the Empire were such that many who advanced later to high posts in the capital city recalled their work in the districts with great nostalgia as the most gratifying of their careers. It was scarcely surprising that the English youth fresh from public school, whose conscious function was to train the ruling class, should be awed by the experience of actually ruling over a district of perhaps a hundred thousand souls on his first assignment. District work was preferred often to staff work largely because it offered the satisfactions of personal rule. The directness of district life—riding into a kampong to receive reports from the elders, try criminal cases, and settle civil disputes on the

3. Quoted in Ralph Braibanti, "Public Bureaucracy and Judiciary in Pakistan," in Joseph LaPalombara, ed., *Bureaucracy and Political Development* (Princeton, Princeton University Press, 1963), p. 395. For a detailed description of the district officer in India, see Philip Woodruff, *The Men Who Ruled India:* Vol. 2, *The Guardians* (New York, Schocken Books, 1964).

spot—provided the deference and feel of power which policy-making in the capital could never match.[4]

If serving as district officer was an awesome experience for the Englishman, it made just as indelible an impression on Malaysians who saw the D. O. on his rounds. Inche' Ja'afar, asked about his childhood ambitions, recalled above all the D. O.:

> My impression in those days—the most important man in the world was the district officer. He was the personification of law and order—of right and wrong—an upright man. It was only later that I discovered there were others. And my ambition in childhood was always to become a D. O. and go to England.

Inche' Ja'afar's experience was fairly typical among the sample. Most of the others first knew colonial rule through the personage of the district officer, and to become a D. O. was a common ambition among them. It was particularly the kingly or praetorian ethos of district rule that made such lasting impressions and captured their imaginations. For many of them, the ambition was eventually fulfilled. What is more, the office did not tarnish in the process, for with few exceptions, they still look on district work as more satisfying than other posts in the administration.

In summary, then, the following aspects of colonial administration, as they were experienced by these men, seem to be most relevant for the political beliefs to be discussed shortly:

1. Initiation into a ruling elite concerned with law and order over development and intensely protective (in the trade union sense) of its own status and privileges.
2. An experience of—and in many cases a participation in—a form of authoritarian rule where the desires of the governed were less important than the judgments of the ruling class.
3. An experience of administrative rule free from popular control and political pressure, with political decisions falling within the confines of the administrative structure.
4. An experience of direct, personal rule as a district officer.

4. Mannoni argues persuasively that colonial rule afforded Western man the opportunity to assuage his inferiority complex by governing a "simpler" society, while the dependence of the colonized on the colonial officer constituted a patron-client relationship natural among the Malagasies. Mannoni, *Prospero and Caliban*, Chs. 1, 2, and 3.

In looking over these aspects of colonial rule, one is struck by the extent to which British colonialism and traditional rule share common traits. To be sure, the legal structure is new and so is the rational, secular basis of decision making, but in other respects the similarity is impressive. Both colonial and traditional politics limit popular participation, both are ruled by individuals or a class that believes in its right to rule by virtue of superior qualities, and both are concerned more with the preservation of an orderly status quo than with social change. Without overlooking the important differences—especially the fact that colonial rule is foreign rule—I would like to suggest that the *style* of colonial rule is perhaps more akin to traditional rule than is popular democracy. Thus, while rejecting its foreignness, the acceptance of the *pattern* of colonial rule may have demanded less of a change in central values than the acceptance of the pattern of liberal democracy. When reference is made later to the attractiveness of administrative rule for these men, it should be remembered that its appeal may stem from its resemblance to traditional government as well as from acceptance of the colonial pattern per se.[5]

The Ideological Deposit of Colonial Rule

The ideal relationship between the people and their leaders, as these men see it, does not differ in many respects from the colonial pattern. They envision a class of people who know best and expect to rule in the interests of the people. As in the colonial system, where a small number of relatively highly educated officials were placed in authority, or, for that matter, the precolonial system of rule by a traditional elite, a small group is expected to rule independently of popular desires by virtue of its superior qualifications. These men would encourage in the masses the traditional belief that this natural elite is best fitted to direct the nation and that only harm could come from following popular whims.

The citizen as a subject. In the paternalistic but authoritarian state these civil servants visualize, the functions of the mass of citizens are quite limited. Having little part in the selection of leaders or the choice of policies, they are expected quite simply

5. If the appeal of an administrative state is strong among the Westernized elites, it would surely be even more familiar and comfortable for the general population, to whom notions of liberal democracy are strange indeed.

to stay in line and follow the instructions of the ruling elite. When these men speak of the "ideal citizen in a democracy," the qualities they mention most frequently are loyalty, respect for law, and obedience. These are the qualities of the ideal "subject," as opposed to the "citizen/participant" qualities of voting, discussing issues, or fulfilling civic obligations.[6] What is required is the passive, compliant subject rather than the active participant who seeks an independent voice, however modest, in political life.

The emphasis on subject qualities was prominent throughout the interviews. When Kamalam was asked what the ideal citizen in a democracy should do, he replied, "The first thing to do—don't break any laws of the country. This is the question of the law-abiding citizen first. If you can do any good, for heavens sake do it—and don't do any wrong." Kamalam's ideal citizen should "do good" when he can, but obeying the law is clearly the most important and explicit obligation of citizenship. By comparison, Inche' Abu Bakar's description of the ideal citizen in a democracy is even more restrictive. "I think he should obey whatever rules there are and keeping [sic] away from mischief." Once Inche' Abu Bakar had finished his sentence, there was nothing more to say. Following the rules and "keeping away from mischief" completely exhaust the functions of citizenship for him. In Inche' Zukifli's answer, the parallel between the traditional pattern and what he desires of the citizen becomes all but explicit.

> We are now in the democratic world—well if the citizen—
> if they just behave like the Tengku [the present prime
> minister] or do what he says, there'll be no trouble. There's
> trouble because the Tengku says one thing and they do an-
> other. They are not patient. The Tengku, though, he believes
> in God, he is patient—but modern people, they're too im-
> patient.

"Trouble" comes from being impatient and not following the instructions of the leader. The ideal citizen, Inche' Zukifli implied, was much more prevalent in traditional society than in the postcolonial Malaysia he now knows.

6. These terms are borrowed from Almond and Verba, *The Civic Culture,* pp. 168–85.

Except where the context makes it explicit, as in Inche' Zukifli's case, it is hard to tell whether the subject qualities desired of citizens flow from a desire to reestablish traditional norms or a desire to retain colonial patterns. The difficulty arises because in both traditional and colonial rule, the citizen is expected to comply with political legislation rather than to express an evaluation of his own. The masses in both systems are expected to acquiesce to a purely subject role and not to pressure or criticize their rulers.

It would be a disservice to give the impression that these men are traditional or colonial in most other respects. For the most part, they see and applaud the steady expansion of education, the growth of industry, and other modern innovations. But when it comes to changing the relationship between ruler and ruled, they are much less sanguine. A majority of those who realize that the broad changes sweeping Malaysia will foster the growth of political groups and create more demands for participation are distressed, for they see the ideal citizen as a law-abiding follower of the rulers in an administrative state.[7]

The obligations of parental rulers. While the people continue as subjects, their leaders are to be paternalistic in the sense that they govern in the ultimate best interests of their clients. The use of the term "paternalism" embraces not only paternal discipline but also the maternal functions of protection and support. There is little need to dwell on the former, since the preference for firm rule to prevent people from acting against the community interests has been treated in some detail. As these men see it, only the cajoling and threats of a strong leader can persuade citizens to cease taking advantage of their fellows. The maternal functions may be less prominent, but they are nonetheless important in the full conception of paternal rule.

When Jeganathan talked of the duties of the prime minister, the protective aspect of paternal rule stood out most clearly:

> Of course the prime minister is worried about the Defense Pact [with Great Britain]. Even though he has his ministers, he is the grandfather of everything. With our prime minister, everyone knows they can go to him and get redress — the

7. This finding conforms with what one would expect from the responses to the "Political Equality" items in the previous chapter, where affirmation of popular capacity for self-rule was the exception rather than the rule.

way it should be. The people have so much confidence in him — it is like hero worship.

The prime minister, as the "grandfather of everything," listens to the grievances of his people and helps when he can. One may look on grievance procedures of this sort as the only acceptable form of political expression in traditional or colonial regimes. In neither are popular demands or protests sanctioned before decisions are made, but the door is always open to those who seek redress for the consequences of state action. Both the Malay sultan and the colonial D. O. are solicitous of the people who gather each morning to await an audience in hopes of redress or assistance. The request for action takes the form of a personal and humble appeal, never a political demand or threat.

Aside from being accessible to personal laments, the paternalistic ruler also sponsors events that both express his support for traditional values and strengthen the bonds between him and his people. Inche' Nordin appeared to have this function in mind when he was asked whether the general public takes enough interest in the activities of government:

> I think it is anyway a policy of the government. It's official routine. We have a Koran contest, and the angle is for religious people to come forward. And we have games, and the angle is for sportsmen to come forward. And then we have festivals to encourage people to be cautious and conscious and everything.

An Englishman who was asked the same question might well cite wider popular knowledge of government decisions, but Inche' Nordin chose to focus on the activities of government that are less manifestly political. Here is the participation without control that characterizes traditional rule and, to a great extent, colonial rule as well.

The style of popular participation. Paternalistic rule requires that citizens remain subjects and emphasizes the firmness and discipline exercised by the ruler. It does leave room for some popular influence and participation; but the form that popular participation takes is quite in keeping with paternal rule in that it either offers largely symbolic rewards or places the citizen in the role of supplicant. Most of the civil servants interviewed consider the representations of the public in much the same light as would a traditional or colonial regime. Humble requests are entirely appropriate, while popular demands or demonstrations are not considered legitimate means of influencing policy.[8] The status relationship seems important here, since appeals and requests imply that one is addressing a superior, while demands are more often addressed to equals or inferiors. When these men talked of their dealings with the public, it became clear that they were more sympathetic to the appeals of the humble subject than to the demands of the citizen. Inche' Mustapha was typical in this respect when he explained the dilemma of not being able to meet a client's request. "There are several types of people. It's easier for me to deal with rural people—they are simple, and if I explain clearly, they are satisfied." Like the others, Inche' Mustapha prefers kampong folk because they are more docile and more easily satisfied than urban residents. He finds the traditional/colonial relationship easier to handle than one between civic equals.

There is another factor at work here aside from the general preference for paternalistic rule. A relationship of equality between bureaucrats and clients might, they feel, jeopardize the impartiality of the civil service and open the door to corruption. As Inche' Ja'afar said when asked whether the public thinks the civil servant is difficult to approach.

> As a matter of fact, in certain spheres you discourage being approached. In the legal and defense spheres, for example, someone may walk in with fruit to the magistrate's house— although that's rare—and you may have to throw him out. Based on that, it may seem we are not approachable—but we are trying to be just and not be accessible to parties.

Mr. Khoo echoed these sentiments in explaining why some people might fear civil servants. "The kampong people fear the civil servant because people in the kampong know that civil servants are incorruptible. But the man on the street doesn't think so." The implication of what both men said is that impartiality becomes

8. The Indian government appears to conform to the same pattern of rejecting demands but listening to private deputations. Weiner, *The Politics of Scarcity*, p. 188.

impossible unless the client retains some fear of the bureaucrat, who for his part remains aloof and relatively inaccessible. Under colonialism it was easy for the British to maintain this social distance between rulers and ruled by virtue of their foreignness, but for Malaysian civil servants a special effort is necessary because of their very closeness to the culture. As Braibanti has written, the bureaucrat in a new nation must "exaggerate the drama of his detachment" in order to shield himself from the claims of kinship and ethnic group that permeate his society; "the mere posture of familiarity inevitably creates a reputation for partiality which leads to actual partiality." [9]

The marked preference for a nonegalitarian relationship with clients—the rejection of demands in contrast to appeals—and the social distance that this implies can thus be viewed from two angles. On the one hand, it maintains a pattern common to both traditional and colonial societies, and on the other, it serves to insulate the civil servant from particularistic pressures, thus retaining the impartiality of colonial administration.

Alienation from popular democracy. From what is known about these men's beliefs, it is hardly surprising that a good portion of them are alienated from democracy as it is now practiced in Malaysia. Both their expectations and their preferences conspire to produce this alienation. First, their abstract, idealized conception of democracy—the politics of principles, civic mindedness, and enlightened leadership—was bound to fare poorly when measured against even the relatively successful democracy of their own nation. Important as they are, the alienation-producing effects of this distortion of the Western model should not be overemphasized, since the actual commitment to democratic norms among Malaysian civil servants is not particularly high, nor is their faith in the capacities of the masses for self-rule.

The second and more crucial distortion of the Western model lies in the direction of a paternalistic administrative state guided by a qualified elite with the acquiescence of a deferential population. While there is an apparent conflict between this distortion toward paternalism and the idealized understanding of Western democracy, it is not a conflict that is consciously perceived. In fact, these men hoped that within a democratic framework the

9. Braibanti, "Public Bureaucracy and Judiciary in Pakistan," p. 394.

population would see that it needed the guidance of the Westernized elite and would thus give this elite their full backing to
govern in the best interests of the nation. Such a solution would
have allowed a form of rule patterned closely on the traditional/
colonial model, but with the consent of the governed as democracy
required.

As it has turned out, however, they could not have their cake
and eat it too. Democracy in Malaysia has meant the rise of less
Westernized politicians, appeals to popular passions, the politicization of primordial groupings, and the race for spoils. Given their
restricted conception of democracy, what is occurring seems but
a crude caricature of what a democratic polity should be and cannot but lead to disillusionment. In particular, though, it is the
decline of respect and deference due the rulers that creates much
of the distaste for political life in the new Malaysia. Inche' Nordin
expressed his unhappiness over the new arrangement quite explicitly:

> [Do people *fear* civil servants?] No, it's unlike before. Before
> the war there was good *respect,* but now it's changed. They
> say you have two eyes and I have two eyes. They're even
> fighting for equality now—there's some women in the Par-
> liament and before the war no women would come forward.
> Before the war they had their own self-respect. They lost their
> self-respect. They think, "you do harm to me, and I'll do it
> to you." [Civil servants difficult to approach?] A few, but
> not many—unlike before. Now everybody is conscious. You're
> equal no matter what your job. A farmer, since he makes good
> money, thinks he's equal to the district officer and says, "I
> don't respect you."

Others put it somewhat differently, but for the most part, their
sentiments were the same. Democracy as it functions in Malaysia
neither measures up to their image of Western democracy, nor
does it retain enough of a paternalistic, noblesse oblige cast to
suit their preferences. Instead of general popular acceptance and
support for rule by the Westernized elite, they see the beginnings
of a revolution of political equality which they reject. Instead of
harmony they hear the din of factions engaged in petty bickering.

Instead of political principles and honor, they see appeals to primordial sentiments and increasing corruption.

Part of their disillusionment is assuredly traceable to the nature of the colonial education system, which promoted a conception of democracy completely torn from its moorings in reality. But for the most part, their alienation from Malaysia's political life stems from a predisposition for paternalistic rule on the traditional pattern—a predisposition strongly reinforced by their experience in a colonial bureaucracy that was, particularly in the prewar period, as strongly elitist and paternal as traditional regimes. They had hoped that after the colonial rulers were thrown out, the new Westernized, indigenous elite could continue to rule in much the same manner with the approval of the masses—a local, popular paternalism to replace a foreign, unpopular paternalism. They were poorly prepared for the fundamental change in the relationship between the rulers and the ruled that has begun to develop since independence; it has left them alienated from the very political system in which they still exercise great power.

Status decline and attitudes toward politicians. Attention has been thus far focused on the style of rule by the colonial bureaucracy and its effects on political beliefs. But the evaluation of a political system is seldom separable from attitudes toward those who are in charge of the system. To complete the picture of how Malaysian administrators view the political life of their nation, it is necessary to know not only what they think of their political system but what they think of their politicians as well.

The view of politicians among these men is colored strongly by the fact that in Malaysia, as in all new nations, administrators have suffered a decline in status vis-à-vis politicians. Before independence, bureaucrats were the rulers, but there is now a new class of politicians whose decisions they must implement. They find themselves reduced from the status of rulers to the position of public servants who must bow to the authority of elected ministers. Whereas they once both made policy and executed it, they have lost much of the policy-making role to an elected elite. Most of the administrators resent this loss of power. Mr. Lim, for example, lamented the subservience of the civil service to politicians when he was asked which group is more important in

national development. "This is—politics do come in here. The
civil service will have to depend on the politicians. They will have
to play the tune of the politicians—unfortunately, I should say."
While the loss of power is regrettable to most, the loss of status
and prestige seems to be much more prominent. No longer must
the citizen look exclusively to civil servants to redress grievances,
for he has acquired a new ally whom he can enlist to bring pressure
on the administration. These administrators are painfully aware
that the power of politicians has reduced their status in the eyes
of the people.[10]

As Inche' Mustapha replied when asked what the "man in the
street" thinks of the civil servant,

> They say they are paid too highly and work too little.
> But there has been a change of attitude recently—even among
> the Malay community. In those days when you were in the
> government service you were very powerful—and now there's
> a more powerful man—like the minister, whom you can
> approach. So government service is not so highly graded as
> before.

Thus while civil servants see the politician as a self-seeker par
excellence because of their general beliefs about human nature,
they also harbor a more specific animus against politicians for
robbing them of the prestige they enjoyed before independence.

Much of their criticism of politicians reflects quite clearly the
basis on which they feel qualified to rule themselves. It was their
education and Westernization that enabled them to rise in the
colonial administration and that they find sadly lacking among
the new politicians. They assume that Western education—which
was the justification of colonial rule—is also the attribute that
should qualify one for rule in the postcolonial society. The politicians as a group are thus denigrated for their relative illiteracy,

10. Pye, in his *Politics, Personality, and Nation Building,* pp. 223–27, suggests
that the *Burmese* administrator has more than just a problem of downward mobility; he shows how politicians have brought the civil servant's loyalty into question
by charging that he collaborated with the British against the nationalist movement.
Though charges of this nature are not unheard of in Malaysia, they are quite
rare because of the relative ease with which Malaya acceded to independence.
In fact, Malayan administrators played an important role in their national
independence movement and, until recently, in local party branches.

their inability to speak English, and their failure to pass their Senior Cambridge Exams.[11]

This generally low view of politicians would be of little note were it not for the fact that it further contributes to a vague feeling that democracy has failed in Malaysia. The colonial bureaucratic experience of administrators and their preference for rule by an intellectual elite make it impossible for them to have confidence in the ability of a less educated, less experienced body of politicians to guide the nation successfully. What are they to think of a political system that through elections has cast up a new political elite so manifestly less qualified than they to rule in the public's best interest? Never very strong to begin with, their belief in democracy is further undermined by the politicians they feel it has produced as well as by the rise of communal, particularistic politics.

THE POSTCOLONIAL BASIS FOR PATERNAL RULE

The nature of colonial rule, then, has tended to create a predisposition to paternal administrative rule on the part of these civil servants. What has not been explained sufficiently, however, is how this preference has survived to the present amidst the spread of democratic beliefs and nationalist populism. The influence of colonial administration and traditional patterns may well account for the *sources* of the preference for paternal rule, but it does not explain the persistence of this preference in postcolonial Malaysia.

As has been found true of other political beliefs throughout this study, the inclination to paternal authoritarian government has a basis in the realities of the environment; like the constant-pie orientation, it represents a more or less rational adjustment to actual conditions. The political beliefs that feed on these conditions must, of course, meet the psychological needs of their supporters. Pye realizes this when he sensitively analyzes the colonial socialization of Burmese administrators, their feeling of being abandoned by the British, and their consequent alienation from the new political life of Burma. What he overlooks, however, is

11. They also criticize politicians for attempting to influence administrative decisions on behalf of their clients and for what they perceive to be increasing political influence over promotions within the civil service. On how civil servants get ahead, Mr. Khoo said, "Some rise on political influence—moving with the right people."

the fact that the yearning for paternal rule on the colonial model, like any belief, contains certain assumptions about the environment. If these assumptions fail significantly to match reality, the belief must eventually change, or it will perish. The failure of communism in England or the United States, for example, has undoubtedly a great deal to do with the failure of its assumptions to match realities as they were experienced by most people.

The durability of the belief in paternal authoritarian rule can, I feel, be explained by the fact that its implicit assumptions about reality conform substantially to realities in Malaysia—or in other new nations, for that matter. In brief, the relative power of the bureaucracy, the political leadership that it actually provides, its domination of voluntary organizations, and, finally, the very real danger of national disintegration all provide an impressive basis for a belief in elite rule.

The Resources of the Bureaucracy

Although the administrative structure in Malaysia no longer enjoys its precolonial complete monopoly of power, it nonetheless represents the largest, most cohesive elite group in the nation. The competing political and commercial elites are neither as well organized nor as experienced in the exercise of power. Fritz Morstein Marx, writing about the role of the bureaucracy in the political development of the West, emphasizes that "It had the triple advantage of greater intellectual resources, elevated social status, and close identification with the government." [12] All three criteria apply equally well to Malaysia as to the West. As far as "intellectual resources" are concerned, the general level of education and special skills is far higher among the administrative elite than in any competing elites. Only at the cabinet level do the educational qualifications of politicians approach that of the higher civil service.

The social status of the bureaucracy is similiarly high. As much as the men interviewed may grumble about the new status of politicians, the civil service remains the group that makes most of the decisions which directly affect the citizenry, and although recourse to political influence is now possible in the event of a rebuff, most

12. Fritz Morstein Marx, "The Higher Civil Service as an Action Group in Western Political Development," in LaPalombara, ed., *Bureaucracy and Political Development,* pp. 66–67.

of the population still looks to civil servants for assistance and advice. In part, this is because the structures that might influence legislation before it is passed are still weak in Malaysia, and it is only at the enforcement stage that many individuals can affect government policy. Influence before bills are passed means dealing with politicians; influence over enforcement requires appeals to the civil servant. Not only must the general population influence policy via the administrative route, but politicians themselves find they must rely on administrators to draw up legislation, formulate development plans, and so forth.[13] Both the location of the bureaucracy in the power structure and its intellectual resources thus serve to enhance the bureaucrats' status in the eyes of both the masses and other elites.

Still another factor greatly enhances the prestige of the administrative elite. The domain of government, until recently at least, has been the domain of the English language, and there has thus been "a positive correlation between skill in spoken English and status in the eyes of the vernacular speaking public." [14] The civil servants' command of English, which is at the same time the badge of their education, makes them the interpreters of the mysteries of English law and regulations to the unschooled masses and contributes to the great prestige they enjoy.

Not only does the Malaysian civil service benefit from "greater intellectual resources" and "elevated social status," which Fritz Morstein Marx ascribes to Western bureaucracies, but it is also, in his terms, "closely identified with government." Given the similarity in social backgrounds of politicians and administrators and the absence of a sharp division between them on policy matters, the administrative corps has retained a great deal of its power and generally enjoys the confidence of the political elite.

The resources of the bureaucracy are impressive whether measured by its expertise, its status, or its share of decision-making power. By and large, it has lost little of the resources or the authority it exercised under the colonial regime. Competing elites have yet to dilute greatly its power. That is to say, its position as an

13. Politicians may complain about the red tape and narrow legalism, but in general they retain a grudging admiration for the administrative service of their nation.

14. Braibanti, "Public Bureaucracy and Judiciary in Pakistan," p. 391.

educated, experienced ruling elite has not been seriously under-mined in post-independence Malaysia. If higher civil servants see themselves as a paternal ruling group, they do not greatly distort reality.

Bureaucratic Leadership and Initiative

The power of the bureaucracy in Malaysia is not at all confined to its administrative role but extends as well into most voluntary associations and interest groups. A good many of the interest groups in the nation were established by administrative initiative, and their leadership is often composed largely of serving or retired civil servants. This pattern is most striking in the rural Malay areas, but is widespread in urban centers as well.

The bureaucratic domination of nongovernmental groups has maintained a pattern characteristic of the colonial regime and has seriously retarded the growth of truly autonomous power centers. What develops is politicization without democratic control, since representatives of the government, in their capacities as officers of these groups, are playing a major role in the formulation of de-mands and appeals to the authorities.[15] Popular participation in these organizations is encouraged, but popular control over na-tional policy is not. The function of these organizations, as the ruling elite sees it, is to generate support for the government's program rather than to create new demands and claims on the nation's resources.

The officers of school boards, religious committees, sporting associations, and charitable groups are drawn heavily from the ranks of the civil service. Division I administrators, in particular, are likely to hold simultaneously posts in a number of such organi-zations. Until little more than a decade ago, even manifestly political organizations were often led by district officers and other bureaucrats. At present, when most civil servants are forbidden to hold political posts, petty officials and retired administrators still hold many local party positions, and higher civil servants often

15. Fred W. Riggs feels that the role of the bureaucracy in guiding these organizations "lays the foundation for totalitarianism." While this conclusion goes further than the circumstances merit, the pattern in Malaysia does certainly imply a "weakening of the prospects for democratic control." Riggs, "Bureaucrats and Political Development: A Paradoxical View," in LaPalombara, ed., *Bureaucracy and Political Development*, p. 141.

act in an ex officio advisory capacity to local branches of the United Malay Nationals Organization (U.M.N.O.).[16]

The pervasive influence of the bureaucracy in extragovernmental groupings is attributable to many factors, but in a real sense, it occurs almost by default. Most of the demands generated in a still largely traditional society are likely to be personalistic in nature, so if associational groups are to exist at all, they are likely to be the creations of the bureaucratic and political elites.[17] In the West, such organizations grew more or less naturally from the general level of social organization and represented the slow growth of autonomous, organized demands. But in a new nation, they tend to be "hothouse" organizations, created and nurtured by the urban educated elite.

It is not as if the Western-educated bureaucrats have ousted local leaders and usurped their positions. On the contrary, local groups have welcomed bureaucratic leadership and guidance for obvious reasons. First, they realize that only this sort of leadership can meet the authorities on an equal footing, with a thorough knowledge of whom to approach and a familiarity with the provisions of the law. Appreciating the considerable resources of status, knowledge, and experience administrators can bring to bear on government, they are willing—even anxious—to accede to official leadership. Second, there is a long tradition of relying on those of higher status to organize political activity, which derives from both the precolonial and colonial periods. This pattern is not confined to Malaysia alone; Banfield has commented on it in southern Italy, and those who have studied Indian efforts at local *panchayat* rule have noted that virtually all the initiative has had to come from the top.[18] Both the relative absence of local organizational initia-

16. For a detailed description of the administrative domination of the most powerful Malay political organization, see Swift, *Malay Peasant Society in Jelebu*, pp. 158–62.

17. To a certain extent the trade unions and business groups *do* represent centers of power which are largely independent of government control and yet not traditionally oriented.

18. See High Tinker, "The Village in the Framework of Development," in Braibanti and Spengler, eds., *Administration and Economic Development in India*. For a superb but inpressionistic view of the failure of local initiative and organization in India as a whole, see Kusum Nair, *Blossoms in the Dust: The Human Factor in Indian Development* (New York, Praeger, 1962). In Malaysia, civil servants are quite aware of the widespread dependence on external initiative and often

tive along modern lines and the traditional reliance on high-status leadership have thus created a situation tailor-made for domination by the administrative elite. Both the bureaucrats and those they guide find this relationship quite natural and appropriate.

One further reason for the prominent role of administrators in public life is related to an important difference between Western nations and new nations at comparable stages of economic development. In most of the West during the early stage of economic growth, the government was not expected to be uniquely responsible for community welfare, industrialization, or employment. Since people did not look to the government for the solution to these problems, there was less need for organized interests to tie in closely with the central government. The pattern in new nations, however, is quite different, since the national authorities have assumed a host of functions that require a much higher level of organized support or compliance. Given the path of development which they have chosen, and the level of social and economic organization from which they begin, these organizational requirements must be met largely through the leadership efforts of the educated governmental elite. In summary, then, the overwhelming resources of the bureaucracy, the popular acceptance of administrative leadership, the weakness of local initiative in forming modern groups, and the need for structures through which the government can push its development program all conspire to perpetuate an environment that leaves few alternatives to bureaucratic leadership.

The Fear of the Retrograde Masses

The preference for a paternalistic state in which the masses are expected to support the policies of an educated elite has yet another, and perhaps more crucial, basis in the environment. The unity of Malaysia is very tenuous, and all of the civil servants are well aware that the entire structure could collapse under the pressures generated by ethnic and religious antagonisms. Already these primordial hostilities have sorely tested the national fabric. The secession of Singapore from the Federation of Malaysia in 1965,

---

wish the people would do more for themselves. As Sundram put it, "That's the Asian attitude toward things. They like to be pushed around, they're not like the English or Americans—they expect things to be done for them."

for example, can be largely attributed to communal tensions. A belief in the fragility of national unity is thus not an idle notion assignable merely to a bureaucratic inclination to Caesarism. It is rather a belief based on a realistic assessment of the forces actually threatening national unity in Malaysia.

First of all, these civil servants see that the skills and knowledge required for modernization are concentrated in the Westernized elite. If modernization is to occur at all, they must play a central role in organizing the support of a largely apathetic and traditional population. Secondly, they recognize that unless there is centralized political and administrative leadership, primordial demands which might well tear apart the nation will come to the fore. Those demands which are organized independently of the government are likely to emphasize the parochial, religious, linguistic, and ethnic identifications that are paramount to most of the citizenry. Should these demands become politicized before the masses are "incorporated into the greater community," [19] the outlook for preserving the integrity of the nation would diminish drastically. These men are not concerned with national unity only because they wish to rule, but also because they appreciate the clear and present dangers to that unity.

All this illustrates the essential dilemma of the Western-educated elites in new nations like Malaysia. It is too simple to characterize them as essentially antidemocratic, for their quandary is much more complex. If they encourage full popular democracy, they know all too well that they are entrusting the destiny of their nation to the most traditional and reactionary forces which threaten to destroy it even now.[20] They recognize that if the Westernized intelligentsia rules, the growth of democracy will be retarded, but this seems a lesser evil than the probable consequences of popular rule now. The fact that the masses are retrograde is thus enough to convince them that they must, for the time being, continue as the oligarchic tutors of an eventual democracy in Malaysia.

19. A. F. K. Organski, *The Stages of Political Development* (New York, Alfred A. Knopf, 1965), p. 43.

20. This dilemma is described in similar terms by Muneer Ahmad in his study of civil servants in Pakistan, *The Civil Servant in Pakistan: A Study of the Background and Attitudes of Public Servants in Lahore* (Karachi, Oxford University Press, 1964), p. 242.

There are, then, persuasive reasons, based on the nature of traditional and colonial rule, for anticipating a predisposition to paternal rule among the administrative class of a new nation. The colony was an administrative state in which citizens were confined to subject roles. Moreover, their experience under the colonial system and the rise of a political elite to dilute their authority have contributed to their alienation from the style of popular democracy and to a distaste for the politician's role. Persuasive as these arguments are, they do not adequately explain the dogged persistence of these beliefs in the postcolonial era.[21]

To account for the durability of a paternalistic ideology, it is necessary to see to what extent the implicit assumptions behind paternalistic rule match the existential base of the society. The realities of Malaysia and most other new nations are quite congruent with the assumptions behind "tutelary democracy." [22] The educated, Westernized elites hold a virtual monopoly of the knowledge and skills needed for modernization, the masses expect and welcome the initiative and leadership of the bureaucratic elite, and, most important, the primordial attachments of the masses, if politicized, would doubtless place the very existence of the nation in jeopardy. Only because tutelary democracy conforms in these essential ways with the realities in new nations is its appeal so irresistible.

POSTSCRIPT: NEW THEMES—A MINORITY CASE

The generalizations made in this chapter hold true for the entire sample with few exceptions. The exceptions, however, are interesting ones. The three, perhaps four, civil servants who see things somewhat differently from the rest are also among the younger group recruited since the colonial period and are university graduates. This is not to say that all the younger, educated civil servants are different from the picture that has been outlined, since as many fit the pattern described as do not. The only exceptions,

21. In particular, they fail to explain a similar tendency among the political elite of many new nations who experienced less of the type of colonial socialization that characterizes the administrative class. See especially Shils, "The Intellectual Between Tradition and Modernity."

22. Shils' term. Cf. Edward Shils, *Political Development in the New States* (The Hague: Mouton & Co., 1965), pp. 60–67.

however, do fall in this category and seem to share certain beliefs and attitudes distinct from the sample as a whole.

This is such a small number of bureaucrats that it would be presumptuous to suggest that they represent the wave of the future. Nonetheless, what distinguishes them from the rest of the sample appears to be related to their postcolonial recruitment and their high education, so that we might anticipate their views becoming more common among the administrative class as their numbers increase. This is the first and only occasion on which a discussion of intra-sample differences has been attempted, and any conclusions we reach are frankly speculative. Two new themes are most prominent in my discussion with this small sub-sample: a more favorable view of popular government and politicians; and a livelier appreciation of underlying social changes which they feel augur well for Malaysia's future.

Politicians and Democratic Politics

Most of the civil servants were not inclined to look favorably upon either the rise of politicians or the increasing participation of the population in political life. Sundram typified the views of this group when he explained that civil servants are more important to national development than politicians. "I think the civil service is the best guide to the politicians. The politicians are just there to please the public. They all want a factory in their own constituency, but the civil servant must decide which is of most benefit to the people."

In this view, politicians are little more than a public relations gimmick to give the populace the appearance of power over decisions without its reality. The three educated, younger civil servants examined here, however, are much more at home in a popular democracy in which politicians play an essential role. Perhaps because they never were a part of the colonial administrative structure, they seem less alarmed at the decline of bureaucratic power in Malaysia. When Inche' Abdul Karim was asked whether administrators or politicians are more essential in national development, his response contrasted sharply with that of Sundram: "I think the government—government here includes the political section—because I think politicians can best assess the needs and requirements of the people, while the civil service merely carries out or implements policy."

The civil service performs an important function, but basic policy is left in the hands of the politicians. Another member of this group, Inche' Zaharuddin, is similarly appreciative of the politician's place in a democratic polity, and he explicitly described the change that has occurred since independence:

> The politicians—I think we must distinguish the functions here—politicians, they make policies. They want to uplift the standards of the people, but the civil service must work it out—how to do it. If the civil service is weak, then the politicians can't do it. That's the difference—before, the civil servants do both things—they are politicians. Now sometimes you find an old officer who served during the British times and can't adjust themselves. They quarrel with the politicians and just order people to do things. In those days the word of the government servant was law.

Inche' Zaharuddin is not only aware of the new and more modest role of the civil service in an independent Malaysia, but he also clearly seems to approve of the wider responsibility given politicians. It is not merely the fact that these younger men did not have *their* power stolen by nationalist politicians which predisposes them to accept the new arrangements in good grace. They also seem to have a firmer commitment to a new relationship between the rulers and the ruled. By and large, unlike most of their colleagues, they applaud the slowly increasing popular participation in political life and favor a relationship with the people in which the civil servant is not perhaps reduced to the commonplace but is certainly no longer the natural ruler of the nation.

In contrast to the others, they do not regard public awe of the civil servant as entirely healthy. Asked if the man in the street respects the civil servant, Inche' Abdul Karim replied,

> I think at the moment, yes—more than enough. [Does public interest help the civil service?] Oh, yes! One thing, it puts you on your toes always. When the general public takes interest in government machinery, they always want better [sic], so you must find ways and means to improve. If not, you get a well-contented and satisfied civil service.

Far from wanting to return to the bureaucratic status of colonial days, Inche' Abdul Karim feels there is too much fearful respect for the civil servant. He looks with satisfaction on the growth of public pressure which prods the bureaucracy to become more effective.

Mr. Tay, the third member of this small group, was quite outspoken in his appreciation of the new scheme of things. He too sees the value of popular access to elected officials in improving the quality of government. His opinion about whether or not the public takes enough interest in government activities was clear and decisive:

> Certainly. For example, in this department alone, if our policies are found to be inadequate, there will be representations to the government. The ministers are so approachable. It is not difficult to see him and air your views. [Does public interest help civil service?] Certainly—those days are gone when, before independence, their views would not even be heard at all. This is representative government—I think it works quite well.

Mr. Tay's preference for representative government is not meant as an endorsement of Malaysian politicians. Like the rest of the sample, all three are in fact full of comments on the shortcomings of their nation's politicians, but unlike the others, their criticism is not part of a general rejection of the politician's role in society. What distinguishes these three civil servants from the others is rather a general satisfaction with a political system in which popular complaints and demands are taken up by politicians. They are certain that Malaysians and their politicians fall far short of making the system work effectively, but they lack the inclination to administrative rule that characterizes most of the sample. Whether this new attitude can be attributed to the fact that these three men were never a part of the colonial administration or to the coincidence that they were all impressionable teen-agers at the height of the nationalist movement, there is no doubt that their conception of the relationship between rulers and ruled sets them apart from the others.

The Cognitive Basis of Optimism

When most of the seventeen civil servants look at political life in Malaysia today, they are struck by the absence of principle, the growth of primordial demands, and the rise of ill-trained politicians feeding at the public trough. The three young, educated civil servants being examined see these disillusioning aspects of Malaysian democracy, too, but they see much more besides. In particular, they see the expansion of education and national loyalty, which in the long run, they expect, will make for a better and more democratic society. They are able to look past the immediate and discouraging to the long-term and hopeful. Thus, when they were asked whether Malaysia is getting closer to an ideal society, they replied optimistically, for they have a longer vision which permits optimism—a vision which the others lack. The importance of education in building an ideal society is apparent in the remarks of Inche' Abdul Karim and Inche' Zaharuddin.[23]

> Inche' Abdul Karim: I think we are getting closer. [Why?] People are becoming more courageous to voice their opinions. This helps make the ideal society come closer. This is closely tied with the educational system, the more educated are the more courageous to voice their opinions. Of course, this expression of opinion should be done with the best of intentions.

> Inche' Zaharuddin: I think we are going closer, at least here in Malaya. [Why?] In the first place the form of government has been changing—it's becoming more representative government. And secondly, with the development of education, the people are becoming more civic-minded—and so they become more conscious of their responsibility towards society.

Education is the vehicle by which Malaysia will approach the ideal society. On the one hand, it gives people political principles on which to stand (Inche' Abdul Karim), and on the other, it promotes national civic consciousness (Inche' Zaharuddin). Throughout my discussions with these three administrators, it be-

---

23. Mr. Tay simply mentioned "knowledge" as the reason why Malaysia is getting closer to the ideal society but did not elaborate.

came evident that they view education as a universal solvent which
will gradually eliminate selfishness, irrationality, and particularistic concerns from the political landscape. As a result of education
or civic training, people will forget their trivial differences and
cooperate in the common interest. Education will bring them to a
closer identification with the nation and assure its solidarity and
cohesiveness.

In a sense, the great faith placed in education as the means of
achieving the civic culture is quite naïve. It reverses the plausible
proposition that democracy does not flourish amidst general illiteracy to say that education will produce democracy. Education is
perhaps necessary for democracy to flourish, but it is surely not a
sufficient condition.[24] Nevertheless, this view does have its virtues,
since it focuses on education as an important prerequisite of democracy—a prerequisite that helps to dilute primordial ties, reinforce civic skills, and replace superstition with knowledge. One
feels that these men are arguing from their personal experiences.
They feel, justifiably, that their own educational experience has
contributed to their national consciousness, their appreciation of
democratic ideals, and their ability to avoid the racial and religious
prejudice that threatens their nation. In fact, it is largely the
educated elite of Malaysia who are committed, however tenuously,
to democratic forms and who have been able to transcend the
strong pull of communal loyalty. Thus when these men pin their
hopes for Malaysia's future on education, they reflect their personal
experience and the experience of their nation.

The ability of these three men to see broad educational changes
as a transforming force is but an illustration of a much more important skill they have acquired—a cognitive skill that is generally
a product of education. Where other administrators see only the
immediate din of communal demands and untrammeled self-seeking, these men are able to look beyond the present and see the
broad social changes that could alter how Malaysians think and
behave. This process implies that human nature is not irrevocably
fixed for all time but is instead tied, at least in part, to environmental factors which, if they could be changed, might affect human

24. Nadav Safram writes that the liberal democrats of Egypt also expected the
growth of education to strengthen the prospects for democracy. *Egypt in Search of
Political Community*, p. 148.

nature itself. Knowledge of this sort is perhaps the distinguishing feature of modern man, and it inevitably suggests that the future is neither immutable nor in the hands of God alone but can be the proper object of collective action. This is the crucial cognitive basis of optimism which these men possess and which is largely absent in the others.

How this cognitive skill changes the nature of problems is apparent in Inche' Zaharuddin's discussion of two problems that confront any new nation. The first is the great gulf separating the urban masses from the rural peasantry in Malaysia. Explaining why kampong people look at national affairs differently from urbanites, Inche' Zaharuddin displayed a considerable degree of sophistication.

> I think the difference stems up from their surroundings. The village people look at—I think they tend to compare—they associate what they see with life in their own village. If, in the village, the social life is different—so they may think the social life in the cities is wrong. [Later] It's because of their surroundings—it's based on what they are used to see or experience.

Most others, when treating the same problem, implied that kampong folk are different from urban people in an irremediable way that has more to do with their basic nature than with their mode of life. Inche' Zaharuddin, however, traced the difference to rural "surroundings," which leaves open the possibility for change if the rural experience is somehow altered. The same understanding of background factors was manifest when Inche' Zaharuddin discussed the cause of poverty.

> I think I tend to agree that inequality is the cause of poverty. If we don't have equality of opportunity because we have poverty—and we have poverty because we don't have quality of opportunity. It is a vicious circle—if you're poor and have no education, you can't get a good job and therefore you have no money and you are poor and you can't get a good education. So it goes round and round.

This is neither a very elaborate nor a very rigorous argument, but there are the unmistakable beginnings of a real sophistication here. Compared to what most of the civil servants have to say about poverty, it is even more impressive. For example, Inche' Zukifli commented, "It's [poverty] because of the head of the country—or the chief doesn't care much about the country." Or Jeganathan: "There're quite a number of causes—one is that you want to take life [sic]—you don't want to struggle for a living and want life on a golden platter." The other two causes Jeganathan suggested were "squandering money" and "keeping up with the Joneses." Inche's Zukifli's statement implies that the only way out of poverty is to have a leader who "cares," while Jeganathan sees no solution as long as people are lazy spendthrifts. In neither statement is there any appreciation of the impersonal causes at work, an appreciation that would provide a basis for optimism and sustained collective action. Inche' Zaharuddin's cognitive skills, on the other hand, allow him to see beyond intractable personal motives to environmental factors which are, in the long run, not beyond human control.

Those who lack the cognitive skills of Inche' Zaharuddin are generally pessimists about Malaysia's future. They look about themselves and see individualism, selfishness, and communal tensions, from which there seems to be no exit. In contrast, the few young, educated respondents who can appreciate both the effects of the environment and the slow but massive changes taking place in Malaysia thereby have a foundation for their faith that a better future is even now being forged amid parochialism and self-seeking. The basis for their optimism is almost certainly the broader cognitive grasp with which their high education has endowed them.[25] Writing about the ways education expands the explanatory resources of men, Lane concludes:

> a central civic function of education is to release men from reliance on personalistic explanations, to enrich their explanatory repertory to include social and impersonal causes. Ignorance personalizes! More than that, it causes men to think of men as autonomous of their environment, permitting

25. Education alone is obviously not a sufficient cause for this cognitive grasp, since two or three other young educated administrators in the sample lack these qualities.

explanations of why they act as they do solely in terms of a series of motives—rage, greed, ambition.[26]

In a real sense, then, these men are the modernizers of a new nation. It is largely they who are able to so analyze the present as to see a viable path to the future—a future that need not depend solely on pure human motives and the good intentions of leaders.

Paternalism: The Present Is Not the Future

The three men under discussion are thus distinguished by their greater commitment to popular democracy, in which politicians are not mere appendages of the administration, and by an optimism about Malaysia's political future which grows from their understanding of impersonal causes.

If colonial socialization and an inability to see more than the immediate and disillusioning aspects of political life were the central factors predisposing civil servants to paternalistic rule, we would expect *not* to find such a preference among these three men—for they differ from the sample in precisely these respects. Yet the inclination to elite rule, albeit milder, is present among this group as well.

Inche' Zaharuddin is perhaps the strongest democrat in the sample, but nonetheless he feels paternal rule by an educated elite is desirable. When asked whether democracy creates confusion and prevents important things from being done, he answered,

> Yes, it does. [Why?] Then it's because the machinery is not functioning well or the people don't reach the standard where the machinery—the democratic machinery may be a little too far-reaching or high for the ordinary people to follow. That's where "guided democracy" comes in.

Again, when deciding whether the people or the elected leaders know what is best for the country, he said, "The elected people because the danger is that—of ordinary people—they are not in a position since their self-interest always dominates their position." In the context of our entire discussion, it became clear why Inche' Zaharuddin thinks Malaysian citizens are not yet ready for their full civic responsibilities. It is because, he said, "The percentage

26. Lane, *Political Ideology*, p. 310.

of the people who can be good citizens in Malaysia is still small."
Those he would include as good citizens are the "civil servants"
and "those with secondary education"—a minute fraction of the
total population. As far as ideal party members are concerned, "in
our society we have far to go," and the same applies for members
of Parliament, too.

Committed as they are to democratic forms, these men are not
blind to what they consider the shortcomings of their nation. They,
like the others, are disturbed by the strength of communal hostility, the narrow concerns of politicians and citizenry alike, and the
tenuous unity of Malaysia. It is therefore inadequate to trace the
penchant for "guided democracy" or administrative paternalism
to colonial socialization or a weakness of vision. In spite of their
democratic views and faith in the future, the future is not the
present. In the Malaysia of today, guided or "tutelary" democracy
appeals because its assumptions about the environment match
much of what these men have observed—the lack of national
loyalty, the absence of much civic-consciousness, widespread illiteracy, and so on. The reality of Malaysia's condition predisposes even
the young, educated administrators to elite rule *in spite of* their
attachment to democratic ideals. Whether one agrees or disagrees
with them, they come to paternal rule via the route of reason, not
out of past prejudice, ignorance, or a lust for power.

11

Reality and Political Beliefs in a New Nation

THE EXISTENTIAL BASE AND CENTRAL BELIEFS

When Western social scientists turned their attention to under-developed nations after World War II, they discovered a host of beliefs and patterns of behavior that seemed quite irrational to them. Political scientists and economists in particular were disheartened by the common failure of Western-inspired institutions to function effectively in the hands of their new owners. The political party, political scientists found, operated quite differently and served functions that its Western counterpart did not; the economic planning group, the economists discovered, either avoided decisions or made them according to criteria that they could not fathom.

Perhaps because of the growing influence of psychoanalysis in the social sciences—especially in anthropology—the explanation for the failure of these institutions was sought in the cultural personality of the Burmese, of the Indians, of the Egyptians, or of whatever peoples were being examined. Since the traditional cultural norms had in every case been subjected to the hammer blows of an imposed Western rule and rapid social change, it was quite plausible to surmise that the elites of new nations were suffering through an identity crisis brought about by this broken pattern of socialization. The political ideology of the elite, in this context, was viewed as an internal dialogue meant to assuage the intrapsychic conflicts of its holder; ideology became a defense mechanism to blame the West for personal failures, to reconstruct a glorious past, and so on. How a personal ideology of this sort might change is never clear—for who is to know when someone suffering from a personality disorder will come to his senses? Realities are unlikely to have any effect on him, since his ideology is constructed as a defense against a painful or threatening reality.

If this study of ideology in a new nation has merit at all, it shows how a person's ideology must in some sense be a reality-serving mechanism rather than a reality-cheating mechanism. A belief which, in the industrialized West, appears to be irrational —appears to misconstrue the existential realities—may well be quite congruent with the environment in a traditional or transitional state. The "pathology," if there is any, is to be sought in the nature of the environment, not in the individual. A man's ideology need never precisely fit his experience; it may change more slowly than the existential base, but it cannot survive long if it consistently distorts essential features of the environment. The Sicilian peasant who immigrates to the United States, for example, gradually realizes that his expectations about interpersonal behavior and about the environment do not give him a reliable picture of reality in his new setting. If he lacks the resources to adjust his ideology to the new environment, then perhaps his children, or his children's children, will make the ideological changes that will equip them for success in their new milieu. This process is not confined to immigrants; it takes place within a nation as its existential base changes, too. Social movements or basic orientations that are no longer congruent with the existential base are likely either to be extinguished or to be transformed so they become more congruent with reality. A society has many realities, of course, and social movements may make implicit assumptions about the environment that substantially match the experience of one sector of the population but not of other sectors. The potential breadth of a social movement is thus in part determined by the degree to which the reality it assumes actually conforms with the experience of the population among which it recruits.[1]

I do not wish by any means to imply that ideology is a mere epiphenomenon—that ideology is a complete and instantaneous product of the environment. If such were the case, the study of ideology would serve no purpose. It is precisely in those instances where the existential base has changed decisively and where past orientations are no longer reliable guides to experience that the

1. It should be mentioned that some beliefs are more directly related to the existential base than others. A belief that community wealth is fixed over time is clearly more amenable to experience than a belief in a supernatural being.

study of ideological transformations is of greatest value. In this instance beliefs conform to a set of circumstances which have largely or entirely disappeared. It would be a serious error, however, to assume that simply because the central beliefs of a people do not "make sense" in the industrialized Western context, they therefore must be explained by resort to pathology. Such beliefs —as strange as they would seem in a setting of abundance and stability—may well seem quite appropriate to an environment of scarcity and instability. The point is simply that beliefs must be evaluated contextually before it can be ascertained to what extent they are reality-cheating and to what extent reality-serving.

Constant-Pie Thinking

Of the basic value orientations that have been discussed, the man-nature orientation is the most significant, since it relates most closely to the environment. Malaysian civil servants have what I have called a constant-pie orientation to nature: they assume a fixed scarcity of desired material goods. The political ramifications of this assumed scarcity are enormous. Much of political and economic life becomes a struggle of one individual, family, group, or nation to enlarge its slice at the expense of other individuals, families, or groups. In the context of a zero-sum environment, concern is focused on the distributive justice of the political system, trust and cooperation are discouraged, and generosity toward other competitors for scarce values becomes an invitation to plunder.

The constant-pie orientation is not the product of individual pathology; it rises rather from a more or less accurate assessment of the limitations of the material environment. Peasant society almost everywhere is characterized by a fixed social product, and even in new nations which, like Malaysia, have experienced substantial economic growth, progress has not been either of the magnitude or the duration that would change basic expectations. The assumption of scarcity as the permanent condition of man is congruent enough with the actual experience of people in the new states to persist as a central orientation. Its origin may lie in the material strictures of traditional society, but it continues to draw sustenance from present conditions.

Social Distrust

The orientation toward human nature of the Malaysian sample is characterized by general social distrust and by the conviction that external control mechanisms are required to restrain man's natural rapaciousness. Both are natural companions of constant-pie thinking; we would hardly anticipate a flowering of social trust in a situation where the gain of one is the plunder of another. The statistical association of misanthropy with constant-pie thinking is a reflection of the underlying Hobbesian qualities of a zero-sum economy.

Pye finds that the Burmese, too, "tend to see each other as individuals seeking personal material advancement or personal political power," but he terms it a "bias in perspective" created by Burmese socialization.[2] Banfield, however, discovers the same pattern among southern Italian peasants[3] (amoral, familism), while Oscar Lewis declares that social distrust and cynicism are typical of the urban poor of London, Paris, Harlem, Mexico City, and Glasgow.[4] In spite of the diverse cultural backgrounds of these peoples, they share an existential base of poverty. Poverty itself involves, for those who experience it, what must seem to be a struggle against others for scarce, fixed resources—a struggle that does not encourage the growth of interpersonal trust or cooperation. The connection between poverty and misanthropy is further confirmed by studies showing that social trust increases with affluence, both across cultures and within a culture over time.[5] Social distrust, though it may have other causes, too, is thus reinforced by a zero-sum economy and weakened by steady economic growth.

The effects of misanthropy on political ideology are considerable. Politicians are expected to exploit every opportunity for personal gain, civic concerns are greeted with suspicion and disbelief, and, above all, the function of government is not to serve

2. Pye, *Politics, Personality, and Nation Building*, p. 202.
3. Banfield, *The Moral Basis of a Backward Society*, passim.
4. Oscar Lewis, "The Culture of Poverty," in Novack and Lekachman, *Development and Society*, pp. 252–61.
5. Cf. last portion of Ch. 6.

men but to control them, to prevent the strong from exploiting the weak by limiting freedom and punishing transgressors. The logic of a belief in man as an asocial self-seeker leads directly to partisanship and to a preference for coercive rather than persuasive strategies. Social distrust, sustained by the rigors of a fixed social product, is what lies behind the failure to create effective and durable groups for common goals in new nations.

Short-Term Goals

Traditional society manages to contain the centrifugal forces of a fixed social product by virtue of its cognitive and normative consensus and its established social control mechanisms. In the new nations, however, these cultural "rules of the game" have been eroded or completely washed away by a flood of social change and new values. The breakdown of stable expectations in this new setting contributes to a heightened apprehension about the future and greater interpersonal suspicion. The environment seems more and more Hobbesian.

Uncertainty and anxiety about the future in a new nation are not the creation of individual or collective fantasy; they are based on an accurate estimate of reality. The businessman adapts to this situation by maintaining high liquidity and investing largely in commercial transactions with a rapid turnover. He may even try to protect himself against the uncertainty of the environment by bribing key government officials. The politician adapts, too: he exploits the rewards of his office while he can and clings tenaciously to the status he has achieved. He learns that loyalty to persons rather than to ideals, while appealing to tradition, too, is likely to promise more security in an uncertain environment. The Burmese may, as Pye says, "prefer not to think too far ahead" because of early training,[6] but it is equally true that long-term strategies require a measure of environmental stability that is absent in most new nations. There is no a priori reason to deny a measure of rationality to the politicians, bureaucrats, and citizens which we are only too willing to grant the businessman.

When transitional man is placed in his environmental context, many of his central orientations acquire a certain realism. In the affluent, stable West, constant-pie thinking, great social distrust

6. Pye, *Politics, Personality, and Nation Building,* p. 204.

(such as amoral familism), and a short-run "exploitationist" time orientation could justifiably be considered examples of deviant pathology, for the environment is fundamentally different. But what is pathology in Great Britain may well constitute, in Malaysia, a successful adaptation to the existential base.[7]

THE EXISTENTIAL BASE AND DEMOCRACY

Democracy, for the new nations, represents both an institutional and an ideological import. Whether it maintains its uncertain purchase on the political cliffs of the new states depends, in part, on the extent to which it is congruent with the central beliefs of the host culture, and in part also, on how deeply democratic beliefs have penetrated—on the firmness with which they have been adopted. On neither of these two closely related points is there much basis for optimism.

The basic value orientations already examined hardly provide a hospitable climate for democratic beliefs. The assumptions that man is narrowly selfish and lacking in restraint, that economic life is a zero-sum game, and that only short-run gains are possible conflict sharply with the long-term cooperative strategies and civic qualities that characterize a democratic style. Moreover, primary socialization promotes both a situational morality and a reliance on authority quite at variance with the stereotypical "democratic personality." Such primary influences could conceivably be counteracted by experiences in school and in voluntary organizations, but in Malaysia, as in most new nations, neither the authority patterns nor the participation style that these structures encourage contributes to a civic culture.

Bereft of both the experiential and characterological support that sustain democratic forms in much of the industrialized West, democracy in the new states must rely on the slender resources of manifest political training and, above all, on the ability of democratic government to satisfy popular desires effectively. The demise of democracy in many new nations has occurred partly be-

7. The same holds true with equal force for "authoritarianism" in many non-Western areas. It may represent deviant pathology in the West, but often in the non-West the environment actually resembles what the pathological authoritarian is supposed to imagine it to be. Someone who is actually being followed may exhibit all the symptoms of paranoia, but he does not need a psychiatrist; he needs a change in reality!

cause during a crisis of effectiveness the system lacked the "capital" of legitimacy that might have enabled it to weather the storm. Since crises of effectiveness are, for obvious reasons, endemic in underdeveloped nations, we can scarcely be sanguine about the democratic potential of the new states.

Like many foreign beliefs, democratic notions have penetrated the minds of the postcolonial Westernized elites in a highly selective fashion. Freedom of speech, for example, seems more firmly embedded than the more subtle, but equally important, cannons of due process. Both beliefs are, however, quite formalistic and tend to crumble when they encounter the existential base and when they conflict with more deeply held values. They have great range but little weight; they are quickly abandoned when they appear to endanger national stability and unity. Thus, not only do Malaysian elites less often support democratic norms in the abstract than do Americans, but Malaysians are also more willing to cast them overboard when the ship founders.

An interpretation of the weakness of democratic beliefs in new nations must again refer to the existential base. Crises of unity and stability are vastly more compelling to the elites of Malaysia than they might seem to Western elites. Malaysians live constantly in the shadow of communal tension and have experienced, in their lifetime, the Japanese occupation, an internal communist insurrection, and a war with Indonesia. If they are more prone to deprecate their people's ability to make wise, democratic choices, it is important to remember that the electorate they are evaluating is in fact less literate and more bound by primordial loyalties than its Western counterpart.

Quite apart from the fact that the preference for democracy is weaker in new nations than in the West, there is every reason for the elites in new states to be discouraged—even cynical—about the prospect for democracy. First, the manner in which they learned about democracy under colonialism has produced an overidealization of the Western model that inclines them to cynicism when they measure their nation's performance against it. This cognitive distortion is, however, by no means the only basis for their disappointment. Their assumptions about human nature and the environment, both of which derive from an existential base, do not lead them to expect either the political tolerance or the cooperation that would help sustain a democratic state. Finally, they have reason to be disappointed in the performance of democracy as they have experienced it. The race for spoils, the illiteracy and narrow loyalties of the masses, and the tensions and social distrust that often accompany rapid change have in fact been serious obstacles to the growth of a civic culture in the new states. The Westernized elites in these areas are thus disappointed over the very real handicaps that popular government faces among their people. Democracy, like any other form of government, contains implicit assumptions about the environment—assumptions which in the new nations, at least, are not congruent with the existential base.

THE EXISTENTIAL BASE AND PATERNALISTIC ELITE RULE

In contrast to the weak resources for democracy, the resources for firm rule by a benevolent elite are considerably more impressive. Paternalistic elite rule is quite consonant with the pattern of both colonial and traditional regimes. Each limits popular participation and rejects demands while accepting popular entreaties; each is guided by an elite that believes it rules by virtue of its superior qualifications; and each considers the populace subjects rather than citizens—what the people want is less central than what the elite knows is best for them. It was the foreignness of colonial rule more than its style that aroused the wrath of the colonized people.

Postcolonial experience has, if anything, enhanced the attractiveness of strong, paternalistic rule. The Westernized elite holds a virtual monopoly on the education, technical skills, and experience necessary to run a modern state. Furthermore, the traditional masses for the most part look to the Westernized elites with their knowledge and organizational skills for leadership. It is not a question of the educated elites usurping the role of traditional leaders; popular acceptance of, and deference to, the Westernized elites—particularly civil servants—is the rule rather than the exception.

By far the most important basis for strong, elitist rule in new nations, however, is the painful realization that full popular rule might tear the nation apart. In Malaysia, racial antagonisms have

more than once threatened the nation's existence. Should the
primordial loyalties and traditional preferences of the masses become politicized in advance of any strong identification with the
national community, there is every reason to believe that national
unity would perish in the ensuing violence. To say that the elites
of the new states are not democrats is in part true, but as an
explanation of why they incline to nondemocratic solutions, it
fails to do justice to their fundamental dilemma. The fact is that
paternalistic, elite rule—or tutelary democracy—makes implicit
assumptions about the environment that are roughly congruent
with reality in new nations, while the implicit assumptions behind liberal democracy simply do not match these realities.

The reader who is familiar with Malaysia will no doubt feel
that I have failed to do justice to many of the historical and
contemporary factors that affect political ideology in that nation.
This is a shortcoming to which I readily confess. In this study,
I have purposely avoided Malaysia's uniqueness and sought, instead, to explore that portion of elite political ideology that Malaysia might share with other new nations. This special focus of
attention has necessitated an emphasis on the common effects of
alien Western rule, of poverty, of traditional culture, and of rapid
social change as experienced by the new states. In the process,
Malaysia's unique brand of multiracial politics, her economic
successes under gifted and wise political leadership, and her
struggle to make liberal democracy work have all been short-
changed—unfortunately, but unavoidably.

Malaysia's democratic system has been sorely tested in the
ten years since her independence. In spite of the accretion of
special emergency powers by the central government, she has
managed to remain a democracy amidst the inevitable Caesarist
temptations, and a large measure of credit must be given to her
experienced, restrained, and talented elite.

This elite, to speak for once of Malaysia's peculiarities, has
ironically profited from the very situation that many observers
imagined would surely cause its collapse. I am referring to the
more or less delicate balance of power between the Malays and
the Chinese. As with the Lebanese balance between Muslims and
Christians—glossing over the subdivisions—or perhaps even the

Swiss division between French Catholicism and German Protestantism, the Malaysian parity has meant that neither the Malays nor the Chinese can achieve utter dominance over the other community. The Swiss example is particularly instructive, since communal compromise was hammered out with France and Germany waiting in the wings; in Malaysia the modus vivendi is occurring in the shadow of Chinese and Indonesian imperial ambitions. Had the racial balance in Malaysia been more lopsided, its history might have taken quite a different turn; as it is, cooperation is less terrible to contemplate than its alternatives. Although this compromise is not without its strains—and it could collapse if the Malays, who have a slight power edge, should ultimately conclude that the costs of sharing power are greater than the risks of imposing total domination—it has now endured over a ten year period. For the time being, then, democracy is the institutional framework that assures each community that its rights and freedoms will not be abrogated by the other. In this context, dictatorship has virtually come to be perceived as the hegemony of one racial group over the other, and democracy has come to mean an uneasy balance between Malays and non-Malays.

The mere persistence of a democratic form of government is of some importance here, too. For over a decade now Malaysia has had a democratic system of rule, and the longer it lasts, the more problems it successfully overcomes, the more practice its political elite gains in operating democratic institutions, the greater the chances are that it will become a durable political framework. Unlike Ceylon, however, Malaysia has not yet peacefully exchanged one political elite for another through the electoral process, and it is difficult to speak too optimistically until this has occurred. Endowed as it is with a comparatively large stratum of educated, Westernized personnel, both within the government and outside, Malaysia's chances of remaining a democracy are perhaps greater than most new nations.

Another factor of equal or greater importance has contributed to the tenure of democracy in Malaysia. In a word, its government has proved *effective*. First, it has contained the fissiparous tendencies of a perceived constant-pie environment in much the same way traditional regimes contained them. The Alliance government has alternately striven to soften the demands of the communities it represents and to grant what it considers the essential core demands of each. The coalition has been largely successful in imposing a "group focused image of change," of which I spoke earlier, by convincing each contending group that the others would not be allowed to advance at its expense. To the extent that the Malaysian government can continue to persuade its people that it is effectively managing the struggle for the constant pie, it will help ensure its own survival.

The equilibrium that has been achieved is a tenuous one. Social distrust and a constant-pie orientation, compounded by the endemic uncertainties of a transitional society, place the entire structure in constant jeopardy. If persuasive strategies have been more effective in Malaysia than in other new nations, much of the credit is due to the decade of steady economic growth which more or less favorable world prices for rubber and tin have made possible.[8] Thus, in spite of the centrifugal potential of constant-pie thinking, economic expansion has helped create the impression that the government has been distributing the slices equitably. An economic setback or a period of stagnation would end this successful game abruptly and force an increasing reliance on sheer strength and coercion. The painfulness of the distribution crisis would then make peaceful adjustment all but impossible.

For as long as the constant-pie orientation dominates the social landscape of transitional societies, the use of force to contain the incivism that it promotes will prove difficult to resist. This dilemma is inescapable in the short run. Over time, however, these nations must place their faith in a gradually expanding economy, where the struggle for scarce values evolves from a zero-sum battle into a variable-sum game, where the experience of economic growth creates the expectation of progress, where trust and limited generosity can replace suspicion and opportunism, and where cooperation is a surer road to advancement than plunder.

This is the nature of the journey the Malaysian people have so successfully begun.

8. See Ness, *Bureaucracy and Rural Development in Malaysia,* pp. 62–69, 223.

Appendixes

Appendix A
Interview Guide

The following is a truncated version of the interview guide used to structure conversations with the sample of seventeen Malaysian civil servants. Roughly one-half of the first section concerning the respondent's administrative life is borrowed from Murroe Berger's study, *Bureaucracy and Society in Modern Egypt* (Princeton, Princeton University Press, 1957). The remainder of the first section was developed on the basis of pilot interviews in the field. Parts two through five of the interview guide were borrowed, with extensive modifications where appropriate, from Robert E. Lane's questions used in research for *Political Ideology* (Glencoe, The Free Press, 1962).

PART ONE

1. Title of post.
   Ministry.
   Grade.
   Department.
2. Year of birth and place of birth.
3. Education through to the university.
4. What is the mission and function of the ministry in which you are employed?
5. What part does your post play in realizing the aims of the ministry?
6. What civil service positions have you held prior to your present post? Starting from the most recent and going back to the beginning, which did you like most and why? Which did you like least and why?
7. How old were you when you first thought of entering the civil service?
8. How did you first obtain your initial civil service job?
9. How did you first learn about the first civil service post you obtained?
10. Why did you prefer the civil service to a nongovernment job?
11. Did you hold any jobs before coming to the civil service? What were they? Did you like them?
12. Have you ever thought that you might leave the civil service entirely for some reason?
13. How would you describe the ideal civil servant? What qualities

should he have? What sort of person should he be? (Probe for specific qualities.)

14. What do you like about government work?
15. What do you dislike about government service?
16. Do you read the newspapers regularly? Which ones?
    a. Which section of the newspaper do you read most often and spend most time on: the news, feature articles, sports?
    b. When you read the news, would you say you skim the headlines, read part way through the main news stories, or read all the main news stories all the way through?
    c. What kind of news interests you most? (Probe.)
    d. Do you have a television? If so, do you watch often? What are your favorite programs and why?
17. What magazines do you read more or less often? Can you recall an article that interested you recently in a magazine?
18. Imagine the following situation: A department head in the civil service asks one of his staff members, an economist, to prepare a memorandum in support of a certain policy which has been followed for some time. In studying the matter the economist finds that he can defend this policy only if he presents arguments that differ with what is generally accepted by most economists in and outside of government.
    a. Can the department head expect this civil servant to prepare such a memorandum?
    b. What do you think this civil servant ought to do in view of his obligation to the government and his obligation as a professional economist? Should he prepare the report or should he refuse to prepare it?
    c. Why do you think so?
    d. What will other economists think when they find out he has prepared such a report for his boss?
19. Do you think civil servants should have their own protective society as doctors, lawyers, and engineers have? Why do you think so?
20. Arrange the following reasons people have for thinking highly of a certain post or occupation in what you think to be their order of importance:
    a. Good salary and working conditions.
    b. Skill required to do the job.
    c. Opportunity to meet important people.
    d. Opportunity to serve the public.
    e. Opportunity to serve the nation.
21. Imagine the following situation: A civil servant is assigned to

factory inspection; his duty is to ensure that factories conform to safety laws. In one factory he sees a floor that looks as if it might collapse under the weight of a large machine. According to usual procedure, he telephones his superior but finds that his superior is away on political business and will not return that day. The inspector examines the floor again and is not certain that it will hold up for more than a few hours. He tells the factory owner about his fear. But the owner tells him that there is no basis for such fear since the chief inspector approved the factory only two weeks ago in the same condition. The owner shows him the certificate of approval, but the inspector is still doubtful and, taking the initiative, he orders the factory closed.

   a. Do you think the factory inspector acted properly in closing the factory? Why?

   b. Do you think the inspector's superior *should* discipline him?

   c. Do you think the inspector's superior *will* discipline him?

   d. Suppose they find out the next day that the inspector was wrong and there is nothing wrong with the factory floor.

22. When a new government takes office after an election, do you think it should be able to dismiss higher civil servants and replace them with its followers? If not, how can the loyalty of the civil service to the new government's program be ensured?

23. If you were asked to advise an intelligent young man on his career, what sort of career would you advise him to follow? (Probe for views for or against the civil service.)

24. If a young man wants to become a civil servant, what would be the best way for him to do so?

25. Does your post place you in much personal contact with the public?

26. In order to get an idea now of your daily routine, consider the last three persons, not in the civil service, who came to see you on business. Beginning with the most recent, what was the person's problem, or what was the reason for which he had to consult you? How did he learn you were the person to see? How did you dispose of his case?

   a. Is this fairly typical of your daily routine? or

   b. What is your usual daily routine?

27. Consider the following list of posts and occupations and rate them as the general public would, placing the number 1 beside the occupation the general public thinks most highly of, number 2 for the next, and so on.

   a. Factory worker   c. Doctor

   b. Small merchant   d. Government clerk

    e. Landowner   h. Factory owner

    f. Bank director   i. Peasant

    g. Lawyer   j. Government bureau chief

28. Do you think the general public takes enough interest in the activities of government?

    a. Why do you think so?

    b. What should the general public do to show a proper interest in the activities of the government?

    c. Do you think the civil service would be improved if the general public took more interest?

29. What do you think the man in the street thinks of civil servants? (Allow for autonomous response.)

    a. Do you think the man in the street has enough appreciation of the job the civil servant does? If not, why not?

    b. Does the man in the street *respect* civil servants? Why?

    c. Does the man in the street *fear* civil servants? Why?

30. Does the man in the street consider the civil servant difficult to approach or easy to approach? Why is that so?

31. Imagine the following situation: A civil servant is officially informed that he is to be transferred from Kuala Lumpur to a new post in another state. He has no objection to service in another state but feels he must be near his aged parents, who cannot be moved away from Kuala Lumpur, where they receive medical treatment. He therefore goes to the permanent secretary in the ministry, who is a close friend of his, and asks the permanent secretary to keep him in Kuala Lumpur.

    a. Can this civil servant expect the permanent secretary to keep him in Kuala Lumpur?

    b. What should the permanent secretary do?

    c. If the civil servant's request were refused, and he thought the situation serious enough, would he be justified in enlisting the support of a friend or relative who knew the permanent secretary?

32. What are the most important ways in which the civil service serves the nation? (Probe to see if development or legal functions considered more important.)

33. Which group is more important to national development, the politicians or civil servants? Why is that so?

34. When members of the public come to your department to ask for information or to make a request:

    a. Do they come as individuals or do they come on behalf of organized groups?

b. What do those who come on behalf of groups usually want?

c. Do people usually come alone or in groups of two or three? Why is that, do you suppose?

d. What do these people do if you are not able to help them? (Probe for anger, recourse to another official, threats, and so on.)

35. Do you think that those who come on behalf of an organization are really interested in the organization or in their own interests?

36. Do you find that members of the public who come to a government office to make inquiries or requests generally know what they are talking about, or must you usually tell them even the simplest things which they should already know?

a. Are they generally capable of understanding government regulations?

b. Are they generally capable of understanding your problems? If not, why do you suppose that is?

37. How can citizens play a role in influencing important decisions which affect them when such decisions are highly technical and complicated and therefore very hard for anyone but the experts to understand?

38. How easy or difficult is it for civil servants to persuade farmers to adopt a new seed which is better than the kind they have been using? Why is that so?

a. What is the best way of getting them to change?

b. Do most civil servants go about it this way?

39. What are the reasons why some people get ahead in their jobs and others do not? (Probe deeply.)

From the following list of some possible reasons why people get ahead, choose those factors you think are most important and explain why.

a. Ambition

b. A stroke of good luck

c. Efficiency

d. Honesty and high principles

e. Intelligence

f. Ability to mix easily

40. How difficult is it for young civil servants to get ahead these days as compared with the past? Why is that so? How do they feel about that?

41. Are some civil servants too much interested in promotion only?

a. Are there too many like this?

b. How can you tell they are mostly interested in promotion?

42. Since in any organization there are occasionally arguments, can you recall the last one and what was it about?

a. How many people were involved?

b. How angry did people get? How could you tell?

    c. Who finally won the argument? Why?

    d. Are there any bad feelings left over from the argument?

43. At work, how do people usually get along with one another?

    a. Are there some who do not get along very well with others? If so, why is that so?

    b. Is it possible to make friends with two people who are not on good terms with one another? If not, why not?

44. Do some superiors treat their subordinates too severely?

    a. How is that? Why do they do it?

    b. How should authority best be exercised?

    c. Is it usually exercised in this way?

45. Can you remember what you did on the last day that you felt you accomplished more work than usual? (Probe for appointments, decisions, reports, and so on.)

46. Do you feel that your job is quite a heavy load for one man to handle alone? If so, why is that?

    a. Would any special training have eased the load?

    b. Do you feel that you have too much routine work and not enough time to carry through new ideas? If so, what new ideas do you have in mind?

47. What do the people you work with like to talk about together when they are not talking about work?

    a. Who joins these discussions?

    b. Do superiors and subordinates often talk together like this?

48. What do you do when you go on leave or a long vacation? (Probe.) Have you thought about what you will do and where you will live when you retire? (Probe.)

49. How are the important decisions made in your office?

    a. Mostly by the highest official?

    b. Do you discuss decisions before making them with others?

    c. Who is part of this discussion?

50. Why is there sometimes corruption in the civil service of other countries? (Probe to find out whether it is the result of bad people or of a bad situation.)

PART TWO: LIFE HISTORY

I. *Chronology*

    A. Parents and grandparents: place of birth, personalities, styles of life, occupations, respondent's feelings in describing them.
       Would you say that you have been able to get farther in life than your father?

B. Infancy and preschool years: punishments, victories over others, deaths, fights, sibling rivalry, parental attitudes.

C. Grammar school years (5–12)

Home life, learning experiences, attitudes toward school, peers, teachers, subjects, playground, discipline, bitter memories, happy events, mobility, and so on.

D. Junior high and high school years (12–17)

1. Neighborhood: gangs, sports, parties, bullies, feelings of acceptance or rejection, scrapes with police, sex experiences, and so on.

2. School: same as above.

3. Home: relations with parents in adolescence, siblings, nature of conflicts, feelings of parental approval or disapproval, development of ambitions, career goals, parental attitudes toward girls, religious influences, and so on.

E. College years—if any, same as above.

F. Adult Life

1. Social life: friends and acquaintances, duration of friendships, parties, visits, hangouts, dating, courting, marriage.

2. Avocations: hobbies, movies, television programs, sports, reading pattern.

3. Present family:
   a. Wife: interests, personality, compatibility, subordination, love of husband, and so on.
   b. Children: number, attitude toward, ideas of rearing, and so on.

II. *Focused Discussion*

A. Sociological aspects of family

1. Parents' national antecedents, occupations, education, religion.

2. Standard of living: sense of want, cars, house, standard of living of neighbors, and so on.

3. Inter-group relations: friends of parents, parents' organizational memberships, parents' recreational patterns, and so on.

B. Personal aspects of family

1. Images of parents
   a. What sort of person was your father; your mother?
   b. What things do you admire most in your father; in your mother?

    c. Assuming that people are not perfect, what human frailties did your father and mother have?

    d. Which parent do you take after? Which one do you like the most? Which one were you most influenced by?

2. Power relations between father and mother

    a. How did your parents get along together?

    b. In what ways were your parents most alike? Most different?

    c. Who usually made the decisions in your family?

    d. Did any disagreements ever arise in your family that you can recall?

3. Siblings

    a. Could you tell me a little more about your brothers and sisters?

    b. How did you get along together?

    c. Who was your favorite brother? Your favorite sister? What did you like about him? About her? What did he mean to you? What did she mean to you?

    d. Could you tell me a little more about the quarrels you had with your brothers and sisters?

4. Image of self as child

    a. Would you say a little more about what you were like as a child?

    b. What things about your childhood do you remember with most pleasure?

    c. What things did you worry about most as a child?

    d. Since almost everybody has had some recurrent bad dreams as a child, what kind of bad dreams did you have?

    e. What were your chief ambitions as a child? Do you think your parents approved?

5. Relations with parents

    a. Which parent did you feel closer to when you were, say, six? When you were in high school? Now?

    b. What were the main satisfactions in your relations with your father? With your mother?

    c. Which parent exercised the discipline in your family? If they were to get angry, which one would you fear most?

    d. What kind of discipline did your parents use?

    e. What kinds of things did they discipline you for mainly?

6. What would you say your major problems were as a child? And as an adolescent?

7. If you had your school years to live over again, what would you change?
8. Health and physique
   a. What did you do when you had a bad cold?
   b. Were you well as a child?
9. Youthful rebellion
   a. When they are teen-agers many sons rebel in small ways against their parents. Did you experience any of these feelings? How? In what way? What was your parents' reaction?

C. Major events
   1. Could you tell me if any of the following events in any way affected your thinking:
      a. The Depression: what did it mean for your family? Who was responsible?
      b. World War II and the Japanese Occupation: what do you remember?
      c. The nationalist movement and independence.
      d. The Emergency.

D. Money and income
   1. What is the most important thing money can give a person?
   2. Is it easy for you to save money, or difficult? Do you have enough to make ends meet or not?
   3. Some people like to take chances and have a "win a lot, lose a lot" attitude; then other people are more cautious about money. What is your attitude about this?
   4. Do you think that people who are very rich are happier than people who are just average? Why is that?
   5. What do you think is the best way to teach a child to handle money?
   6. What do you miss most that your present income does not allow?

PART THREE: PERSONAL QUALITIES

I. *Social Relations*
   A. How important are friends in a person's life? How do you mean?
   B. What attracts you in a friend? Give an example.
   C. How do you choose friends? For example?
   D. What do you enjoy doing with your friends?
   E. Are you the sort of person who has a few close friends or do

you tend to have a lot of friends? Which do you think is better?

F. What are the occupations of your best friends outside of work? What do you do together? How did you meet?

G. Think back to the last time you were out in the evening and had a good time. What was it that made it a good time for you?

H. If your job made it necessary for you and your family to move to some other city, how would you feel about leaving your friends here? Whom would you miss most? Why is that?

I. In a group of friends would you describe yourself as "the life of the party," a "good listener," or what?

J. What do you find offensive, annoying, or objectionable in other people?

K. Do you have any close friends of other races? If so, how did you meet them? What sorts of things do you usually talk about?

II. *Self-Image*

A. How would you describe yourself to someone who did not know you at all the way you really are, both your good and bad points? (Cover skills, intelligence, knowledge, temperament, exceptionality, task orientation, orientation to others, leadership, ability to follow, weak-strong dimension, anxiety.)

III. *Temperament in Concrete Situations*

A. When you go to a sporting event do you get excited, do you get right in there playing the game in your imagination, or do you remain pretty calm? (Emotionality.)

B. Can you remember the last time you lost your temper? What happened? Impatience? Irritability? Did you have tantrums as a child? (Anger.)

C. Are there any recent events which have made you feel very unhappy and like crying? What were they? (Does he turn to other people, to action, or to solitude when unhappy?) (Sorrow.)

D. What kinds of things do you worry about? For example? Do you lie awake at night worrying? Do you worry about things that are not likely to happen? (Anxiety.)

E. Some people think they can plan their lives and aim for

long-range goals, such as what they will be doing ten years from now. Others say, "whatever will be, will be," and they take things as they come. What do you think of this? (Ego strength, external dimension.)

F. Have you ever made any long-range plans either for yourself or for others? How did this work out?

IV. *Values*

A. What would you say have been the most important lessons of life for you?
B. What makes people happy?
C. What are the things you believe in most, or think the most important?
D. What is the main point of life? Why are we here?
E. Personal values: when boys are growing up they often have rather farfetched ambitions and ideas about what they are going to do with life. Could you remember what your ideas were of that sort when you were, say, 18 or 20?
   1. How did things work out? Did events lead you to change your ideas?
   2. What are your main ambitions now?
   3. How hopeful are you about them?
   4. What kind of people would you like your children to be when they grow up?
F. Social values: the ideal society
   1. What do you think the perfect community would be like?
   2. How would people behave?
   3. What would people do for a living? Would they have to work?
   4. What kind of government would there be, if any?
   5. What kinds of things that you have to do now would you not have to do in an ideal society?
   6. Are we getting closer to this ideal society? In what ways?

V. *Attitudes toward Leadership—General*

A. Are there any political leaders either living or dead whom you especially like? Who are they? Why do you like them? Are there any others?
B. Are there any political leaders either living or dead whom you especially dislike? Who are they? Why do you dislike them?

C. What might make a person want to run for political office?
D. How would you describe most politicians? What about their skills, motives, backgrounds, intelligence?
E. What would you say makes a man a politician?
F. Would you have more respect for a man if he were the mayor of a big city, the chancellor of a university, or the head of a large industry? Why?
G. Let us talk for a moment about two political leaders we all have some idea about: Nehru and Churchill. What do you think of Nehru?
   1. Do you think he was sincerely interested in people like you?
   2. Was he the sort of person you would have felt at ease with if you had to spend some time with him?
   3. What sort of man was he? What kind of personality did he have?
   4. What was his influence on his country? What achievements?
   5. What kind of politician was he? Why?
   6. What kind of war leader was he?
   (The same questions for Churchill.)

VI. *Group Memberships and Identifications*

Many people belong to some voluntary organizations. Do you belong to any? Which ones? (Probe for religious, professional, neighborhood, social, sports, old boys' association, and so on.)
   1. Could you tell me a little about what you do in these groups?
   2. What do you like most about these organizations?
   3. What do you feel you have in common with other members of these groups?
   4. Do you think some voluntary groups should play a role in election campaigns? Which groups? Why? Do you pay attention to what groups think in an electoral campaign or do you not pay any attention to them?

VII. *Religion*

A. What does your religion mean to you?
B. How important is it to you in your daily living? Do you think about it much? How about prayer?

    C. Does religion help a person stay honest and on the right track, or doesn't it make any difference?

    D. How do your religious beliefs differ from those of your parents?

    E. Do you feel differently about people who belong to different religions? How so?

    F. How active are you in your religion?

    G. Do you think that people should all take their religion seriously, no matter what religion it is? I mean, should they go to the temple or church or mosque regularly?

    H. What role do you think religion should play in political life, if any? (Probe general principles, moralism, selection of leaders.)

    I. Is there any conflict between science and religion?

VIII. *Origins*

    Do you think it sometimes helps to understand others when you know what group they belong to? Is it important whether they are Chinese, Malay, Indian, or whatever? Why is that?

PART FOUR: ATTITUDES TOWARD SOCIAL DIVISIONS

  I. *Social Class*

    A. Sometimes one hears the term "social class" as in "middle class" or "working class." What do you think people mean by that term?

    B. What class would you say you belong to?

    C. Do you think it is hard to go from one social class to another?

    D. How would you describe the people who belong to your own social class? To others?

    E. How important do you think social classes are in Malaysia today?

  II. *Age*

    A. Do you think there are any important differences in the way younger voters think as compared to older voters? How do you mean?

      1. Are younger (older) voters more liberal or more conservative?

      2. Which group is more judicious in temperament?

      3. Do you think much about whether people are older or younger than you? Do others?

      4. Are most of your friends your own age, younger, or older?

III. *Sex*

What is the difference in the way men and women look at politics? Do you think that women have somewhat different points of view, or do they simply follow their husbands or fathers?

IV. *Urban-Rural*

What are the differences, if any, between the people who live in rural areas and in kampongs and those who live in the city? Do you think these different groups of people have different ways of looking at public affairs? How so? In what ways? (Probe for differences in need for government services; differences in temperament or personal qualities; conflict in interests; whether the respondent looks upon himself as a city man; which is more important in politics, urban or rural.)

PART FIVE: ATTITUDES TOWARD POLITICS

I. *Roles*

A. Citizen: What would an ideal citizen in a democracy be like? Regardless of whether there is such an ideal person or not, what kinds of things would he do? What kinds of attitudes toward politics would he have? How close do most people come to this ideal?

B. Party man: What are your ideas about what a good party man would be like? What kinds of things would he do? What kinds of attitudes would he have? How close do most party members come to this ideal?

C. Nationalist: What is the ideal nationalist? What kinds of things would he do? What kinds of attitudes would he have? How close do most people come to this ideal?

D. Member of Parliament: How would you describe an ideal member of Parliament? What qualities do you think he would have? How would he behave? How close do most members of Parliament come to this ideal?

II. *Democracy*

A. What is your understanding of democracy?

B. What are the advantages of democracy as compared with some other system?

C. What would happen to you if you lost your democracy?

D. What kinds of things would you consider undemocratic? Why?

E. Do you think that sometimes in a war crisis there is need for a temporary dictatorship?

F. Do you think that sometimes democracy creates confusion and prevents important things from getting done? What things?

G. Are the voluntary organizations to which you belong democratically run? How do you mean?

H. In general, do you think that the people or the elected leaders are more likely to know what is best for the country? Why?

I. Democracy, according to some people, means that everyone, no matter how ignorant or careless, should have an equal vote. Do you agree with that?

J. Some people say that in a democracy most people like to vote for the ordinary man rather than the person with greater ability than themselves. How do you feel about this?

K. Do you think that sometimes the government must force people to do things against their will? What? Why?

L. What do you suppose people mean when they say "a government of laws and not of men?"

M. The future of democracy in the world is generally bright, isn't it? How about Malaysia?

III. *Equality*

A. What is your understanding of the phrase, "all men are created equal?"

B. In your own personal life are there some people whom you regard as not really equal to you? How?

C. How would you feel if everyone received the same income, whatever his job was?

D. Do you think generally people would not work so hard under these conditions, or would it not matter?

IV. *Freedom*

A. What does the word "freedom" make you think of?

B. Some people think there should be more freedom, others think there should be less. What do you think? What kinds of freedom?

C. What are the dangers of too much freedom? Too little? What happens when people feel too free?

D. Do you sometimes feel that listening to all the different points of view on a subject is too confusing and that you would like to hear just one point of view from someone who knows? For example?

E. Do you think there is any special way of bringing up children in a democracy? How?

F. Are there any subjects which you think would be better discussed privately instead of in the newspapers and on the radio where anyone can see and hear them? What kinds of subjects?

G. Can freedom of speech go too far? How?

V. *Government*

A. Would you say that you are more interested in international affairs, national affairs, or local affairs? Why?

B. Which part of the government is the most important: Parliament, the courts, or the civil service? Why?

C. Do you think there is any difference between those who work for the government compared with those who work for a large business organization? Why is that?

D. How would you describe the job of a member of Parliament?

E. How would you describe the prime minister's job?

VI. *Interest and Involvement*

A. Would you say that you were very much interested in following the last general election campaign? What part of the campaign most interested you? Why?

B. Why do most of the people go to the polls and vote? How would you describe them? What about nonvoters? How would you describe them?

C. How did you feel the last time you voted? What thoughts went through your mind as you stepped up to vote? Did you feel your vote made much difference?

D. Do you think a person should go about trying to convince his friends to vote the way he thinks right, or should he be more silent about this and let others make up their minds by themselves?

E. If you had the time for it, would you enjoy a political career? Why? Why not?

F. If there were some issue in an election which you felt was very important—and you were not a civil servant—would you go out and work for what you thought was right on that issue, or would you think it was better to leave this up to the political experts?

VII. *Environment and Discussion Style*

    A. Do you find it difficult or unpleasant to have a political discussion with someone who disagrees with you? Why?

    B. Do you like to discuss national political events with your friends outside of work? And at work?

    C. When a topic or discussion in a group turns to subjects such as an election or something that happened in Parliament, how do you feel?

    D. Would you say that in your experience it is more useful to have a person in a political discussion who jokes and keeps things from getting too serious, or to have a person who knows a lot about the subject and can give the answers? Why is that?

    E. It is sometimes said that it is useful to have someone in a discussion who tends to criticize other people's ideas because it makes for a better discussion and better answers. Other people say that this kind of person is just a nuisance and keeps things from getting decided. How do you feel about this?

    F. Would you rather be respected for your independent opinions or for your ability to get along with people well?

    G. When a person changes his mind after a political discussion, do you think this is likely to mean that he does not have any principles or that he has principles but is willing to be persuaded by a better argument?

    H. Do you think that most groups tend to be hard on a person who does not agree with the group on something like politics, or do you think it does not matter in most groups? What examples? Why?

    I. If you had your way, would most of the people you know have the same political opinions as you?

    J. What is the good of political discussion among friends, anyway?

VIII. *Political Information*

    A. Does the ruler who is chosen to be the Yang di-Pertuan Agong [king] continue to rule in the state from which he comes?

    B. How many members of the Dewan Negara [senate] are there? How are they chosen?

    C. Can you describe the way Kuala Lumpur is governed?

D. Could you give me the rough totals of party representation in Parliament presently?

IX. *Current Events*

A. Do you remember some of the things Parliament did last session?

B. What has the *Tenku* (Abdul Rahman, the prime minister) been doing recently?

C. Can you recall what has been going on at the United Nations Organization recently?

D. Has anything your state government done recently caught your attention?

X. *Persons*

Could you tell me the names of some of these persons?
1. The member of Parliament from your district?
2. His opponents during the last election?
3. The head of West Germany?
4. Malaysia's ambassador to the United Nations and to the United States?

XI. *The Ropes*

If you wanted to get something done in your city—such as having a traffic light installed at a dangerous intersection—how would you go about it? How do most people go about it?

XII. *General Focus of Attention*

What do you think are the major problems in Malaysia today? What should the government do about them? What should ordinary citizens do about them? Who is to blame for this situation? Which of these problems is the most important?

XIII. *Areas of Emotional Involvement*

A. Has there been anything in the news in the last two years which made you really mad? (For each event probe with: Why did it make you mad? Was it anybody's fault? Did you do anything about it at the time? Do you think anything could have been done about it? Anything else?)

B. Has there been anything in the news in the past two years which gave you a great deal of satisfaction? (For each event probe with: Why is that? How did it happen? Who should get the credit?)

XIV. *Broad Orientation*

    A. What do you think causes wars? Will there be any more wars?

    B. What do you think causes poverty? Will there always be poverty in this country?

XV. *Flexibility*

Do you often change your opinions on national or international questions, or don't you change your opinions very easily? If you do change your opinions, what is the cause, usually?

XVI. *Parties*

    A. What is the purpose of a political party in your mind?

    B. In general, do you think political parties are good or bad things?

    C. Do you think that elections give political leaders a pretty good idea what the people want to have done by the government, or do you think that elections are too vague to tell the political leaders anything the people want? (How do you think the political leaders decide what to do?)

    D. If there were an election in your city and you did not happen to know anything about the issues, to whom would you most likely go for advice?

    E. Do you feel strongly that all citizens should belong to a political party and be loyal to it? Why? Why not?

Appendix B
Attitudinal Measures

Part One: Scales Administered to Higher Civil Servants
Who Were also Intensively Interviewed.

I. Authoritarianism: ten items (five reversed) from "F" Scale used by Argus Campbell, Philip E. Converse, Warren E. Miller, and Donald E. Stokes in *The American Voter* (New York, Wiley, 1960). On each item the respondents were asked to check one of the following:

—Agree a lot   —Disagree a little

—Agree a little   —Disagree a lot

A. The artist and the professor are probably more important to society than the businessman and the manufacturer.

B. The findings of science may someday show that many of our most deeply-held beliefs are wrong.

C. Human nature being what it is, there must always be war and conflict.

D. People ought to pay more attention to new ideas, even if they seem to go against the *accepted* way of life. ("*American* way of life" in original.)

E. What young people need most of all is strict discipline by their parents.

F. Most people who don't get ahead just don't have enough will power.

G. It is highly unlikely that astrology will ever be able to explain anything.

H. Sex criminals deserve more than prison; they should be whipped in public or worse.

I. An urge to jump from high places is probably the result of unhappy experiences rather than something inborn.

J. Bosses should say just what is to be done and exactly how to do it if they expect us to do a good job.

II. Faith-in-people: five items, from Morris Rosenberg, "Misanthropy and Political Ideology," *American Sociological Review*, *21* (1956), 690–95.

A. Some people say that most people can be trusted. Others say you can't be too careful in your dealings with people. How do you feel about it?

—Most people can be   —You can't be too careful in
   trusted   your dealings with people

B. Would you say that most people are more inclined to help others or more inclined to look out for themselves?

—Inclined to help   —Inclined to look out for them-
   others   selves

C. If you don't watch yourself, people will take advantage of you.

—Agree   —Disagree

D. No one is going to care much what happens to you, when you get right down to it.

—Agree   —Disagree

E. Human nature is fundamentally cooperative.

—Agree   —Disagree

III. Social and neurotic anxiety: twenty-four items adapted for Robert Lane by David Sears from an unpublished scale developed by Seymour B. Sarason and Irving L. Janis.
Social anxiety:

A. How nervous or afraid are you when you have to talk in front of a group of several people?

—Very nervous   —Hardly nervous at all
—A little nervous   —Not nervous at all

B. When you are doing a job, how much does the fear that you might not be doing too well keep you from doing your best?

—It never does   —It often does a little
—It sometimes does a   —It often does a great
   little   deal

C. In comparison with other men your age, how much do you worry when your boss or superior tells you to come to see him without telling you why he wants to see you?

—I worry a great deal   —I get a little worried
—I get quite worried   —I don't worry at all

D. How much do you worry about how well you get along with people?

—I worry about it   —I worry about it a
   quite a lot   little
—I worry about it   —I worry about it
   quite a bit   hardly at all

E. How much do you worry about the job you hope to have next?

—A lot   —A little
—A good deal   —Not at all

F. When you have been in a situation in which you have done poorly, or felt embarrassed, or made some mistake, how much do you keep on worrying about it?

—I worry about it   —I forget about it
   for a long time   pretty quickly
—I worry about it   —I forget about it
   for a short time   right away

Neurotic anxiety:

A. How afraid are you when you hear thunder or see lightning?

—Never feel afraid   —Often afraid
—Sometimes a little   —Always afraid
   afraid

B. When you go to a dentist, how much do you find yourself worrying about the pain you will feel?

—Always worry   —Sometimes a little worried
—Often worry   —Do not worry at all

C. How often do you have trouble going to sleep because you are worrying about something that has happened to you or some thought you have had?

—Very often   —Sometimes
—Often   —Never

D. How often do you feel restless or uneasy on days like Sundays or holidays, when you have nothing in particular to do?

—Never feel uneasy   —Often feel uneasy
   or restless   or restless
—Sometimes feel uneasy   —Always feel uneasy
   or restless   or restless

E. When you are in a high place, how frightened are you when you look down?

—Very frightened   —A little frightened
—Quite frightened   —Not frightened at all

F. How often do you feel uneasy or uncomfortable without knowing why you are feeling that way?

—Very often   —Sometimes
—Quite often   —Never

G. How often are you afraid when you find yourself in a small closed place or when you think about finding yourself in such a place?

—Almost always   —Sometimes
—Often   —Never

H. In comparison to other people you know, like friends or relatives, how much do you worry about your physical health?

—A good bit more   —A little less than others
  than others
—A little more   —A good bit less than others
  than others

I. When you go to the doctor (or when he comes to you) because you don't feel well, how worried are you about what the doctor will say is wrong with you?

—Not worried at all   —Quite worried
—A little worried   —Very worried

J. How often in the past year have you had nightmares or dreams from which you have awakened feeling nervous or frightened?

—Never   —Sometimes
—Very rarely   —Quite often

K. How much do you worry about your mental health, in comparison to other people you know, like friends or relatives?

—A good deal more   —A little less
—A little more   —A good deal less

L. How often do you find it hard to pay attention to your work because disturbing or frightening thoughts come into your mind?

—Very often   —Sometimes
—Often   —Hardly ever

M. In comparison with other men of your age, how nervous do you feel about fighting with someone?

    —A good deal more   —A little less
    —A little more   —A good deal less

N. How afraid are you when you are alone in the dark?

    —Not afraid at all   —Somewhat afraid
    —A little afraid   —Very much afraid

O. How often do you find yourself worrying about a particular person, situation, or happening, even though you know that there is little reason for worrying?

    —Never   —Often
    —Sometimes   —Very often

P. How afraid of drowning are you when you are near a body of water, in swimming, or in a boat?

    —Not afraid at all   —Quite worried
    —A little nervous   —Quite frightened

IV. Dominance: eleven items selected by Lane from sixty items used in Harrison G. Gough, Herbert McClosky, and Paul E. Meehl, "A Personality Scale for Dominance," *Journal of Abnormal and Social Psychology, 46* (1951), 263–69. On each item the respondents were asked to check one of the following:

    —Strongly agree   —Disagree
    —Agree   —Strongly disagree

A. I must admit I try to see what others think before I take a stand.
B. In a group, I take responsibility for getting people introduced.
C. I have to stop and think before I act, even in trifling matters.
D. I am embarrassed with people I don't know well.
E. I would rather not have very much responsibility for other people.
F. When in a group of people, I have trouble thinking of the right things to talk about.
G. I have a natural talent for influencing people.
H. There are times when I act like a coward.
I. I hate to tell others what to do.

J. I like to give orders and get things moving.

K. I do many things which I regret afterwards.

V. Anomie: four items from Leo Srole, "Social Integration and Certain Corollaries: An Exploratory Study," *American Sociological Review, 21* (1956), 709–16. On each item the respondents were asked to check one of the following:

—Strongly agree   —Disagree

—Agree   —Strongly disagree

A. Nowadays a person has to live pretty much for today and let tomorrow take care of itself.

B. These days a person really doesn't know who he can count on.

C. In spite of what some people say, the lot of the average man is getting worse, not better.

D. It's hardly fair to bring children into the world with the way things look for the future.

All scales scored on a straight 0-1-2-3 basis except for faith-in-people scale (0-1).

Part Two: Scores for Respondents on Above Measures

Scoring:	high = most authoritarian	low = least authoritarian
Authoritarianism	high = least faith-in-people	low = most faith-in-people
Faith-in-people	high = most social anxiety	low = least social anxiety
Social anxiety	high = most neurotic	low = least neurotic
Neurotic anxiety	anxiety	anxiety
Dominance	high = most dominant	low = least dominant
Anomie	high = highest in anomic	low = lowest in anomic
	feelings	feelings

Part Three: Questionnaire items administered to 110 civil servants not members of the sample intensively interviewed. Scales not accompanied by a reference to their origin were developed in the field by the author. On each item the respondents were asked to check one of the following:

—Strongly agree   —Disagree

—Agree   —Strongly disagree

I. Authoritarianism scale: seven items used by Joseph W. Elder and reported in his article, "National Loyalties in a Newly Independent Nation," in David E. Apter, ed., *Ideology and Discontent* (Glencoe, The Free Press, 1964), pp. 77–92.

	Authoritarianism	Faith-in-People	Social Anxiety	Neurotic Anxiety	Dominance	Anomie
	Score	Score	Score	Score	Score	Score
1. Sundram	28	4	8	15	18	5
2. Md. Anim	27	4	10	24	18	5
3. Khoo	26	4	6	10	18	7
4. Nordin	27	2	4	9	19	4
5. Hussain	27	4	6	17	16	7
6. Ismail	26	4	7	12	17	2
7. Abdul Karim	25	2	7	15	17	3
8. Tay	26	3	3	7	23	3
9. Lim	28	4	5	12	14	11
10. Jeganathan	28	3	8	11	12	12
11. Zukifli	28	4	8	16	17	9
12. Zaharuddin	22	4	3	13	14	3
13. Abu Bakar	27	4	16	24	13	8
14. Ja'afar	24	2	6	19	17	4
15. Kamalam	27	4	8	18	14	5
16. Mahalingam	23	5	5	7	18	5
17. Mustapha	31	3	10	18	18	3

A. An insult to one's honor should always be punished.

B. Human nature what it is, there will always be wars and conflict.

C. Nothing can really be predicted by astrology.

D. It is not good to think too much.

E. Nowadays the courts give more punishment to lawbreakers than they ought to give. (Reversed from original.)

F. People can be divided into two classes: the strong and the weak.

G. There are so many evil people nowadays that it is dangerous to go out alone.

II. Other-directedness: six items. (From various sources.)

A. One should not become a close friend of someone who does not pay any attention to the common social customs of the group.

B. A person should strive to be successful even if it means he will be unpopular and others will be jealous of him.

C. It is important not to dress or act very differently from other people or else you will lose their respect.

D. My opinion is almost never swayed at all by editorials in the newspapers I read.

E. The negative opinion of others often keeps me from seeing a movie I had planned to see.

F. As long as a person does what he thinks is right, it does not matter at all what his family, friends, and community think of him.

III. Constant-pie orientation: four items.

A. Even in a rich country, if population grows rapidly, there is great danger that there will soon not be enough wealth to go around.

B. Those who get ahead usually get ahead at the expense of others.

C. When an individual or group gains, it usually means that another individual or group loses.

D. Any government that wants to help the poor people will have to take something away from the rich in order to do it.

IV. Entrepreneurial attitudes: eleven items used by David C. Mc-Clelland and found to discriminate effectively between industrial managers and administrators in cross-national research. Reported in McClelland's *The Achieving Society* (Princeton, New Jersey, Van Nostrand, 1961), pp. 496–97.

- A. I would prefer to work on a project that I could see was getting somewhere, even though it was far from where I usually live and work, and among people very different from me.
- B. An article for sale is worth what people will pay for it.
- C. Seniority should be given greater weight than merit in giving promotions.
- D. Incentive pay should not be used because workers will overwork and ruin their health or destroy jobs for others.
- E. Workers should not be promoted to managerial jobs even if they are qualified because it would destroy the respect for authority which the workers must have toward management.
- F. Part of the price which one pays in joining any organization today is the sacrifice of individual, personal decision making, and I, for one, am not willing to pay that price.
- G. The amount of education a person has should be a major factor in determining his pay scale.
- H. I approve of a career or job outside the home for married women.
- I. A good son should try to live near his parents even if it means giving up a good job in another part of the country.
- J. The most important factor in the success of a commercial firm is the establishment of a reputation for the excellence of its products.
- K. A man with money cannot really learn how to behave in polite society if he has not had the proper upbringing.

V. Risk-taking in decisions: two items.

- A. In an important decision, you should not wait until everyone is agreed. It is better to make a few people angry than to delay the decision until it is unanimous.
- B. Usually, it is better to get on with the job and perhaps risk making a mistake rather than to delay a long time until you are certain there can be no mistakes.

VI. Control over future and environment: two items. (From various sources.)

- A. Planning only makes a person unhappy, since your plans hardly ever work out anyway.

B. When a man is born, the success he is going to have is already in the stars, so he might as well accept it and not fight against it.

VII. Superiors as vindictive and threatening: three items.

A. A subordinate who questions his superior's decisions will usually find that his superior will hold a grudge against him thereafter.
B. Most subordinates are somewhat afraid of their superiors.
C. Once a person gets a little authority over others, he is apt to use it to boss around others and to show what a big man he is.

All the above items were administered to the following groups:

Group	Number	Sector
1. Settlement officers and senior hand clerks	24	Public
2. Audit Department examiners	27	Public
3. Telecoms trainees	16	Public
4. Bank Negara (National Bank) trainees	20	Public
5. National Productivity Centre management trainees	23	Private
Total respondents	110	

Part Four: dogmatism and politics questionnaire items administered to 116 civil servants *not* members of sample intensively interviewed. On each item, the respondents were asked to check one of the following:

—I agree a little   —I disagree a little
—I agree on the whole   —I disagree on the whole
—I agree very much   —I disagree very much

A. Dogmatism: thirty-six items found significant in discriminating the dogmatic from the nondogmatic in Milton Rokeach, *The Open and Closed Mind* (New York, Basic Books, 1960), pp. 73–80.

1. Most people just don't give a "damn" for others.
2. Nations which have opposing ideologies have nothing at all in common with one another.
3. It is only natural for a person to be rather fearful of the future.
4. Once I get involved in a heated discussion I just can't stop.

5. In a heated discussion, I generally become so involved in what I am going to say that I forget to listen to what others are saying.

6. If a man is to accomplish his mission in life, it is sometimes necessary to gamble "all or nothing."

7. It is better to be a dead hero than to be a live coward.

8. I would like it if I could find someone who would tell me how to solve my personal problems.

9. Even though I don't like to admit this even to myself, my secret ambition is to become a great man like Gandhi, Einstein, or Shakespeare.

10. A person who thinks primarily of his own happiness should be hated and despised.

11. The main thing in life is for a person to want to do something important.

12. There are two kinds of people in this world: those who are for the truth and those who are against the truth.

13. In a discussion I often find it necessary to repeat myself several times to make sure I am being understood.

14. If given the chance, I would do something of great benefit to the world.

15. There is so much to be done and so little time in which to do it.

16. In the history of mankind, there have probably been just a very small number of really great thinkers.

17. There are a number of people I have come to hate because of the things they stand for or believe in.

18. Fundamentally, the world we live in is a pretty lonesome place.

19. Unfortunately, many people with whom I have discussed important social and moral problems do not really understand what is going on.

20. Man on his own (by himself) is a helpless and miserable creature.

21. The highest form of government is a democracy, and the highest form of democracy is a government run by those who are most intelligent.

22. A person who gets enthusiastic about too many causes is likely to be a "wishy-washy" or indecisive sort of person.

23. To compromise with our political opponents is dangerous because it usually leads to the betrayal of our own side.

24. I get extremely angry whenever a person stubbornly refuses to admit he is wrong.

25. It is only natural that a person would have a much better knowledge of the ideas he believes in than with ideas which he opposes.

26. In times like these, a person must be pretty selfish if he considers primarily his own happiness.

27. Even though freedom of speech for all groups is a good goal, it is unfortunately necessary to restrict the freedom of certain political groups.

28. Of all the different philosophies which exist in the world, there is probably only one which is correct.

29. A group which tolerates too many differences of opinion among its own members cannot exist for very long.

30. Most of the ideas which get printed nowadays are not worth the paper they are printed on.

31. In the long run, the best way to live is to choose friends and associates whose preferences and beliefs are the same as one's own.

32. It is often desirable to reserve judgment about what is going on until one has had a chance to hear the opinions of those one respects.

33. The worst crime a person could commit is to publicly attack the people who believe in the same thing as he does.

34. It is only when a person devotes himself to an ideal or cause that life becomes meaningful.

35. The present is all too full of unhappiness. It is only the future which counts.

36. Most people just do not know what is good for them.

B. Rules of the game: eight items selected and adapted from Herbert McClosky, "Consensus and Ideology in American Politics," *American Political Science Review, 58* (June, 1964), pp. 361–82. Where items have been adapted, McClosky's original version appears in parentheses.

1. People ought to be allowed to vote even if they cannot do so intelligently.

2. I do not mind a politician's methods if he manages to get the right things done.

3. It is all right to get around the law if you do not actually break it.

4. In dealing with subversives, sometimes you cannot always give them all the legal rights which peaceful citizens have, otherwise many will escape the law. (If congressional committees stuck

strictly to the rules and gave every witness his rights, they would never succeed in exposing the many dangerous subversives they have turned up.)

5. We might as well make up our minds that in order to make the world better a lot of innocent people will have to suffer.
6. Very few politicians have clean records, so one should not get excited about the mud-throwing that sometimes takes place. (so why get excited about the mud-slinging that sometimes goes on?)
7. There are times when it almost seems better for the people to take the law into their own hands rather than wait for the machinery of government to act.
8. To bring about great changes for the benefit of mankind often requires cruelty and even ruthlessness.

C. Support for freedom of opinion and speech: seven items selected and adapted from McClosky. Original version appears in parentheses where adaptations have been made.

1. People who hate our way of life should still have a chance to talk and be heard.
2. Nobody has the right to tell another person what he should and should not read.
3. Unless there is freedom for many points of view to be presented, there is little chance that the truth can even be known.
4. No matter what a person's political beliefs are, he is entitled to the same legal rights and protections as anyone else.
5. Freedom of conscience should mean the freedom *not* to believe in God (to be an aetheist) as well as the freedom to worship in the religion of one's choice.
6. I would not trust any person or group to decide what opinions can be freely expressed and what must be silenced.
7. You can't really be sure whether an opinion is true or not unless people are free to argue against it.

D. Applications of freedom of speech and procedural rights: six items selected and adapted from McClosky. Original version appears in parentheses where adaptations have been made.

1. Freedom does not give anyone the right to teach foreign ideas in our schools.
2. A book that contains wrong political views cannot be a good book and does not deserve to be published.
3. If a person is convicted of a crime by use of evidence which is

not legal (by illegal evidence), he should be set free and the evidence thrown out of court.

4. In dealing with dangerous enemies of the nation (dangerous enemies like the Communists), we can't afford to depend on the courts, laws, and their slow and unreliable methods.

5. When the country is in great danger, we may have to force people to do certain things against their will, even though it violates their rights. (Force people to testify against themselves, even though . . .)

6. A man ought not to be allowed to speak if he doesn't know what he is talking about.

E. Political equality: four items selected from McClosky.

1. The main trouble with democracy is that most people don't really know what's best for them.

2. It will always be necessary to have a few strong, capable people actually running everything.

3. Political "issues" and arguments are beyond the understanding of most of the voters.

4. Few people really know what is in their own best interest in the long run.

F. Economic equality: four items selected and adapted from Mc-Closky. Original version appears in parentheses where adaptations have been made.

1. The government ought to make sure that everyone has a good standard of living.

2. I think the government should give a person work if he cannot find another job.

3. There will always be poverty, so people might as well get used to the fact (idea).

4. Every person should have a good house, even if the government has to build it for him.

G. Cynicism toward politics: six items selected from McClosky.

1. There is practically no connection between what a politician says and what he will do once he gets elected.

2. I usually have confidence that the government will do what is right.

3. To me, most politicians don't seem to really mean what they say.

4. Most politicians are looking out for themselves above all else.

5. No matter what people think, a few people will always run things anyway.
6. Most politicians can be trusted to do what they think is best for the country.

H. Political futility: three items selected from McClosky.

1. It is no use worrying my head about public affairs; I can't do anything about them anyhow.
2. Nothing I ever do seems to have any real effect on what happens in politics.
3. Political parties are so big that the average member has not got much to say about what goes on.

All the above items were administered to the following groups:

Group	Number	Sector
1. Postal service trainees	23	Public
2. Financial administrators	18	Public
3. General Staff administrators	28	Public
4. Senior clerks	19	Public
5. Senior Financial administrators	14	Public
6. State Assembly members	14	Politicians (all Alliance
Total	116	Party members)

Appendix C
Constant-Pie Correlations

Correlations between constant-pie orientation and other attitudinal variables (number of respondents is given in parentheses).

A. Authoritarianism: $N = 56$

	Low in constant-pie thinking	High in constant-pie thinking
Low authoritarian	69% (20)	48% (13)
High authoritarian	31% (9)	52% (14)
	100% (29)	100% (27)

Chi² = 4.22   1 df $p < .05$

B. Superiors as vindictive or threatening: $N = 66$

	Low in constant-pie thinking	High in constant-pie thinking
Superiors as less vindictive or threatening	56% (18)	38% (13)
Superiors as more vindictive or threatening	44% (14)	62% (21)
	100% (32)	100% (34)

Chi² = 3.63   1 df $p < .06$

C. Faith-in-people: $N = 35$

	Low in constant-pie thinking	High in constant-pie thinking
High faith-in-people	56% (10)	29% (5)
Low faith-in-people	44% (8)	71% (12)
	100% (18)	100% (17)

Chi² = 3.93   1 df $p < .05$

D. Control over the future: $N = 57$

	Low in constant-pie thinking	High in constant-pie thinking
High control	79% (22)	31% (9)
Low control	21% (6)	69% (20)
	100% (28)	100% (29)

Chi² = 24.10   1 df $p < .001$

Index